Esther

Esther ▪ ▪ ▪

HER MURDER HAUNTS A
SMALL TOWN IN OKLAHOMA

LEONARD SANDERS

A JOHN MACRAE BOOK
HENRY HOLT AND COMPANY   NEW YORK

Author's Note: A portion of the profits of this book
will go to the Esther K. Steele Scholarship Fund,
administered by Deanna Reeves, Route 1, Willow, Oklahoma 73673

Henry Holt and Company, Inc.
Publishers since 1866
115 West 18th Street
New York, New York 10011

Henry Holt® is a registered
trademark of Henry Holt and Company, Inc.

Library of Congress Cataloging-in-Publication Data
Sanders, Leonard.
    Esther: her murder haunts a small town in
Oklahoma/Leonard Sanders.—1st ed.
        p.   cm.
    "A John Macrae book."
    1. Steele, Esther K.   2. Murder—Oklahoma—Granite
—Case studies.   3. Homicide investigation—Oklahoma—
Granite—Case studies.
I. Title.
HV6534.G75S747   1994
364.1'523'09766443—dc20   93-38503
                                              CIP

ISBN 0-8050-1050-5

Henry Holt books are available for special promotions
and premiums. For details contact:
Director, Special Markets.

First Edition—1994

DESIGNED BY PAULA R. SZAFRANSKI

Printed in the United States of America
All first editions are printed on acid-free paper. ∞

10   9   8   7   6   5   4   3   2   1

For Florene,

who first suggested
this book

And for Esther,

who inspired it

Acknowledgments

I can think of no greater tribute to Esther K. Steele than the overwhelming response I encountered everywhere in researching the events surrounding her death. I emerged obligated to scores of gracious people who gave freely of time and emotion. To all I am deeply grateful. But some were imposed upon even more than others. I especially wish to thank former OSBI agent Jerry Sunderland; O. C. Kruska; Special Prosecutor Charles V. Williams; Judge Alan Markum; OSBI agent Richard Goss; the Rev. Mr. Wilbur D. and Edna Mease; OSBI criminologist Mary Long; Daisy Brown; Jan Wingo Locklear; William and Joyce Manning; H. C. Ford, Jr.; Penny Kruska Hook; the Rev. Mr. Charles Horton; Charles Jones; Doris Broiles Post; Tal Oden; and jurors Bonnie Steiner, Barney Brown, and Otis Ray Martin.

Leonard Sanders
Fort Worth, 1994

Acknowledgments

1 ∎ ∎ ∎

A COLD NORTHER HAD STRUCK EARLIER in the evening, and as Charles Horton brought his sermon to a close strong gusts battered the brick walls of the church. Horton pushed aside a growing concern. He and his wife were expecting their second child at any moment. She had come to Granite with him. He was apprehensive, thinking of the sixty-five-mile drive home to Cheyenne in the cold wind along the bleak stretches of blacktop road.

But the church sanctuary was filled with a warmth not entirely attributable to the furnace. Horton was pleased with the way the evening had gone. The congregation had been unusually attentive on this, the next-to-final night of his four-day revival, and he was encouraged to see so many young faces. In these small towns of western Oklahoma, populations tended to be old. Church attendance was dying off with them. Tonight the congregation of First United Methodist Church contained many teenagers and young adults.

Horton ended his two-hour service with a prayer. At the conclusion, while the congregation gathered coats and wraps, he moved up the sloping center aisle to the foyer and the front door. There he said good-night, individually, to the departing congregation. Each time the door opened, cold blasts of frigid air penetrated the church.

Gradually the sanctuary emptied. After the last of the congregation shook his hand and went out into the cold, Horton turned away from the door.

Resident pastor Wilbur D. "Bill" Mease, his wife, Edna, and three members of the local congregation—Esther Steele, Daisy Brown, and Gertrude Hawkins—stood talking with Horton's wife in the fellowship area, where earlier the women of the church had served refreshments.

Esther Steele called across the foyer to Horton. "We haven't put the punch away yet. We thought you might like a cup before you go."

Horton appreciated her thoughtfulness. After two hours in the pulpit, his throat was indeed dry.

As he crossed the foyer to join the group around the punch bowl, he reflected once again that Esther Steele was a remarkably striking person. He remembered that many years ago he and his wife had discussed her, and wondered about her, upon first seeing her briefly at a church conference. She was that impressive. She was tall, and moved with athletic grace. She often wore her black hair pulled straight back into a youthful ponytail or chignon. She could be taken for a well-groomed woman in her indeterminate fifties. But through the years Horton had picked up clues that she must be older. Yet with her lively dark eyes, high cheekbones, and classic features, she remained a vibrantly attractive woman. Her rich contralto voice and strong personality invariably dominated her surroundings. As she

ladled the punch for Horton, Esther adroitly initiated a conversation, asking about a mutual acquaintance, a member of his congregation in Cheyenne.

Horton fell easily into the small talk. But he was remembering
that on the previous evening Esther had paid him a highly valued
compliment. She had said she was canceling previously made plans
so she could attend the final night of his revival.

"I have tickets for the symphony in Oklahoma City," she had told
him. "But I've enjoyed your revival so much, and it's making such a
difference in our church, that I want to stay and be a part of it."

Concerned about the late hour and the drive ahead of him,
Horton glanced at his watch. It was ten fifteen. Pastor Mease and his
wife had invited him to dinner at their pastorage before the concluding service the following night. With an hour-long drive home tonight, and another hour-long trip back tomorrow, that appointment
was not far away. Esther and the other women had yet to put away
the dishes. Mease was waiting to lock up the church.

As soon as he could do so gracefully, Horton finished the punch,
said good-night to the group, and escorted his wife out to their car.

Esther Steele, Daisy Brown, and Gertrude Hawkins could not hold
back exclamations as they walked out of the church and into the
boisterous, cold wind. Hugging their coats about them, they hurried
to Esther's Cadillac. The sky was devoid of clouds. A full moon hung
two hours high, bathing the mountains to the north and west of
town in soft pale light.

The trip home had become routine. Esther drove north the few
blocks to Gertrude's house. On the way, the three women discussed
the refreshing appeal of Horton's low-keyed, well-reasoned sermons.

"I believe his way is so much better than the hellfire and brim-
stone sermons we used to have at revivals," Gertrude said. "He really
makes you think."

"I was watching some of the young people tonight," Esther said.
"I could see that he was reaching them."

"He's doing so much good for the church," Daisy said. "I haven't seen such interest in years."

"It's a genuine revival," Esther agreed.

They arrived at Gertrude's house. Gertrude slid out. Esther and Daisy waited until she was safely in her door. Then Esther drove east on Mountain Avenue and south on tree-lined Main Street to her home.

She stopped in the drive. Daisy's house was next door. Both women were widows, living alone. Sometimes they played cards for a while after evening church services. But tonight Daisy felt drained of energy.

"Esther, I'm just too tired for cards tonight," she said. "I hope you don't mind."

"I should be getting to bed," Esther said. "I may go to the City in the morning. I don't know yet. If I do, I'll just have to turn around and come right back."

Daisy assumed that Esther was delaying a decision, waiting until morning to see if she felt like making the five-hour round-trip. Esther's next comment tended to confirm this impression.

"It's been a long day," Esther said. "I'm exhausted."

The remark concerned Daisy. Earlier in life Daisy had served as office nurse for a doctor. She had developed the habit of listening for nuisances of health.

If Esther said she was tired, perhaps something was wrong. At seventy-three—nine years younger than Daisy—Esther was one of the most active people Daisy knew. Esther maintained a busy schedule, with responsibilities and interests that took her all over the state. Often Daisy had seen her return home well after midnight, only to be up and going at dawn. Daisy could not remember a time in decades when Esther had been ill.

They said good-night. Daisy stepped out. Esther started the car and drove on past her house and into her garage.

As Daisy walked to her own door, Esther's last remark lingered in her thoughts. She had known Esther Steele almost all of their lives.

She was fully aware that Esther was an extraordinary person. There was no one Daisy admired more.

Yet Daisy sometimes grew exasperated with her. During the last few weeks Esther had received several obscene—even threatening— phone calls. Esther had not mentioned them to Daisy, apparently not wishing to alarm her. But Daisy had heard about them through mutual friends.

Esther had been urged to report the calls to the authorities. She had refused, saying she thought she knew who it was. She had seemed more irritated than concerned.

Even more alarming to Daisy, twice in recent months Esther had heard someone in her house at night.

Only a few weeks ago Esther had awakened one night just as someone stepped into her bedroom. Still half asleep, and registering the faint odor of cigarettes, Esther had thought in her confusion that her sister Lenore and brother-in-law Blackie, who smoked, were visiting, and that Blackie had gotten up in the night and mistaken the door to her bedroom for that of the adjacent bathroom.

"Blackie?" Esther had asked in the darkness.

The dim form backed out of her bedroom and moved down the hall. A moment later Esther had heard the back door close.

Daisy and other friends had begged Esther to start locking her doors. Esther refused.

She said she would not allow such a contemptible person to dictate how she lived her life. She explained that her nieces and nephews sometimes came by unannounced to spend the night.

"I want them to think of this as their home," she said. "I want them to know they're always welcome. I don't want to go through the awkwardness of handing out keys." And, laughing, she said she wanted to catch whoever it was.

Daisy had been appalled. But she knew that after forty years of teaching in public schools, Esther possessed a supreme confidence in her ability to handle any situation.

Until recently Daisy had seldom locked her own doors. Crime

had never been of much concern in Granite. But now, as she prepared for bed, Daisy made certain her own doors were locked.

Esther was tired but not sleepy. There still was work to be done as
long as she had the energy to do it.

She went down the hall to her bedroom, tossed her purse onto
one of the twin beds, removed her coat, then walked back through
the house.

Her Easter cards lay in rows on the dining table, some ready for
mailing, some not. Their preparation was time-consuming, for she
always included a personal note with each to keep in touch with
friends, relatives, and former students.

Today was Tuesday. Sunday would be Easter. The cards should
be in the mail. But another matter was even more pressing. She
walked on to the rear of the house, into her den.

Each year the Retired Teachers Association awarded scholar-
ships. Winners were chosen on the basis of essays. This year's entries lay on the sofa, where she had been reading every spare
moment during the last few days.

She sank onto the sofa, picked up her reading glasses, and
resumed judging the essays. She keenly felt the responsibility. Many
times through the years she had seen an occasional, seemingly unex-
ceptional student blossom remarkably from a minimum of special
attention. One of these essays might be from such a student. The
proper choice could change the entire course of someone's life. She
read carefully, paying close attention to grammar and syntax, yet
going beyond, seeking the elusive spark that might await discovery.

She regretted she would miss the symphony concert in Oklahoma City the next night. She had been looking forward to it for
weeks. Yet she was glad she had changed her plans. The revival in
her church not only had been an exhilarating experience, but also
was meaningful in a personal way.

Horton had opened the revival Sunday night by saying that all
Christians need "a time apart," sufficient solitude to get away from

the rush of the world about them, in order to refocus on their relationship with God. From the first Esther had liked Horton's message and his style. But it was on the second night that his sermon seemed chosen especially for her. That evening Horton spoke on the Kingdom of God, as revealed in Christ's parable of the sower whose seeds mostly went to naught. Quoting from the Book of Mark, Horton had talked of distractions of the day-to-day world that choked out the Word of God, just as the seeds of the biblical sower were choked by weeds.

Horton pointed out that only when the Word fell on fertile ground—the receptive seeker—could it take root, thrive, and bear fruit.

More and more in recent years Esther had found herself tied down by possessions. She wished for more time to devote to her mind and to the service of others. She felt the need for more freedom and independence in her life. Horton's sermons seemed to be showing her a way.

On that second night, as she listened, she had made her decision to cancel her plans to attend the concert. She had already phoned her sister Lenore in Oklahoma City to tell her that she would not be coming up for the symphony.

Esther knew she was not as settled into her ways as some of her friends—and perhaps even some of her family—believed. She long had thought of selling her house in Granite to buy a small condo apartment in a university town, perhaps in Norman near the University of Oklahoma, where she had spent several summers doing graduate work.

She liked to think of her house as forever open to any member of her family. She had encouraged her nieces and nephews to think of her as always available to discuss anything that might be troubling them. Her house had served a purpose.

But the idea of a small apartment was tempting.

Her outlook had changed drastically since her retirement from teaching, and since the death of her husband, Warren. In many ways, these last few years had been the best and most satisfying of her life. Now she wanted more time for herself, and for this new life.

If she were near a university, she would have ready access to a good library, music, drama, dance, and sporting events. She loved seeing young people doing their best in every pursuit. She had long believed that school years were the most important, and most exciting, in everyone's life. She took a vicarious pleasure in seeing young people acquire knowledge.

She had confided her dream of a small apartment to only a few friends. Some had argued against the idea, pointing out that in buying into a condo, one was locked into a partnership that inevitably brought problems, big or little. But her house in Granite contained more space than she needed. Her nieces and nephews were marrying, starting families. Surely they would appreciate receiving furniture and heirlooms now, rather than later.

She had been unable to have children of her own. That had been one of the biggest disappointments in her life. Warren also had desperately wanted children. At least subconsciously he might have harbored resentment about this. While he was overseas during World War II she had faced a terrible decision alone. She had followed the prevailing medical advice of that era and accepted surgery. Not wanting to worry Warren while he was in combat in Italy, she had not written him about it until months later.

Perhaps she had handled it badly. Some of her close friends thought so. Warren had been extremely unhappy that he had been shut out of this crisis in her life—in their lives.

Her childlessness might have been at the core of the troubles in their later years.

After an hour of judging essays, Esther grew sleepy. She placed her reading glasses on the stack of entries and walked back through the house to her bedroom, turning out lights as she went.

The night had grown colder, the wind stronger. A chill penetrated the house. After a quick bath, Esther pulled on a nightgown, spread an electric blanket on her bed, and set the dial on low. She turned out the bedroom light and slipped beneath the covers. The wind moaned through the trees outside.

Spring in this part of the country could be rambunctious—warm one day, frigid the next. She hoped the night would not bring another hard freeze. With the recent warm weather, trees and shrubs had budded. She would not like to see the buds killed and spring delayed.

She thought ahead to her upcoming schedule. Next week she would be in the City baby-sitting her niece Penny's two-year-old son, John, and four-year-old daughter, Leslie, while Penny and her husband, Richard Hook, were away on a business trip. She was eagerly looking forward to that.

She had not bothered to set an alarm clock. She always slept lightly, and never had difficulty in waking on time.

She drifted off to sleep.

Her back door remained unlocked.

The residents of Granite will long remember that eerie night—the full moon, the cloudless sky, the fierce north wind rattling the bare branches of trees.

Shortly after midnight, correctional officer Harry Ellis arrived home from his shift at the Oklahoma State Reformatory, three miles to the east of town. For years Ellis had spent much time with convicts. Perhaps he was more aware of dire possibilities than most of his neighbors. Many of the residents along this stretch of Main Street were elderly widows living alone. Ellis felt an unassigned sense of responsibility for them. He glanced around at the nearby houses.

He saw nothing amiss.

Often when he came home at midnight, lights would be on in Esther Steele's house across the street. She habitually stayed up late.

Tonight her house was dark.

Ellis went on into his house and closed the door.

■ ■ ■

Six miles to the north, in the Lake Creek community, Ruby Neighbors could not sleep. Later she remembered how eerie the night seemed when she rose and walked through the house, into the kitchen, for a drink of water. The wind was moaning in the eaves. The moon was so bright she did not need to turn on lights.

But most residents of Granite slept, never dreaming that Esther Steele soon would be fighting for her life.

For on that night, the first murder in the history of the town was committed. Esther was the victim.

If she screamed for help, no one heard. Her voice might have been lost in the howling of the wind.

2 ▪ ▪ ▪

NORTH OF THE RED RIVER, BACK ROADS are preferable if the time can be spared. Lonely, straight, and seldom traveled, the rural dirt, gravel, and two-lane blacktop roads of far southwestern Oklahoma hug a gently rolling landscape that offers tantalizing glimpses of the past and uneasy intimations of the future.

Fields of wheat—green, golden, or brown in season—lie interspersed amid occasional patches of cotton and stretches of lush Bermuda grass and grazing cattle. Recent seasons have been generous with rainfall. Fences are few. Profuse crops spill out of the fields, spread across the ditches, and threaten to engulf roads. The clash of reality and childhood memory becomes surreal: this land, now so lush and green, once was ground zero of the Oklahoma Dust Bowl.

Today few people live on the land. Owners and operators of the farms and ranches drive out from nearby towns to do whatever needs to be done. When encountered on the remote stretches, they wave, friendly but curious, willing to assume that a passing stranger is not necessarily bent on meanness. In a sense they, too, are intruders here.

Most of the people who once populated this land between the two upper forks of the Red River are gone. Decades ago the young moved away, uprooted by various wars and the ongoing agrarian revolution. They now work and grow old in nearby towns, or in larger, distant cities. Because of a protracted boundary dispute between Texas and the U.S. government, the frontier experience came late to this region, delayed almost until the eve of the twentieth century. Now only elusive traces remain of the pioneers who settled this land within living memory. Scattered foundation stones, stubs of cisterns, gray remnants of abandoned houses, and lonely cemeteries provide ghostly glimmers of an era when each quarter section here nurtured a family and rural schools thrived.

American history as written suggests that the Kiowas and Comanches who once ruled this region were displaced by Anglos in advance of the frontier. But in truth, that displacement was but one of many. Archaeological evidence reveals that early Americans were hunting and living here while Cro-Magnon man still populated Europe.

A leisurely hour north of the river, low mountains—the western end of the Wichita chain—come into view. Even anticipated, they manage to surprise, abruptly breaking the monotony of the undulating plain. From a distance they appear gray-blue. On closer approach, the colors shift subtly with changing light, mauve or soft purple one minute, blending into rosy pink the next.

In size the mountains are not impressive. None rises more than a thousand feet above the surrounding plain. But the huge granite boulders, weathered egg-shaped through a half billion years, kindle a fascination sufficient to endure a lifetime.

The insistent aura of great age is valid. The Wichitas are among the oldest intact geological formations on earth. The Rocky Mountains, created sixty to seventy million years ago, are but new-born pups to these ancient hills.

It might seem that this sense of infinite age would render the span of human life insignificant by comparison. But the opposite is true. The primordial landscape effectively suggests that human life as we know it is rare—and precious beyond measure.

At the western end of the Wichitas, beyond Devil's Canyon, beyond Quartz Mountain, the chain terminates with Headquarters Mountain. To the west rolling plains stretch away unbroken to the Texas Panhandle, forty miles away.

Headquarters Mountain dominates the surrounding landscape and enfolds the small town of Granite at its base.

Comfortably removed from major highways, railroads, and air-ports, and isolated by many miles of rural buffer, this small town long managed to remain essentially unchanged. Like Brigadoon, Granite resisted the passage of time. A few years ago Sher-wood Anderson, William Saroyan, Norman Rockwell, or Mark Twain would have recognized Granite instantly and used his talents to celebrate its basic decency, its simplicity, its contradic-tions, and its human foibles. In those years, when family farms fueled the nation's economy, Granite thrived. Now maps show eleven ghost towns within an hour's drive. And Granite struggles to survive.

Along Main Street most buildings are vacant. But all are painted and neat. Seedling trees shade the sidewalks. Carefully crafted facades convey a disarming impression of newness. It is as if an effort has been made to preserve in amber the best of small-town America and the superior qualities of a vanished way of life.

But the lady seated in the glass ticket booth at Kozy Theater is, on second glance, a mannequin. The Kozy screen has been dark thirty years. Appearances are not as they seem. Dry rot lurks behind the painted facades.

For the last several years, Granite has been contending with more than survival.

In large cities, the full cost of murder in human terms tends to be obscured. Each death sinks into a morass of ongoing crimes. But in Granite, where everyone knows everyone, the ripple effects of Esther Steele's murder are laid bare. The workings of the erratic, balky machinery of justice can be followed in detail.

Granite, forced to take a hard look at what it once was—and what it has become—perhaps serves as a microcosm of a nation in search of solutions.

3

IN THE HOUR AFTER DAWN, DAISY BROWN carried Quai, her rambunctious little shih tzu, out to his pen in the backyard. Quai spent his nights indoors. But during the day he liked to go outside for a while to romp in his pen and do dog things.

The morning air was brisk, but still. Apparently the norther had blown itself out. The grass was lightly sheathed in white rime, not thick enough for a killing frost. Already the bright April sun offered considerable warmth. Once again the perversity of Oklahoma weather had been demonstrated: only hours after the fierce norther, this promised to be a delightful day. The sky was cloudless. The sharp detail of the mountain to the north of town proved that the air was clear.

Daisy glanced next door. Esther's garage door was down. Her car was not in the drive. Usually Esther left the garage door up when she was out on errands, but sometimes she put it down when she left town on longer trips. Daisy assumed Esther had gone to Oklahoma City early, despite her voiced doubts of the night before. Daisy was not surprised. Esther was always on the go.

Daisy hurried back into the house. Three consecutive nights of attendance at the revival had cut into her spare time, and she had much to do. Later in the day, Esther probably would call and confirm that they again would attend the revival together that night.

That thought was still in the back of Daisy's mind when, in midafternoon, she rushed to answer the ringing phone. She recognized the voice of Flora Mae Kruska, Esther's sister-in-law.

"Daisy, have you seen Esther today?"

Daisy thought back. "No, I don't believe I have."

Flora Mae sounded puzzled. "I don't know what to think. I've been trying to call her all day. When I drove by a while ago, I noticed her garage door was down. She must be home. But she doesn't answer her phone."

Daisy was still reflecting. "I can't remember seeing her at all today."

"Well, it isn't important. But if you see her, will you ask her to call me?"

"I will," Daisy promised.

Daisy ended the conversation vaguely disturbed. Not once during the day had she heard Esther's car in the drive. That was most unusual. When in town, Esther was always coming and going. And if she had made the trip to Oklahoma City, she should be back by now.

Daisy felt the first twinge of alarm. She remembered Esther saying last night that she was exhausted, and thinking at the time that it was an atypical remark. She glanced out a window to see if Esther was in the yard tending to her flowers. Daisy saw no sign of activity about the house.

She returned to her work but could not put the worry out of her mind. Could Esther be ill?

She dialed Esther's number. As Esther's phone rang uninterrupted, Daisy made her decision. She hung up the phone and reached for a sweater. She would walk over and make sure Esther was all right.

Afterward, Daisy could not remember whether Esther's back door was standing slightly open or if it was completely closed. But she was sure it was not locked. She encountered no difficulty in opening it and stepping into the house.

She raised her voice. "Esther?"

The house remained silent.

Tentatively, Daisy walked into the house, again calling out. The interior remained deathly still.

Daisy was swept by a strong premonition. She moved on past the den, into the kitchen. The cabinet top was painstakingly neat. Esther never went to bed leaving so much as a saucer out of its cupboard.

Daisy edged on into the dining room, still calling out. The house felt deserted, empty. Esther's dining table, large enough to accommodate her family dinners, was slightly oversized for the room. Precise stacks of Easter cards were arranged on the bare, polished wood. A chair was drawn back from the table where Esther had been seated while preparing the cards for mailing. Not much space was left between the chair and the wall. Daisy eased by and walked on into the living room, again calling out. Nothing seemed out of place.

Thinking Esther might be in the bathroom, Daisy went through the living room and into the hall.

For reasons she could not explain, Daisy suddenly felt even more apprehensive. She moved on down the hall.

The door to Esther's bedroom was open. The blinds were closed, leaving the room in semidarkness. Esther lay under a blanket. Only her right arm was visible, sticking out from her twin bed.

Calling out one last time, Daisy hurried into the bedroom.

A blue electric blanket seemed thrown over Esther at random and lay slightly askew. The effect lacked Esther's customary neatness and gave Daisy the impression that something was wrong. But at the moment she did not focus on these peripheral details.

After years of experience as a nurse, her reaction was automatic. She walked to the bedside and reached to feel for a pulse. From the instant Daisy touched Esther's wrist, she knew Esther was dead. The flesh was cold, the arm rigid.

Daisy did not explore further. Calmer than she would have expected to be, she eased out of the bedroom, hurried to Esther's hall phone, and dialed the office of Dr. Herbert Harold Lenaburg. Not only was he Esther's personal physician, he also was the county medical examiner.

His office did not answer. Daisy knew it was about five o'clock, or perhaps a few minutes after. She dialed the doctor's home. Mrs. Lenaburg answered. She said Dr. Lenaburg was on his way home from the office.

"Would you please have him come to Esther Steele's house right away?" Daisy asked.

Accustomed to emergencies, Mrs. Lenaburg did not ask questions. "He should be there in a few minutes," she said.

While waiting, Daisy reflected that someone from Esther's family should be present. She dialed Flora Mae. Although she allowed the phone to ring for a time, her call was not answered.

She next phoned Viola Cypert, Esther's sister.

"Viola, I'm at Esther's house," she said. "You should come quick. Something has happened to her."

"What is it?"

Daisy did not want to be the one to pronounce Esther dead. She evaded the question. "I've called Dr. Lenaburg. He's on his way. You should be here."

Viola did not press further.

Daisy pushed the button to hurry return of the dial tone for another call she should make. She knew that Esther's adept social manner and quick humor tended to conceal one fundamental fact about her: Esther was an introspective, deeply religious person, committed to the church and to her beliefs. Her pastor should also be here.

Viola arrived first. Daisy heard her car, met her at the back door, and took her arm.

"She's in her bed. Viola, we've got to be strong. I'm sure she's dead."

Viola hurried down the hall to Esther's bedroom. Daisy followed. Viola stood for a moment looking at Esther's extended arm. She did not touch the body or move the blankets. One hand went to her face. She turned away, stood for a moment, then walked into the adjoining bedroom to compose herself.

Dr. Lenaburg arrived a moment later. Daisy met him at the front door and showed him the way to the bedroom.

He took Esther's arm and felt for a pulse. He also encountered the cold flesh and the stiffness of rigor mortis.

Returning to the hall, Dr. Lenaburg called for an ambulance and a medical technician to assist him in the formalities he now was required to perform as medical examiner.

Viola came back into the hall. Dr. Lenaburg was her family physician. But she was under the care of specialists as well, and she had long been battling congestive heart failure and wore a Pacemaker. After noting that she seemed to be holding up well, he returned his attention to Esther's death and the cause of it.

He flipped the light switch in the bedroom. But the ceiling was high, and the bulbs were of low wattage. They did little to alleviate the gloom.

"I'll need a flashlight," he told Daisy. "Do you know where we might find one?"

Glad to be of help, Daisy began a search, opening drawers and digging through them. Viola joined her.

"Do you know Esther's date of birth?" Dr. Lenaburg asked Viola. "I'll need it for the death certificate."

Under the circumstances, Viola could not remember the exact date.

"It would be on her driver's license," Dr. Lenaburg suggested.

Esther's black alligator purse lay on the other twin bed. Viola picked it up and searched through the contents.

"She usually keeps her billfold in her purse," she said. "But I can't find it."

Viola opened drawers and looked through Esther's other purses, scattering them on the empty bed. Dr. Lenaburg joined Daisy in the search for a flashlight. In the kitchen, in a drawer, they found one.

The medical technician arrived with the ambulance. Dr. Lenaburg returned to the bedroom. Esther had been his patient for several years. She had never made a secret of her certainty that her death eventually would come from a heart attack. She believed heart trouble was congenital in her family.

"Just so it's quick," she would say, laughing. "That's all I ask."

Dr. Lenaburg pulled back the blankets, fully expecting to find that Esther had died of a massive coronary, or perhaps of a stroke.

When he saw extensive bloodstains on her arm, he at first was puzzled. The thought came to him that a stomach ulcer might have hemorrhaged, and that perhaps she had vomited in her sleep and strangled. That sometimes happened.

"Did she ever complain of stomach ulcers?" he asked Daisy.

But before she could answer, he moved the flashlight. Streaks of blood also covered her face. He pulled the blankets down to her waist.

Esther lay in a pool of coagulated blood. The blankets and sheets were soaked. Dr. Lenaburg moved the flashlight beam, seeking the source of the blood.

Esther's burgundy nightgown was ripped down the front. A puncture wound was visible just below the neck. Another was evident on the left side. A large clot below the left breast indicated yet another wound.

With the clotting, the exact nature of the wounds was not plain. But to Dr. Lenaburg they appeared to have been made by a .22- or a .30-caliber weapon.

He again moved the flashlight beam. Clotted blood was caked down the wall. Dr. Lenaburg did not explore further.

He raised his voice. "Don't touch anything," he cautioned Daisy and Viola. "I'm calling the police. This was a violent death. Esther has been shot."

For Daisy, the shock of Dr. Lenaburg's words was even greater than that of first finding Esther dead.

This was the kind of thing that happened on television. Not in Granite. Not to people you knew.

Charles Horton had just sat down to dinner with Pastor Bill Mease and his wife, Edna, when the phone rang. Mease excused himself and left the table to answer it.

Horton continued his conversation with Edna but kept one ear cocked, suspecting that the call might concern him. He had been anxious over leaving his wife in Cheyenne so close to delivery.

Bill Mease's voice rose in an exclamation, halting the conversation at the table. A moment later he returned, visibly shaken.

"Daisy just found Esther Steele dead in her bed," he said. "Daisy wants us to go to Esther's house immediately."

The Meases hurried to get their coats, preparing to leave. Horton felt out of place. This was an emergency in Bill Mease's congregation. As a visiting minister, he considered himself an outsider.

"I'll just stay here while you're gone," he said. "I don't want to intrude."

"No! You must come with us," Mease said. "Esther was so enthusiastic about your revival. She would want you there."

Horton acquiesced and accompanied the Meases to Esther's house in the Mease car.

An ambulance blocked the drive. Mease parked at the curb. Horton followed the pastor and his wife up the walk toward the front door.

Just as Mease raised his hand to knock, a medical technician burst through the door. His eyes were wide.

"There's been foul play here," he said to the Meases. "Esther was shot."

He rushed out to the ambulance, leaving the door open. Horton followed the Meases into Esther's living room, more than ever unsure that he should be there. Other people arrived, spilling in the front door. Everyone kept expressing shock and disbelief. Repeatedly they warned each other not to touch anything.

Horton and the Meases moved out of the traffic, into Esther's dining room. Standing there, waiting to learn more of what had happened, Horton recalled a portion of his sermon on the previous night. It was a memory that was to haunt him through the next several months.

In stressing that Jesus Christ had brought a New Testament, Horton had contrasted this message with the "eye for an eye" code of the Old Testament. He had expressed his belief that in the Christian perspective, capital punishment was wrong, even for murder. And now, less than twenty-four hours later, he stood in the home of a murdered woman who had canceled her scheduled trip to the symphony to hear his sermon tonight.

At his side, Edna Mease also was thinking of the previous evening. She remembered that at the start of the service, Esther had crossed the sanctuary, handed Edna a birthday card, and hurried back to her seat.

Inscribed on the card was Esther's handwritten comment that she had a reason for being glad, other than that it was Edna's birthday. April was here. Soon they again would be out bird-watching together.

Gazing down at Esther's unmailed Easter cards, Edna wondered if she could bear to go bird-watching ever again.

Bill Mease also was remembering an outing with Esther. Not long ago Esther had guided the Meases and a select group to a secluded field near a lake just before sunset. As they sat quietly with car windows lowered, birds started arriving, as Esther had known they would—hundreds of birds, perhaps thousands. They had surrounded the group, oblivious to the cars, singing into the sunset. Meadowlarks, mockingbirds, robins, more birds than Mease could readily identify.

That sunset and the serenade of the birds had been a wonderful, moving, spiritual experience. Mease knew he would never forget it.

Somehow, at the moment, the memory seemed fitting.

Police Chief L. D. Williams arrived, made his way past the crowd at the door, and went down the hall to Esther's bedroom.

A moment later he was back. He raised his voice. "Everybody out!" he ordered. "This is a crime scene. The house must be sealed."

Horton followed the Meases back outside. A crowd had now gathered on the sidewalk at the front of the house. Horton was familiar with these small towns. When the hint of trouble or disaster threatens, no one bothers to ask if his or her help is needed. The fire department is all-volunteer and the boundaries of officialdom are vague. Everyone piles into car or pickup and hurries to the scene, prepared to help.

But the authorities had arrived, and Esther was beyond help. Horton and the Meases returned to the church. The sanctuary, filling for the final night of the revival, was abuzz. The congregation was plainly in shock over the news of the murder.

Mease and Horton conferred only briefly.

"There is no way we can conduct services tonight," Horton said. "No one's mind would be on it."

So the concluding night of the revival—and the sermon Esther had remained in town to hear—was canceled.

Most of the congregation left the church and joined the crowd on Main Street.

The news continued to spread. Within an hour virtually everyone in the community knew that Esther Steele had been murdered in the bedroom of her home. More and more people came and stood in front of her house, as if by their presence they somehow could express their shock and dismay.

And close behind the shock came fear.

Who could have done this? Who was the murderer?

The crowd milled, exchanging mutual speculation. Word circulated that Chief Williams had notified Greer County sheriff Alfred Rogers, who was calling in the Oklahoma State Bureau of Investigation—the OSBI.

Daisy Brown returned to her own home. She looked out her front door on an amazing sight. In the last rays of the setting sun, people were standing five and six deep on each side of Main Street, from Mountain Avenue all the way downtown, awaiting the arrival of the OSBI. The whole town seemed to be there.

Daisy had never before seen anything like it. Not in Granite.

4 ▪ ▪ ▪

OSBI AGENT JERRY SUNDERLAND PICKED
up on the third ring. At this time of day, calls
to his home on the unlisted phone invariably
concerned business. He recognized the voice
of Greer County sheriff Alfred Rogers.

"Jerry? You know Esther Steele, don't you?
In Granite?"

"I'm acquainted with her," Sunderland
said. He waited.

"L. D. Williams just phoned. They found
her dead in bed. Nightgown ripped. Shot several times. No weapon at the scene. Billfold
seems to be missing."

The sheriff's words triggered an instant flood of memories. But Sunderland

long ago had learned to shove personal feelings aside while
working.

It was a trick that came with experience.

"They just now found her," Rogers went on. "I haven't been over
there yet. I'm calling you for OSBI assistance."

"We'll respond," Sunderland said. "Consider me on my way. I'll
see you in Granite."

On breaking the connection, Sunderland reflexly logged the time
of the call—5:48 P.M. He was aware that the entry was the start of
what undoubtedly would become a mass of field notes. If all went
well, someday his notes might be used to help convict someone on
murder one.

The procedure on calls for assistance was clearly delineated.
Sunderland dialed his home office and requested a crime scene processing team. He logged that call at 5:50 P.M. The team would have
to drive all the way from Oklahoma City. The sooner they started,
the better.

He then called his partner, Richard Goss, who lived in Lawton,
fifty-eight miles to the east of Sunderland's own home in Altus. That
call also was brief. They did not waste words. In a murder case, quick
arrival at the scene often helped to preserve evidence.

Not until he was on the road for the eighteen-mile drive to
Granite did Sunderland allow his personal feelings to surface.

Esther Steele! Murdered!

That seemed absolutely incredible.

Sunderland had grown up in Granite. As a boy he had played in
Granite's streets and on the surrounding mountains. His parents
had grown old and died there. They were buried there. He knew
most everyone in town.

Driving to Granite was, in a way, a homecoming.

And he was going back there to investigate a murder!

The first shock was that there *had been* a murder in Granite.

The second shock, right on the heels of that, was the identity of
the victim.

Sunderland could not keep from thinking ahead. Involvement in the murder investigation of even the most casual acquaintance was never easy. And he recognized another complication. His wife also had lived in Granite. She also knew Esther Steele. Sunderland could see that this case might bring serious difficulties into his own life.

Yet he could not help but marvel that he was going back to investigate a murder in the place where his career began.

He had always known, from childhood on, that he wanted to spend his life in police work. After his graduation from high school in 1954, and army service, he had worked as a guard at the reformatory near Granite. After six years, he left to obtain his degree at Southwestern Oklahoma State University in Weatherford. To pay his way, he had worked as a policeman for the city of Weatherford. By then he was married and had three children—a daughter, Memory, and two sons, Shawn and Shay.

Carrying a heavy academic load, he had finished college in three years. He had been a full-time student and a full-time policeman, with a wife and three children.

Sunderland and his wife did not see much of each other through those three years. A year after his graduation, he was divorced. He won custody of his three children.

At that time—in the late sixties—unrest was common on college campuses all over the nation. Sunderland was asked to set up a security division at Northeastern Oklahoma State University at Tahlequah.

For the next several years he helped solve those problems.

In 1971, he joined the OSBI as an agent. But from the first he felt the effects of the long hours and heavy responsibilities.

In practice the bureau serves as a major crimes unit for the state of Oklahoma. Its agents are expected to take the investigative lead in cases beyond the capabilities of sheriffs and police departments in smaller municipalities.

As the crime rate rose steadily through the early seventies, Sunderland found himself working increasingly longer hours. For days, even weeks, he was away from home investigating crimes, making arrests, testifying in court.

He wanted to spend more time with his children, so in 1975 he returned to the Oklahoma State Reformatory as warden. His parents were still alive and residing in Granite. He welcomed the chance to be near them in their declining years.

He had relished the challenge of the job as warden. As a boy, working in the fields, he often had looked over at the reformatory across the river and wondered what in the world went on in there, behind those walls. He had never dreamed then that someday he would be there as warden.

He always felt that perhaps no one who has not held the job of warden can understand the full weight of the burdens. A warden is responsible not only for the lives and safety of a prison full of convicts but also for the large staff hired to control them. With so many violent men in unnaturally close confinement, the danger is inescapable. And the job also imposes a hazard of a different sort: in time, every prison administrator becomes overwhelmed with the futility of it all. Prison populations kept expanding and budgets kept shrinking. Wardens were expected to do more with less. Everything had changed. With new court rulings and new laws, such traditional disciplinary tools as solitary confinement and mail restrictions had been taken away. The courts had given the inmates law books, and now all of them considered themselves to be legal experts. In effect, they were running the prison system.

Sunderland endured as warden for nine years. He left in August 1984 and returned to the OSBI.

His father died in 1984. His mother now had been dead only three months.

Sunderland thought ahead to the coming investigation.

This one promised to be different.

He had always felt that newspaper headlines and television dramas tended to give the public a false picture of murder. Contrary to the impression fostered by the media and screen dramas, only a small fraction of murders involved random violence. Of residential homicides, eighty-five percent still remained family- or friend-related.

So that is the way an investigator thinks, going into a case.

He starts with the family.

But Sunderland knew Esther's family. He had been well acquainted with her husband, Warren. He knew her brother, O. C. Kruska. He had dated one of Esther's nieces in high school. Esther's nephew, Jay Kruska, was his dentist.

He knew them all!

Sunderland kept turning over possibilities as he drove to Esther's house, trying to imagine who would commit such a crime.

In *Granite!*

The bright sun had warmed the late afternoon into the lower seventies. Flora Mae had gone out to work for a while in her flower beds, to enjoy what was left of the springlike day. She did not hear the phone ringing inside the house, and had missed Daisy's call.

Lucille and Raymond Massey, close friends and neighbors, came with the news that something terrible had happened to Esther, that the ambulance and police cars were at her house.

O.C. had gone out to one of his farms to move a center-pivot sprinkler system. Raymond said he would go get O.C.

Flora Mae and Lucille hurried to Esther's house.

The policemen at the front door refused to allow them to enter. So they stood for a time in the crowd, gathering what information they could.

O.C. and Raymond arrived a few minutes later. Chief Williams refused to let O.C. go into his sister's house to see firsthand what had happened to her.

"That was silly," O.C. felt. "There were a dozen deputies and emergency people plunking around all over. If there had been any evidence, they had already tromped it down. Most of them didn't know what the hell they were looking for in the first place."

The sun had set. Dusk was deepening. Still in shock, and unable to do anything at the scene, O.C. and Flora Mae drove back home to start the notification of out-of-town relatives.

They called their grown children. Then cousins phoned cousins so someone would be present when the news was relayed to Esther's other sisters: Lenore, in Oklahoma City; Rosalie, in Fort Worth; and Polly, in Sherman, Texas.

During a break in the calling, the phone rang. Flora Mae answered, assuming that the call would concern Esther.

But it was one of her own sisters, conveying more shocking news: Flora Mae's brother, Carl Warner, and his wife, Lavada, visiting their grown children in California, had been involved in a head-on collision earlier in the afternoon. Carl, Lavada, and their daughter Sherry were in intensive care, not expected to live.

News of the two family tragedies had hit O.C. and Flora Mae in less than thirty minutes.

The situation on the West Coast was in the hands of God and the medical doctors.

But Esther's death left a question that rapidly became an obsession: Who could have killed her?

In his shock, grief, and anger, O.C.'s mind kept returning to that question.

He knew that time would take care of the shock.

The grief, too, could be handled.

But from that first day, O.C. knew he would spend the rest of his life contending with the anger.

Sunderland turned onto Granite's Main Street at 6:29 P.M. Darkness had fallen. As he passed the business district and approached Esther's house, his headlights raked over a large crowd awaiting his arrival.

He drove the last block with his car surrounded by people. Everyone knew him. Some were shouting his name. He knew all of them. The instant he stepped out of his car, he was mobbed. Some were trying to tell him about the murder. Others wanted to find out what he knew.

Sunderland pushed his way through the throng to Esther's front door.

Sheriff Rogers and Police Chief Williams were still on the scene, along with their staffs.

"Sheriff, couldn't we at least clear the yard?" Sunderland asked.

He knew it was a useless gesture. If footprints had existed, they were now gone.

He went into Esther's bedroom and made a preliminary inspection of the body and of the crime scene. He took notes with professional objectivity:

Observed victim to be a white female approximately 74 years of age, lying on her back in a twin bed on the west side of the bedroom. Victim's red nightgown appeared to be torn and pulled down, exposing both breasts. Appeared to have been shot at least three times in the chest area. Punctures looked like .22 caliber. Electric blanket was set on Number 3.

House appeared exceptionally neat, with no indication of any burglary having taken place. Victim's 1986 Cadillac was parked in garage with keys in vehicle. Garage was not locked. Kleenex in seat similar to two lying on floor near victim.

When his partner, Richard Goss, arrived a few minutes later, Sunderland was ready with a gloomy assessment.

"The crime scene is totally destroyed," he told Goss. "The victim's purse, everything the killer might have handled, has been handled by others. People have been going in and out the doors. They've been into every drawer in the house hunting a flashlight, hunting her billfold. At least twelve or fifteen people have been in the house. Maybe more. God knows how many were in the bedroom. People have been all over the grounds, front and back. Partner, that's what we have to work with."

Younger than Sunderland, Goss had been married only four days. And now, with the start of a murder investigation, he could assume he would not be seeing much of his bride through the next several days, if not weeks.

Sunderland and Goss were different in temperament and in appearance.

In many ways, Sunderland is the antithesis of the stereotypical detective. He gives the impression of a man who has spent much time behind a desk, yet who could turn physical if the situation demanded. At five eight, he is heavyset, full-faced, with a tendency toward jowls. He approaches people with an easygoing manner and a loquaciousness atypical for one in his profession. But he is not a back-slapper. He simply possesses an intensity that makes people feel he considers his dealing with them the most important thing he could be doing at that moment. This riveting attention seems to work especially well with women.

"I don't know what women see in Jerry," a friend confided. "But they sure see something."

And one phrase is voiced almost everywhere his name is mentioned: "You can't help but like ol' Jerry."

In contrast, many people consider Goss aloof, even abrasive. Women invariably describe him as strikingly handsome. He is tall. His thick black hair is combed straight back, and he has quick, intelligent eyes. He grew up in Lawton—Oklahoma's third largest city—where he earned a degree at Cameron University. He had worked eight years with the Lawton Police Department before moving to the OSBI in October 1984.

People react in different ways to his cool, taciturn manner. Some like his quiet dignity. Others find him standoffish. He is good at staring down suspects and in cross-questioning them into inconsistencies and admissions of guilt.

Sunderland and Goss often worked the good-cop, bad-cop routine to perfection.

Sunderland's first priority was an interview with Daisy Brown, apparently the only person to view the crime scene in its pristine condition. And she was the last person to see Esther alive, other than the killer.

But her house was now full of people milling about, discussing the murder. He could not interview her there. And he did not want to take her back to the crime scene.

As a last resort, he escorted her through the crowd to his car. He closed the car doors, rolled up the windows, and he and Daisy sat in the front seat, surrounded by the crowd.

Sunderland began at the beginning. "How did you come to go over to Esther's house?"

Daisy explained. "Flora Mae called and asked if I'd seen her. I said I hadn't. Then I got to thinking. I hadn't seen her all day. That was unusual. I was afraid maybe she was sick."

Sunderland was aware that Daisy had the reputation of being flighty—in the best Southern sense of the word. But he was pleased to see that she was bearing up well and seemed to have a good grip on her emotions.

"You went in the back door?"

"Yes."

"Was it open or closed?"

Daisy hesitated, thinking back. "I'm not sure. It might have been open a little. But it wasn't latched. I'm sure of that. I went right in."

She explained that she and Esther were accustomed to entering each other's houses by knocking and calling out, rather than going through the formality of phoning.

Sunderland knew that was a widespread community practice. He wanted to get the matter of the doors out of the way.

"Did you close the door behind you?"

Again Daisy hesitated. "I really don't remember. I probably did."

"When Viola Cypert came, did she come in through the front or the back?"

"The back."

"And Dr. Lenaburg?"

"The front. That door was locked. I'm positive. I remember turning the bolt to let him in."

Sunderland reconstructed Daisy's entry into the house. She told of making her way through the kitchen and dining room, calling out.

"Did you see anything out of place?"

"No. I'm sure I would have noticed. There was a chair pulled out from the dining room table, where Esther sat to work on her Easter cards."

"Did you move it?"

"No. I remember turning sideways to get by it. There wasn't much room between it and the wall."

Sunderland had noticed the narrow passageway. Daisy's observation was valuable. She confirmed that the chair had not been moved during the search for a flashlight, or later by the people who entered the house.

Daisy described her progress through the living room and down the hall. She said the moment she saw Esther's outstretched arm she knew for certain something was wrong, and hurried to the bedside. She described the way the electric blanket was thrown over Esther, slightly askew.

"Did you touch the body?"

"Only her wrist, to see if there was a pulse. Of course the instant I felt her skin, I knew she was dead."

"You didn't bother the bedclothes, anything like that?"

"No."

"Were the lights in the bedroom on or off?"

"Off. Dr. Lenaburg turned them on. But the bulbs were too small. With that high ceiling, they didn't do much good. That's why we were hunting for a flashlight."

"Did you look under the blankets? Examine her face?"

"No. I went to the phone in the hall and called Dr. Lenaburg."

Sunderland took her back over it, approaching the questions from different angles. Daisy remained adamant on what she saw and did.

Sunderland questioned her about the previous evening. She told him the trip home from church had been routine.

"So you went into your house, and she went into hers?"

"Yes."

"Did you see anyone around on the street?"

Daisy thought back. "No."

But she said Esther had told earlier of hearing intruders. Daisy described the incidents as related by Esther. Daisy said Esther also had received obscene phone calls, but she did not know about them because Esther had not mentioned them to her. She had learned about them from mutual friends.

Sunderland took down the names of those friends, to follow up on later.

"When you came home from church, did you see any strange persons around?"

"No."

"Did you hear anything unusual during the night?"

"No."

Sunderland concluded the interview by telling her he probably would be talking further with her later. He escorted her back through the crowd to her house.

By now he was convinced that Esther's murder would not be solved quickly. Family and acquaintances would be routinely checked. But he sensed that perhaps he should jump ahead, widen the scope into the community.

One trick investigators often use is to determine if anything else unusual occurred in the same time frame, and to seek connections.

Sunderland went to Chief Williams. "Who worked the midnight shift?"

"Alan," Williams said. "Alan McCormack."

Sunderland found McCormack and took him into Esther's kitchen, where they could talk.

McCormack was well over six feet tall, and big, an overgrown teddy bear. He towered over Sunderland.

"I'm told you worked the midnight shift," Sunderland said. "Anything unusual occur?"

McCormack did not hesitate. Apparently he, too, had been thinking along those lines. "Two things. There was a wild party at Terry

Rhine's house. People were coming and going there all night. Then, toward morning, two guys from Mangum wrecked their pickup about four miles southwest of town."

"Two from Rhine's party?"

"Might have been. But I don't think so."

McCormack told what he had seen and heard of the party. A lot of yelling. Cars arriving and leaving. Considerable activity all night.

To Sunderland's ear, the party sounded promising. The host, Terry Rhine, was an ex-convict with a well-earned reputation for meanness. He hung out with a motley crowd.

Sunderland knew Rhine, and his background.

Everybody knew Terry Rhine.

Paroled from a ten-year sentence for armed robbery in Harmon County, he had returned to Granite and purchased a home next door to the post office where he lived with his wife, Susan Carol, and, if rumors were to be believed, a house full of snakes.

Furthermore, the location of Rhine's house offered easy access to Esther's home. A rock-lined drainage ditch ran behind Esther's house, straight south to within a stone's throw of Rhine's place. The ditch was four to five feet wide at the bottom, and five or six feet deep. As a boy, Sunderland had played along these streets. He was familiar with the ditch.

It could have provided the murderer with concealment from Rhine's house almost to Esther's back door.

And Sunderland considered Rhine perfectly capable of murder. Big and beefy, with long, scraggy hair, he seemed to take pride in resembling one of the menacing background hulks in a B-grade biker movie. He also lived the part. He usually roared in and out of town several times a day on his big motorcycle. He claimed to be a member of Hell's Angels.

Already Sunderland could see that Rhine and his party guests deserved quick attention, before they had a chance to assemble and agree on alibis.

"Alan, I'd appreciate it if you could give me a list of all the people you saw coming and going at that party," Sunderland said.

McCormack said he would work on it.

"Now, tell me about the wreck."

"Well, I'd gone home to eat. Along about four, Murley called me. He'd found this subject staggering along Main Street. This subject said he'd been in a wreck and that his friend was still out there, hurt. I went down to talk to him. He was pretty drunk. Couldn't even talk. Every time I'd ask him where the wreck was, he'd just point. I got him in the car and we drove out in that direction. I finally got out of him that it was close to a cemetery, and I knew it must be the Lutheran, so we finally found it. His buddy had been thrown through the windshield. The pickup was laying on its side. I called for an ambulance and notified the Highway Patrol. Both subjects were taken to Mangum Hospital."

Sunderland knew that Murley was Mitchell Dwayne Murley, who worked security in the kitchen at the reformatory. He would have been due at work at 4:00 A.M.

Sunderland made notes. He would talk to Murley, get his impressions.

"These two in the wreck. Were they bad hurt?"

"They looked more drunk than hurt. The one that went through the windshield was cut up some."

"Who worked the wreck?"

"Pettingill."

That would be Kerry Pettingill, Highway Patrol trooper. Sunderland knew him. "Who came with the ambulances?"

"Doug. Hayden. Eddie Graumann. Alan Gibbs. Johnny Wilson. Guy Brooks."

"Doug" would be Douglas McCormack, Alan's brother and an emergency medical technician. Charles Lynn Hayden would have been the ambulance driver. The others were emergency personnel, some better trained than others.

All needed to be interviewed.

Already the case was expanding exponentially.

At 8:30 P.M. the forensics team arrived. The four OSBI agents now on the scene—Sunderland, Goss, senior specialist Bruce

Richard Spence, and forensic chemist Alan Cornelius—had worked many cases together. Little conversation was required. Quietly they started processing the crime scene.

Spence made color photographs of Esther's body and of the bloodstains on the wall behind the bed. He photographed each room in the house, taking care to show detail and the route of access presumably followed by the killer.

After completing the photography, Spence dusted the entire house for fingerprints.

He did not find many. The house was neat, all surfaces well cleaned. The few latent prints he found lacked ridge detail. But from the inside left facing of the front door he lifted a well-defined partial palm print.

Cornelius vacuumed carpeting throughout the house, harvesting hair and fiber. He cut samples from the carpets. He did not take swabbings or fingernail clippings, or hairs from the bedding. That would be done later in Oklahoma City, where better facilities were available. But he carefully bagged each hand at the wrist to preserve any evidence.

Goss also took photographs. Then, while Spence and Cornelius continued their work, Sunderland and Goss carefully went over the house and grounds, seeking the murder weapon, any evidence that might help them put together the story of what happened.

The crime scene analysis would not be complete until reports came in from the medical examiner, from the various labs, and from FBI profilers.

But Sunderland and Goss agreed that at this point certain surmises could be made. The facts that the electric blanket switch was on, that Daisy had found the lights off, and that Esther was wearing a nightgown confirmed that she had gone to bed before she was killed.

And the murder could be placed within a loose time frame. Daisy had left Esther in the driveway about ten thirty or a quarter till eleven. Daisy had said Esther was an early riser. This would place the time of the murder between 11:00 P.M. and dawn. The medical

examiner probably would not be able to narrow that time frame sig-
nificantly, considering the complications caused by the warmth of
the electric blanket.

On visual examination, Sunderland and Goss agreed with Dr.
Lenaburg's impression that the wounds had been made with a small-
caliber firearm. But they did not move the body to search for exit
wounds, and they did not explore beneath the coagulated blood.

That was the job of the state medical examiner.

Room by room, square foot by square foot, Sunderland, Goss,
Spence, and Cornelius processed the crime scene, working on into
the night.

At a late hour, the investigators were surprised by the arrival of
H. Russell Wright, the district attorney, who had driven down from
Elk City.

After viewing Esther's body, Wright seemed especially incensed.

"Find the murderer," he told Sunderland and Goss. "I promise I'll
go for the death penalty."

Outside, the crowd had thinned only slightly.

As so often happens in the first hours after a death, the victim's
friends and acquaintances were just beginning to understand the
extent of what they and the community had lost. Esther's many contributions and good qualities were evaluated as perhaps never
before.

Throughout Esther's thirty-three years with the Granite school
system, she had been among those teachers who went far beyond all
anyone could expect of them. She routinely invited students into
her home for sessions of personal tutoring. Often she called on
friends to help take a student bird-watching, in an effort to make the
student's visit seem more social than remedial.

And for more than thirty years—through class after class—Esther
had sponsored an Audubon Club, taking students on weekly field
trips to study birds, animals, and nature. She always knew where to
find the different varieties of wildflowers. She knew where rare birds

nested. She seldom mentioned it, but some of her friends knew that nationally known ornithologists consulted her on bird counts, sightings, and migrations.

Esther's marriage had been an enigma to everyone. Esther, so warm, thoughtful, kind, and generous, was in many ways the opposite of Warren. Often a sentimental man, and fiercely loyal to a fault, Warren was still known for his snide and sarcastic remarks, especially while drinking, which for many years was much of the time.

Esther was intellectual. Warren was not. He objected to her keeping books and magazines on view in the house. He felt intimidated by them. Yet he took tremendous pride in Esther's scholastic attainments and endured many summers alone while she went off to various universities for seminars, short courses, and postgraduate work.

Both were hard workers. In addition to operating a service station, Warren distributed gasoline and oil in wholesale quantities to ranchers and farmers who maintained their own underground tanks. Usually he made these deliveries after closing the service station. Often he did not arrive home for dinner until late in the evening.

Esther was always neat and impeccably groomed. Warren usually wore rumpled khakis and the grease stains of his work. Somehow, Warren and the oil truck he drove never seemed to fit with Esther's immaculate housekeeping and her spotless big car. Yet the marriage apparently worked, at least for many years.

Eventually, Esther had filed for divorce. Most friends blamed Warren's drinking. Later they had remarried. Warren's long illness with colon cancer had been a tremendous burden on Esther. But she had stuck with him until the end.

"Esther was a tough lady," a close friend remarked after her death. "She had to be, to put up with Warren all those years."

Upon her retirement from teaching, and after Warren's death, Esther not only continued her many activities but took up more. She was active in the Oklahoma Arts Institute at nearby Quartz Mountain, where nationally known actors and actresses came to teach. Friends recalled an evening when institute administrators and government officials from all over the state had honored Esther. On this "Esther Steele Night," visiting dignitaries made speeches in her praise.

Esther never seemed to stop. She regularly took senior citizen groups on hikes to bird sanctuaries and to fields of wildflowers. She traveled in Europe and elsewhere. She seldom missed a home football game at the University of Oklahoma, and sometimes attended the out-of-state games as well. She was a patron of the arts in nearby Altus. She regularly attended concerts and performances there, in Oklahoma City, and on the OU campus at Norman. She thought nothing of driving across the state—at night, alone—to keep pace with all she wanted to do.

She was active in the Oklahoma Retired Teachers Association. She was enthusiastic about explorations into space and attended summer sessions at the University of Oklahoma to discuss how best to prepare young students for this exciting future. She was secretary of her church and attended all district meetings and conferences. In the hours after her death, stories of how much Esther had done for others abounded—driving the elderly to the doctor or shopping, or arranging outings for the infirm.

And beyond all this, she was intimately involved with her family. She routinely participated in the lives of her brother and sisters. She doted on her many nieces and nephews.

Lamentations over her murder invariably contained the observation that few persons had ever contributed as much to the community.

Inevitably, all discussion returned to one salient question:

Who could have murdered her?

Sprinkled among the throng in front of her house were individuals closely related to local policemen, sheriff's deputies, and emergency personnel. The crowd was receiving enough accurate information to fuel speculation. The fact that her nightgown had been ripped down the front became general knowledge and suggested that this was a sexual crime, adding to the horror.

As various scenarios were explored, one observation found consistent agreement: In her supreme self-confidence, Esther could be careless.

Some theorized that perhaps in the last few weeks, in her frequent late-night travels across the state, Esther might have stopped somewhere for gasoline or coffee. Maybe her killer recognized the possibilities—an older woman, well dressed, driving a large car, flashing a billfold presumably filled with credit cards and cash. Her killer might have followed her home and staked out her house for a future visit.

Or could she have angered someone?

Esther could be outspoken. She was strongly opinionated. She was forever quick to step into disputes to set things right. If two adults became embroiled within her earshot, she might enter the fray, as if stopping a dispute between two kids on the playground.

Or perhaps there was a psychological basis behind her murder. Maybe her authoritative, schoolmarmish manner had triggered some psychotic. She easily might have represented an authority figure, an unyielding older woman, from the killer's past.

Or could she have had a boyfriend, an affair turned sour?

Those who knew Esther well sensed that she kept her life compartmentalized. She was many things to many people.

But an affair?

Surely she was too involved with her groups, organizations, and helping others to be conducting an affair on the side. When would she find the time?

Other theories seemed more plausible.

Esther never met a stranger. Her uninhibited personality, high humor, musical voice, infectious laugh, and sincere interest in others might be mistaken as flirtatious. Perhaps an otherwise innocent encounter progressed to the point that it got out of hand and turned into a fatal attraction.

That was possible. Sometimes Esther called attention to herself by entering overheard conversations. If she had stopped at an all-night café for coffee and the talk at a nearby table concerned University of Oklahoma football, pro or con, Esther absolutely would not have kept quiet.

A more realistic possibility was voiced: with overcrowding at the reformatory, more than two hundred convicts now slept in dormitories outside its walls.

Could an inmate have slipped away after bedcheck, walked the three miles into town, murdered Esther, and returned before morning roll call?

But word soon passed that Police Chief Williams had looked into that possibility. None of the reformatory inmates was missing. None had blood on him or was marked in any way.

As the various theories and scenarios were explored, a terrible realization began to build: the murderer must be one of Granite's own.

All indications were there. The murderer had known the location of Esther's bedroom. And he had made his way through the dark house at night without bumping into furniture.

The prowler Esther had heard in her house in recent weeks was discussed. That, too, pointed to someone local. Anyone on the streets of Granite late at night would draw attention. Surely no one would prowl Granite at night unless he knew places to duck into to keep from being seen.

The obscene phone calls were discussed. It was agreed that they also were no doubt local. No one would be dumb enough to make such a call via long distance, with the exact time and calling number automatically recorded.

Gradually all speculation concluded that the murderer must be homegrown. And as that assumption became general, fear mushroomed.

More than a dozen elderly widows lived within two blocks of Esther's house. As the news of the murder continued to spread, relatives phoned from distant cities, urging the women to come visit for a few days, at least until the murderer was found.

All declined.

Some agreed to double up, in an impromptu buddy system. All were frightened. But just as Esther would not allow a prowler to force her to lock her doors, they refused to be driven out of their homes by an unknown killer.

Shortly after midnight, the crime scene processing was completed. The evidence, bagged and labeled, was ready for transport to the OSBI labs in Oklahoma City.

Bill Greer of the Greer Funeral Home in Mangum arrived with a hearse. Agent Alan Cornelius carefully placed the blue electric blanket, the yellow blanket, and the multicolored sheet in a bag, sealed it, and tagged it with his initials to preserve the chain of evidence.

Sunderland, Goss, Greer, Cornelius, and Spence gathered at the bedside. The mattress cover and blue sheet were folded over Esther's body.

With all helping, the entire mass was guided into a body bag.

At 12:30 A.M. the body was loaded into the hearse for the trip to Oklahoma City and the morgue of the state medical examiner.

At 1:15 A.M., the OSBI agents sealed the house.

For Sunderland, the familiar, gnawing intensity of an ongoing homicide investigation had taken firm hold.

Esther's killer was out there somewhere. The longer he remained free, the less likely it was he would be caught. Sunderland insists that the sense of urgency an investigator feels in such circumstances is beyond description.

"Until you work a homicide, you can't realize the concentration and the activity. Especially during the first few days."

And he felt other pressures.

"I had grown up there. Everybody knew me. They expected me to *do* something."

Also, in his spare moments, he worried that Esther's death might contribute to his wife's deteriorating condition.

Paula's trouble had begun eight years before, when she was divorcing her former husband, Steve Toole, a reformatory correctional officer. Sunderland had been over and over the details until he knew them by heart.

"They'd been to court that day. The judge had ordered Paula to give Steve some dishes and sheets and things like that. They left the courthouse in Mangum, and they lived in a house trailer in Granite. They went to the trailer. They had the baby with them. Paula was getting silverware out of the cabinet, and she heard the front door close. She looked around, and Steve had put the baby out on the front porch and locked the door.

"She said, 'Steve, what did you do that for?' And he raised his shirt up and pulled a gun out and said, 'I'm going to kill you.'

"He shot her five times. Twice in the head. And the last one, he had the gun right at the back of her head, and it went into her brain.

"The bullet fragmented. It was a .22. They got what they could out, but they had to leave a lot of fragments in there because they couldn't disturb the brain."

Steve also shot her twice in the back. One bullet remained lodged next to her spine.

He then shot and killed himself.

With five wounds, Paula survived.

And for a while, Paula's troubles seemed endless.

"There were a lot of rumors, a lot of bad feelings. Steve's mother accused Paula of killing Steve and then shooting herself. That's ridiculous! How could she shoot herself twice in the back and then in the back of the head?"

Sunderland, single and warden at the reformatory at the time, also was aware of the rumors that he and Paula were having an affair that precipitated the divorce.

"That is totally untrue. I knew Paula, but I didn't know her that well. I just knew her, basically, because Steve worked for me. I didn't come to know her well until she was out of the hospital and was coming out to the reformatory to see one of my deputies to get her insurance. We worked with Paula, collecting Steve's insurance for her. That's when I started dating her."

After his marriage to Paula, Sunderland took her two daughters to raise.

Now, eight years after the shooting, Paula's medical condition was worsening. She vividly relived the shooting in nightmares. She suffered from severe headaches. She often experienced difficulty breathing. And she was still troubled by intestinal problems as a result of the bullet wounds.

Sunderland had taken her to a number of specialists. None had been of much help. Her doctor—the one who had treated her initially—made periodic X-ray studies.

He thought the bullet fragments in her brain might be moving, causing the headaches.

Paula currently was under medication for severe depression. And she had known Esther.

"Not well. They didn't visit back and forth or anything like that. But Paula thought a lot of her."

Sunderland was deeply concerned over what effects Esther's murder, and his involvement in the investigation, might have on Paula.

5 ▪ ▪ ▪

THE FACT THAT ESTHER'S MURDER HAD been the first in the history of Granite was confirmed by Palmer Briggs, whose memory encompasses the entire life span of the town—and of the state of Oklahoma.

Palmer was born in April 1893 at Comanche Springs, five miles to the northeast of Headquarters Mountain. He was seven years old when the founder of Granite, K. C. Cox, staked out the first town lots.

He was fourteen when Oklahoma became a state.

"Time and dates become ridiculous," he insists from his vantage point of a hundred years of living. "I was born in Texas. My brother and sister were born in Oklahoma. All at Comanche Springs."

Today Palmer is a rare historical source. Most Texans have forgotten that the Lone Star flag flew for more than three decades over the Delaware-sized chunk of land between the forks of the Red River. In Texas the matter usually is relegated to no more than a footnote in history texts. Amidst the crazy quilt creation of Oklahoma— with scores of land rushes, lotteries, and collapsed Indian reservations—the story of Old Greer County also receives short shrift.

But Palmer knows the story. He was born into it.

His father, George W. Briggs, had been on his way west to the Texas Panhandle to join the great buffalo slaughter when, south of the Red, his wagon became hopelessly mired in mud. He saw two men nooning in the shade of a tree. He approached them to ask for help. One offered him a job. Already disillusioned with buffalo hunting before he started, George Briggs switched careers on the spot. He became a Texas cattleman.

The man who hired him was Dan Waggoner, the now-legendary Texas rancher.

Soon Briggs was foreman of a million-acre spread.

By 1880 the Chisholm Trail, ninety miles to the east, had become crowded. Many Texas ranchers, including Waggoner, began sending their herds via a shortcut up the North Fork of the Red River to the new railhead at Dodge City. Soon that trail, too, became crowded. Herds became mixed, and larded with strays. Tempers flared.

In 1881 Waggoner and other ranchers incorporated the four-year-old Texas Cattle Raisers Association and sent George Briggs into the disputed land as brand inspector, armed with sufficient authority to settle all disputes.

Briggs established his base camp at Comanche Springs. In his first year as range traffic cop, he counted more than 450,000 Texas cattle passing between Headquarters Mountain and Comanche Springs on their way to the Kansas markets.

Texas had laid claim to the land, and had named it Greer County, Texas, but the U.S. government insisted that the region was part of the Louisiana Purchase, and consequently U.S. territory. The controversy had been taken before the U.S. Supreme Court.

With the land unsettled and in legal limbo, Texas Panhandle ranchers moved huge herds in for permanent grazing. The trail cattle coming up from the south were immune to the diseases they carried. The Panhandle cattle were not. Again tempers flared. Briggs the peacemaker was instrumental in working out an agreement creating a trail corridor through the permanent range.

But with fall gluts on the Kansas markets, some south Texas ranchers began holding their herds in Greer County to await spring and a better price. The Panhandle ranchers were furious over the usurping of land they had usurped first. They placed advertisements in Texas range publications warning all trail drivers: "We're armed, and we mean business."

Again Briggs helped to keep the peace.

When the trail closed, and his duties with the Waggoners at last ended, Briggs remained at Comanche Springs. There he established his own ranch, and there Palmer was born and spent his boyhood.

"We saw more Indians than whites," he remembers. One Indian who visited often was Quanah Parker, the last great chief of the Comanches—and the last to surrender.

George Briggs had represented the Waggoners in leasing Comanche land. In fact, Briggs was Quanah's host in the famous incident in Fort Worth when Quanah's companion, Yellow Bear, was asphyxiated through unfamiliarity with gas lamps. Briggs had accompanied Quanah back to the reservation to help Quanah explain that Yellow Bear's death was not his fault. Quanah was forever grateful. Quanah and Briggs became close friends, and Briggs helped to teach Quanah the white man's language and ways.

"I can't really say I remember Quanah Parker," Palmer Briggs says. "I was about three or four the last time he visited Comanche Springs. I remember the talk about it. But I can't really say I remember him."

No schools existed in those days. George Briggs hired a private tutor for Palmer, his brother, and his sister. But in 1903—three years after Granite was founded—the Briggs family moved into town.

The Rock Island railroad had arrived. Palmer remembers the excitement.

"With three cotton gins humming, the monument works hammering, the gristmill grinding, and bawling cattle being loaded at the new railroad, the noise was almost overwhelming."

A two-story resort hotel had been built at Sulphur Springs on the eastern edge of the mountain. Visitors came great distances over the new railroad to bathe in and to drink water that smelled like rotten eggs. The town maintained a full-time professional band to entertain the guests.

Palmer remembers the immediate effect of statehood in 1907: Granite's seven saloons and twenty-one gambling houses were closed by padlock. Prohibition was implicit in the Oklahoma constitution.

Today Palmer drives his own car, does his own shopping, his own cooking. He has lost much of his hearing, but his mind remains sharp. A few years ago he fell and broke a hip. After surgery in Oklahoma City, the medical people wanted to warehouse him in a convalescent home.

Palmer would have none of it. He called his friends in Granite to come get him.

He hung onto ownership of Comanche Springs all through the years. He has no living descendants. His only son, Eddie, served in the navy during World War II and was among the first recalled for the Korean War. With three years of service already invested, Eddie decided to make the navy his career. He was promoted to full commander not long before his death of a heart attack.

Palmer still mourns the loss.

The land around Comanche Springs has never known a plow. Palmer wanted it kept just as it was. Recently he sold the land to his friend H. C. Ford, Jr., who shares his philosophy.

Palmer remembers a few face-to-face shootings in Granite. He remembers a violent death—in 1901—resulting from a barroom brawl.

But he is certain that Esther Steele was the town's first victim of cold-blooded murder.

． ． ．

For relatives, friends, and the hundreds of students Esther taught through the years, memories offered the only solace. Often it was the small, caring gesture that came to mind.

Her nephew Kenneth Lemke—Rosalie's son—remembered that when he was entering the military, he misjudged the time between resigning his job and his departure. The unexpected interval without income temporarily placed him in a serious financial bind.

"I don't know how Aunt Esther knew," he said. "But she did. She didn't ask. She just sent me some money."

His sister, Paula Branch, remembered that when she lost almost everything in a house fire, her Aunt Esther was the first to track her down by phone.

Esther did not waste time with lamentations or amenities.

"What do you need?" Esther asked. "What can I do to help?"

Some of Esther's caring gestures were done with such subtlety that the recipient hardly noticed.

"Right after I was married, Esther asked me to grade some scholastic papers," recalled Jan Wingo Locklear, publisher of the *Granite Enterprise*. "Looking back, I realize she was helping me find work, make some money when I needed it. I've never forgotten that kindness."

Esther's financial habits were an enigma to her brother, O.C. At times she could be exasperatingly tightfisted. Unexpectedly, she could be remarkably generous.

Edna Mease, the pastor's wife, remembered such an act of generosity.

"When we first came to the church, Esther was with a committee refurbishing the parsonage. The committee had bought two new chairs for the living room. But the new furniture just made the old sofa look worse. On her own, Esther bought a matching divan. She didn't say anything to anyone about it. She just did it."

Some of her extravagances were almost whimsical.

"When we were kids, she bought a boat, just to take us water-skiing," Kenneth Lemke recalled.

O.C. also remembered the boat. "Warren and I tried to talk her out of buying it. We knew the work involved, keeping a boat. But she went ahead and bought it. I guess maybe she was right."

But some of Esther's most lasting gifts were not monetary.

"One of my sons was in her class," said Gene Hahn, Granite's city clerk. "He's grown now. But to this day he can identify birds a block away. He can name them just from their songs. Esther awakened that interest in him. He never lost it."

Years before, Esther selected fifth-grade student Mark Thomas as reporter for the Audubon Club. She showed him how to prepare releases for the county newspapers. He saw his words in print.

"That was the start," Thomas remembered.

He studied journalism, became a newspaper reporter, and went into advertising. He is now with the Oklahoma Press Association in Oklahoma City.

"I wish I had let her know how much she helped me," Thomas said in retrospect. "She guided me into a career."

He reminisced on the high standards she set.

"My science project in her class was a display of the different types of granite. One side of each had to be polished perfectly smooth. I spent hours and hours on it. That was the year the astronauts landed on the moon. She made sure we didn't miss a thing."

"Aunt Esther never settled for mediocrity," agreed her niece Penny Kruska Hook.

When Penny was an infant, and her brother, Jay, was three, her father, J.C., died in his sleep of a massive heart attack.

Their mother later remarried. But Esther always seemed to devote special attention to Jay and Penny.

Jay, now a dentist, remembered the childhood birthday parties Esther tossed for him.

"She'd say, 'You bring your friends over, and we'll spend the night at my house.' And we'd have a slumber party. She would do all kinds of stuff like that."

He also remembered that Esther somehow managed to impose a certain discipline on him and on his sister, Penny.

"Somehow, she made work enjoyable. She did that with a lot of people, and I think with Penny and me especially. She was like another mother to us."

On her graduation from Duke University, Penny won a Rotary International scholarship for two years of postgraduate study in Berlin.

Penny's quest for knowledge eventually took an unusual turn. After completion of her postgraduate work, she became an apprentice baker. For two years she lived with bakery families in small villages in southern Germany and in Austria, learning the art of baking bread.

Most of Penny's family considered the apprenticeship a giant step backward for a person of her academic attainments.

"For them, education was highly desirable, of course," Penny remembered. "But at some point you were expected to stop and put it to practical use. Like in a good job."

Esther traveled to Germany to give Penny moral support. Penny talked Esther into cashing in her structured tours, and the two roamed Germany and Europe, utilizing the skills Penny had acquired for mingling with the populace. They took in Oktoberfest and traveled into then-verboten areas behind the Iron Curtain.

"I can't believe some of the things they did," Jay said. "I just can't imagine Aunt Esther doing that."

Afterward, Penny spent two years with World Vision in Ethiopia and Somalia. She emerged with a true world vision.

In her perspective, learning the art of baking bread and feeding the hungry were a logical extension of the wheat fields of home.

Like so many others, Penny received the news of Esther's death with a devastating sense of personal loss.

"Aunt Esther was the only one who really understood."

6 ∎ ∎ ∎

ESTHER'S BODY WAS PLACED UNDER
refrigeration in Oklahoma City at 3:10 A.M.
Five hours later, Dr. Fred Jordan, chief medical examiner for the state of Oklahoma,
arrived at the morgue and donned his sur-
gical gear preparatory to conducting the
autopsy.

The burgundy nightgown, mattress cover,
and top layers of bedding that came with the
body already had been bagged and moved to a
storage area to await pickup by OSBI personnel. Photographer Jerry Peters was at work at
the steel autopsy table, photographing the
body, completing preliminary documentation
of wounds and abrasions, and the patterns of

bleeding. His color photographs would become a part of the permanent record.

Dr. Jordan waited until Peters had finished. He then moved forward to begin his work.

During his eighteen-year career as a forensic pathologist, Dr. Jordan had performed at least six thousand autopsies, perhaps as many as ten thousand; he often was asked to estimate, but he had never bothered to count.

Of medium height, with a lean, trim frame, Dr. Jordan still retained an athletic appearance. His thin mustache, short hair, and glasses lent him a scholarly demeanor, supported by his self-confidence and relaxed manner.

He began with the external examination, dictating his notes into an overhead microphone.

"Height five-ten. Weight one hundred and forty-five. Rigor mortis has come and gone. At least I find none present. Livor mortis is poorly defined."

He wondered for a moment about the lack of livor mortis, the settling of blood after death. Apparently the lady had lost most her blood before dying.

He paused to make diagrams depicting abrasions around the mouth and across the nose. He noted that the neck was bruised, but not extensively.

Reports from the field had indicated that this was a shooting victim. But on examining the wounds, Jordan encountered a surprise.

The lady had been stabbed.

Clearly, the punctures had been made by a sharp, narrow instrument. Dr. Jordan explored their locations and depth, logging each into the record.

The first stab wound, to the abdomen just below the navel and slightly to the left, was almost superficial. The second, high into the left side of the chest, just under the clavicle, was deep. The third, under the left breast, had penetrated into the chest cavity in the area of the sixth rib. The fourth, lower on the left side, also had penetrated deeply. The fifth, also on the left side, had fractured the seventh rib. The sixth, high at the back, fractured the third rib, which apparently partially deflected the blow. There the sharp instrument had not entered the chest cavity.

Dr. Jordan also found an entrance and exit wound in the fleshy portion of the upper left arm. He noted that the wound lined up perfectly with the one on the lower left chest.

Apparently both were made with the same thrust. The blade had gone completely through the arm and into the chest.

He examined the hands. The inside of each thumb bore deep lacerations.

The lady had put up a battle. She had grabbed the knife, or whatever sharp instrument was used. The thumb cuts were classic examples of what lawyers call "defensive wounds."

He examined the eyes. There he found telltale petechial hemorrhage.

The lady had been partially asphyxiated.

Whether that came before or after the stabbings, he had no way of determining.

While his assistant drew blood for typing and toxicity tests, Dr. Jordan prepared the labels.

Since the start of the AIDS epidemic, the autopsy procedure had changed. Now they were more watchful in guarding against contamination. Dr. Jordan applied the appropriate label to each specimen his assistant handed to him.

The assistant took samples of scalp and pubic hair, and clipped the fingernails. Dr. Jordan made swabbings from the interior of the anus and mouth.

Using a speculum, he assembled swabbings from the cervix and vagina.

Each item of evidence was carefully bagged, labeled, and initialed. Some of the swabbings would go to his own lab. Others would be sent to the OSBI lab.

Still speaking into the microphone, Dr. Jordan observed that the vagina was badly bruised.

"An area of an inch or more is a deep reddish blue, indicating that the lady was raped at some time before her death."

He then opened the body and began the internal examination.

Probing, he determined that the sharp instrument the murderer had used was exceptionally narrow, sharp on one side, and dull on the other. He estimated the width of the blade at three-quarters of an inch maximum. A precise measurement was not possible. Straight-in and straight-out stabbings are rare. Usually a blade moves to some degree laterally. Dr. Jordan estimated the length of the blade as about six inches. But that, too, could not be determined accurately. The chest expands and contracts. A knife thrust on exhalation would penetrate deeper than the same thrust at the peak of inhalation.

He explored the path of each thrust and examined the internal damage. The highest frontal wound on the torso, near the left clavicle, went across soft tissues and into the upper right portion of the right lung. The next, just below the left breast, went upward into the left ventricle of the heart. The third, lower down, injured the left lung, ruptured the diaphragm, and penetrated the right ventricle of the heart.

As he had assumed from his external examination, the abdominal wound was not deep. Perhaps the lady had partially fended off the blade on that thrust.

The stab wound on the lower left, where the seventh rib was broken, cut into the pleura of the lung. The thrust high on the back had struck the third rib and did not penetrate the chest cavity.

He checked the airways. The throat showed some petechial hemorrhage, about what he would expect after examining that in the eyes. But he could find no major hemorrhage into the airways. Certainly not enough to account for the partial asphyxiation.

The lady had either been smothered, perhaps by a pillow over her face, as the abrasions about the mouth and nose might indicate, or partially strangled, as indicated by the neck bruises.

The exact cause could not be determined with certainty.

The sac around the heart still held about 150 cubic centimeters of blood.

Attorneys always asked Dr. Jordan to define measurements in lay terms. He had devised a graphic definition for 150 ccs of blood.

"That's about a coffee mug full," he often told jurors.

The left pleural cavity contained about 500 to 700 ccs.

"That's about what you give when you donate blood," he usually explained to jurors.

The lady had been a fighter. Even with extensive damage to both ventricles of the heart, a punctured lung, a ruptured diaphragm, painful penetration of the pleura, and partial asphyxiation, she had remained alive long enough to do considerable bleeding.

He knew that if the lady's killer was ever brought to trial, he probably would be asked to estimate the length of time she suffered before death. He felt he safely could say that she might have lived as long as five minutes after the stabbings.

Carefully he dissected the organs to be biopsied. He opened the cranium, examined the brain, and made biopsies.

The work was tedious and time-consuming. He did not finish until just before noon.

He had other work to do. An assistant would apply the fixative to the slides he needed to study under a microscope, and he would look at them the first thing tomorrow.

In the meantime, his preliminary findings would be sent to OSBI agents in the field.

Dr. Jordan's initial report—revealing that Esther had been stabbed, not shot—came as a complete surprise to the OSBI agents in Granite.

"I wish we could keep that quiet," Sunderland said to Goss. "It'd give us an edge. But I guess that'll be impossible."

It was. Local authorities had to be informed. Within hours the information spread through the community.

Six OSBI agents were now on the case. A room had been set

aside for their use at the back of Granite City Hall. A phone provided access to their home office—and to the many tips coming in.

Although Jerry Sunderland had received the initial call from
Sheriff Rogers, and had been first on the scene, his caseload was
heavy. Richard Goss was named case agent.

Goss and Sunderland agreed that priority should be given to
Terry Rhine and his all-night party.

But other individuals also needed to be interviewed. Goss and
Sunderland sat down and made a list that included people known to
be at the party, members of Esther's family, Esther's neighbors and
close friends, and everyone in town known to have been out running
around that night.

The list was broken down, assignments were made, and the
agents spread out to conduct the interviews.

Goss brought in Terry Rhine. Despite his size and reputation,
Rhine offered no resistance. To the contrary, he was effusive in
pledging his full cooperation.

He was aware that most everyone in town considered him the
prime suspect.

"I was home all night," he told Goss. "I never left the house. I was
with people every minute. Just ask them."

He gave Goss a list of everyone who had attended his party.

The first of the party guests Sunderland interviewed—a young
high school student—indeed provided Rhine with a strong, if unwill-
ing, alibi.

She said Rhine had been incessant in his efforts to get her into
bed all night.

The young woman was from Arizona, residing in Granite with
her grandparents while attending high school. She told Sunderland
that when she attempted to leave the party, Rhine had grabbed her
by the arm, held her, and invited her to stay and sit on his face.

She said that when she attempted to pull free and leave, Rhine
struck her. Her face was bruised.

Sunderland and Goss urged her to file a complaint. An assault
charge would allow them to jail Rhine for a couple of days and per-

haps put some pressure on him. If nothing else, it would keep him off the streets while they sorted out the sequence of events at his party.

But after her encounter with Rhine, and after Esther's murder, the young woman was badly frightened.

"I'm going back to Arizona," she said.

And she did.

After the first series of interviews with party guests, the OSBI agents returned to the back room at City Hall and compared notes. They pored over them for hours, pitting each version against the others, hunting for discrepancies.

Then they went back out for further interviews, focusing on those discrepancies.

In the wake of the preliminary report from the state medical examiner, Goss and Sunderland decided to launch an immediate, massive search for the murder weapon, for Esther's missing billfold, and for any other clues that might be found.

Sunderland phoned his successor at the reformatory, Warden Dave Miller. Every off-duty correctional officer came into town to help. Members of the Sheriff's Department, the Granite Police Department, and volunteer officers from surrounding towns and counties took part.

They joined forces and walked every square inch of ground for blocks around Esther's house. They examined the rock ditch inch by inch. They canvassed the town on foot—the alleys, the yards. They sifted through the garbage in the town's fifty-two Dumpsters.

The daylong search was unsuccessful.

Except in fitful moments of exhaustion, sleep became a lost art for O.C. His every waking moment was filled with one question: *Who?*

At times anger threatened to consume him. The injustices done to Esther were now being compounded almost hourly.

Her murder had made the front page of the *Daily Oklahoman*, and was treated on every television newscast. Yet none of the television stations or newspapers had made the slightest effort to find out anything about her, who she was, what she did, or what she had meant to the community.

In every news account, she was written off as "a seventy-three-year-old retired schoolteacher." The implication seemed to be that she had been half dead anyway.

And they kept calling her "an easy target."

O.C. knew Esther had not been an easy target. She had been physically strong. Not long ago friends had told of seeing her leading a bunch of panting schoolkids up a mountain trail, lecturing all the way. She exercised routinely in her home. She also drove to Altus to maintain a regular schedule of workouts at a spa. When she became drowsy on her cross-country trips late at night, she would stop her car at some lonely spot and run up and down the road to fight sleep.

O.C. had caught her at that.

She might have been too overconfident, too careless, and exceedingly foolish in her refusal to lock her doors.

But an easy target? Never.

O.C. also rankled under the inactivity now imposed upon him. He had to force himself to remain quiet and allow the police to do their work. He limited his participation to trips down to City Hall to observe those brought in for questioning, to offer what help he could to the OSBI agents.

Ordinarily, he would have been preoccupied with the details of Esther's funeral. But that, too, had been put on hold. No one could tell him when her body might be released. It had been explained to him that results of various lab tests were awaited, to determine if they needed to be repeated or if further studies would be required.

He had contacted Esther's lawyer. Her will named O.C. executor of her estate. But there again he was stymied. Her house remained sealed. He could not even examine her account books and make an inventory of her possessions.

And no one could give him an estimate on when the house might be released.

Flora Mae was spending much of her time on the phone. Her brother, sister-in-law, and niece were still clinging to life. The doctors said that if they survived, each would face a long series of operations, that their lives would never be the same.

In his frustration, O.C. was relieved when Richard Goss came to interview him.

Earlier, he had thought that since he knew Jerry Sunderland, he might feel more comfortable talking of personal matters with him rather than with a total stranger. But from the first, O.C. liked Goss's no-nonsense manner and quiet concentration.

Goss even seemed attuned to O.C.'s feelings and seemed to understand his anger.

Goss asked O.C. many questions he already had asked himself. He did not need to ponder over the answers. No, he could not think of anyone in Esther's life who might wish this calamity upon her. He could not imagine anyone around her capable of committing such a crime.

O.C. gave Goss a summation of Esther's background. He explained that the family—the Kruskas—had always been close, perhaps because on their father's side they were first-generation Americans.

Their father had landed in Texas from Germany at the age of six, accompanied by his parents, a sister, and a brother. Their mother, a music teacher, had been a true "Texas fraulein," the daughter of a rancher near Somerville.

O.C. explained that in those years before World War II, large sections of central and south Texas contained German enclaves where English was the second language. Born and reared in America, their mother had spoken English with a German accent throughout her life.

Their parents married in 1910. The bride was thirty-three, the groom thirty-eight. It was the first marriage for both. They quickly made up for the late start on a family. Lenore was the oldest. Esther was next. Then came Viola, Olga (called Polly), Rosalie, and the two boys, J.C. and O.C.

O.C. was the youngest.

Their father had bought a farm south of Granite in the new state of Oklahoma. There the Kruskas settled in 1910. So Esther was born in Oklahoma. But when she was eight, the family moved back to Corpus Christi, Texas, where she grew up and finished high school. She was graduated from Southwest Texas State College at San Marcos in central Texas.

The family returned to Granite in 1934, in the depths of the Depression. Esther began her teaching career at Liberty, a rural school south of Granite. In those difficult years, sometimes the school did not have the money to pay her the promised thirty dollars a month.

Later she taught in the Lone Wolf school system, six miles to the east of Granite. Then, at the start of World War II, she started teaching at Granite.

In all, she had taught school for forty-two years.

And she still kept in contact with many of the hundreds of students she had taught.

O.C. explained to Goss that Esther had remained busy in many areas—the arts, the church, retired teachers, nature groups, the universities. He said he could not begin to name all her friends and acquaintances.

"But she was well known and widely respected. She wasn't just a seventy-three-year-old retired schoolteacher," he concluded.

To Goss, O.C. confided a theory that had been building ever since the murder.

"Richard, she was physically strong. She was active. I know she would have fought with all of her strength. It would have been a job keeping her on that bed. I'm convinced that either it was a large man, or else there were at least two of them."

Goss asked about the obscene telephone calls, the prior entries into her house.

"She identified the person who had been coming into her house,"

O.C. revealed. "She didn't tell me until after the man died, because she knew I'd have done something about it. But that's the way she was. She wouldn't say anything bad about anybody."

The man had been a hard drinker. O.C. said that as far as he knew, the man's death had been natural.

And to Goss, O.C. voiced his frustration: "Not a month ago I asked Esther to do two things. First, I begged her to take it easier, to get more rest, to take better care of herself. And second, I asked her to lock that damned door. She did neither."

Only one full day into the investigation, Sunderland already was regarding the murder as the hardest he had ever worked. To begin with, it was the first where everyone in town knew him—and singled him out to voice suspicions.

Each time he started out to conduct an interview, he was stopped by a delegation of elderly gentlemen who advised him whom he should go talk to, even whom he should arrest.

He had known most of the old gentlemen all of his life. He did not feel he could just walk away from them. And besides, they knew the community. Their tips and observations might be valuable. He felt he must stop and listen to what they had to say.

Most wanted Terry Rhine arrested.

Sheriff Rogers and Police Chief Williams concurred.

But Sunderland and Goss resisted community pressure, for by the end of that first day they had become almost totally convinced that Rhine and his party had had nothing to do with the murder.

The agents met repeatedly in the back of City Hall to go over the results of their interviews. Rhine's party had been fueled by drugs and liquor. But all witness accounts dovetailed; alibis appeared unshakable.

And while it seemed unlikely that Rhine's wild party had taken place only one block from a murder and that the two were uncon- nected, the intense investigation had failed to find a link.

The agents felt frustrated that after all their work they had come up dry. But much had been accomplished in twenty-four hours. The entire town had been searched for the murder weapon and for the missing billfold. Mangum authorities had been contacted concerning the two young men who had wrecked their pickup southwest of town. Neither had a record of consequence. Esther's neighbors and all members of her immediate family had been interviewed. Many tips had been checked out.

Yet nothing solid had been developed.

Clearly it was time to expand the scope of the investigation.

At the end of that first long day, Sunderland was exhausted. He had not slept since receiving the sheriff's call more than twenty-four hours earlier.

He drove home to Altus and collapsed in exhaustion. But only a few minutes after he dropped off to sleep, his phone rang.

"Terry Rhine just called," said the policeman on duty at Granite City Hall. "He said he has some information on the murder."

Sunderland dressed and drove back to Granite.

At City Hall, Rhine was waiting, excited. Sunderland took him into the back room and closed the door. Rhine lowered his voice and told his story.

"Me and Steve Barton get together just about every week to drink Jack Daniel's and listen to some good music. Last night Steve came by, and we got to talking about the murder. Steve was laughing about Esther Steele getting herself *stabbed*. Everybody I'd talked to said she was *shot*. But when the television news came on, they said it'd just been learned that she had been *stabbed*. Now how did Steve know that? Before it was announced?"

Sunderland doubted that Barton's foreknowledge was significant. The medical examiner's findings had spread through town quickly after receipt much earlier in the day. As the community's prime suspect, Rhine was simply out of the loop and the last to know.

But Barton's whereabouts on the night of the murder probably should be checked out. Sunderland added Barton's name to the growing list to be interviewed.

Sunderland fully understood Rhine's motive for turning in his drinking buddy. As the town's prime suspect, Rhine was as eager to see the crime solved as anyone. Sunderland thanked him for the information and promised to check into it.

Relishing the role of good citizen, Rhine was magnanimous. He said the television station had posted a reward for information. "I don't want the reward," he said. "Just take the money, buy some locks for these old people around here, and teach them to use them."

7 ∎ ∎ ∎

DR. FRED JORDAN ARRANGED THE SLIDES from the Esther Steele autopsy in their proper sequence. He adjusted his microscope and began work, recording his observations.

Swabbings from the mouth and anus revealed nothing he would not normally have expected. And the swabbings from the vagina showed exactly what he had anticipated, considering the torn nightgown and vaginal bruising. Under his microscope he saw sperm, some with tails intact, some now tailless.

And there were a lot of them.

The biopsies of soft tissues proved normal. Alcohol and toxicity tests were negative.

All results were in. He now could say without equivocation that Esther Steele died from multiple stab wounds made by a sharp instrument about six inches in length and three-quarters of an inch maximum width.

She also had been partially asphyxiated.

And, at some indeterminate time immediately prior to her death, she had been raped.

If OSBI criminologist Mary Long and Esther Steele had met in life, they would have discovered much in common. Mary Long's expertise with comparison microscopes, antigens, and the structure of human hair would have fascinated Esther, who was sufficiently schooled in science to have asked the right questions.

And if their mutual interest in science had waned, there was still Oklahoma football. Mary Long also is known as a sports fanatic.

That meeting of Esther and Mary Long in life was not to be. Yet, in the months after Esther's murder, their close association was inevitable.

In a lab on the lower level at OSBI headquarters, Mary Long explored the evidence in the Esther Steele murder case even beyond the findings of Dr. Jordan. The medical examiner's job required him to determine only the *cause* of death. It was Mary Long's responsibility to gather sufficient scientific evidence to identify the killer beyond a reasonable doubt. Or, as she often liked to point out, possibly to clear the innocent.

If Mary Long and her associates found solid evidence to support the conclusions of agents in the field, criminals went to prison. And, even more frequently, their findings guided agents in the field in the right direction to make an arrest.

It was a symbiotic relationship that, more often than not, proved effective.

Mary Long is a tall, attractive woman with long, dark hair and a quick mind. During her eight years with the OSBI, she had testified in two hundred criminal cases. Among defense attorneys she had established a reputation as a formidable opponent. Prosecutors always stressed the depth of her training. She held bachelor's degrees in both forensic science and chemistry. She also had completed the special course on forensic evidence offered by the FBI Academy.

As she began work on the material forwarded to her by the medical examiner and by OSBI agents in the field, she kept extensive notes, aware that if the killer was found, she would be called upon to testify on the evidence. As she worked, she evaluated the worth of that evidence.

She determined that Esther Steele's blood was type B, and that she was a B-antigen secretor. The semen on the vaginal swabs also tested B-antigen.

That was not good. The rapist *might* be a B-antigen secretor, or he *might* be a nonsecretor. The semen *might* have been contaminated by Esther's own bodily secretions. There was no way to know for sure.

Along with the swabs and whole blood received from the medical examiner were samples of Esther Steele's scalp and pubic hair, and fingernail clippings. A separate bundle held the nightgown, a pillow, a pillowcase, a blue bedsheet, and a mattress pad. Agent Cornelius had already hand-delivered the rest of the bedding—a yellow blanket, a blue electric blanket, and a multicolored bedsheet. All were bloodstained.

Mary Long labeled, initialed, and logged each item to preserve the chain of evidence.

At the end of a large worktable hung a big roll of white paper, much like butcher wrap except that it was not waxed. She pulled a strip out to cover the table. She then placed one of the sheets from Esther's bed on top of it.

With tweezers in hand, she began a square-inch-by-square-inch search, looking for hair and for stains from bodily secretions.

Occasionally she stopped her search to place a find in an envelope. She labeled and initialed each. From time to time she stopped to snip a small portion of sheet to be studied under the microscope and submitted to chemical tests. The process was slow and painstaking. But in the end, the results were promising.

On the two blankets and multicolored sheet she found thirty-four hairs. That was not an unusual number. Most people simply never notice how many hairs they gather regularly with the laundry.

On the blue sheet, she found fourteen hairs.

She mounted each on a slide and moved to the comparison microscope.

Those that were long and pipelike she immediately identified as scalp hair.

Others—flat and ribbonlike, with waves and buckles—were pubic hair.

Some, with less definition, could not be classified as either. These she designated as body hair. Most were of uncertain origin.

She first needed to determine which hairs found on the bedding came from Esther Steele and which came from someone else.

After mounting a known sample of Esther Steele's scalp hair received from the medical examiner, she began her comparisons.

The work was more complex than most people realized. After years of testifying as an expert witness, Long had devised a simplified explanation of the disciplines involved.

"Under the microscope, scalp hair usually looks much like a pencil," she often explained to jurors. "The scales—the outside part that protects the hair—is like the paint on a pencil. The wood part of the pencil would be the cortex, which varies greatly among people because it contains the pigmentation, and tends to differ widely with race. The lead of the pencil is the medulla, which has characteristics of its own.

"In all, there are fifteen to twenty points of comparison that I look for under the comparison microscope. And if I don't find *all* of those points of comparison, I can't say that two hairs are microscopically consistent."

One by one, she moved through the hairs from the bedding, comparing them with the samples collected by the medical examiner.

Most of the hairs from the bedding were microscopically consistent with the known samples.

But when she had finished, she was left with four hairs from the bedding that were *not* consistent with those from Esther Steele.

Those four hairs were from someone else. She labeled and preserved each. If a suspect was found, those four hairs might help to convict him.

In another part of the lab, forensic chemist Alan Cornelius studied the fingernail clippings. Nine were devoid of evidence.

But on the tenth—the clipping from the middle finger of Esther's left hand—a red cotton fiber was caught in a crack in the nail.

Cornelius checked the fibers gathered from his vacuuming of the house and from the bedding. He found nothing remotely similar.

The tiny thread suggested that Esther's killer wore a reddish article of clothing during the rape and murder.

In the search for those who knew Esther well, Sunderland was given the name of an Altus attorney, Tal Oden.

The tip was fortunate. Few people had been in a position to see as many facets of Esther in life.

Like most people who had lived in Granite, Sunderland had seen Esther's constant coming and going, without knowing exactly what she did. Oden was able to provide the answer. He was analytical and observant, and spoke with a lawyer's eloquence. He explained that he was chief lay person of the United Methodist Church in Oklahoma.

"That's an office, in a sense. But it really is a function that just says I'm interested in the Methodist tradition in public and private life."

He said he first came to notice Esther years ago while serving in his lay capacity at various operations of the church. He gradually became aware that he saw Esther everywhere—at state conventions, at general conferences, and at meetings of planning boards, missions, the Women's Missionary Society, poverty ministries, and other church agencies.

"Usually, even leading church members participate in only one or two of these areas," Oden said. "They consider that their personal contribution to the church.

"Esther was active in all."

Oden said that Esther had once told him that her parents and most of her family were Lutherans but that in the years after she was born no Lutheran church was near. So her parents had attended a Methodist church. She had grown up in that tradition and felt more comfortable with it.

"My contact with Esther was over a long period of time, for very short periods of time," Oden told Sunderland. "Five minutes, or maybe a church meeting for an hour or two. My wife and I have sat together with her at dinners on a number of occasions and had long discussions. These are just things I picked up through the years. I had such an appreciation for her."

Oden said he had been impressed by the way Esther's life was planned and organized.

"I've never seen her look drab. She always wanted to look very good. Her appearance was very important. She always dressed nicely. She kept her hair black and, though she'd followed the elaborate fashions of the sixties and seventies, she seemed to prefer simpler, classic styles. She was extremely alert and intellectual. She was a sophisticate. She knew what plays were on Broadway, what was in Dallas or Oklahoma City, who were conductors of the symphonies. She always drove a nice car—a four-door car big enough to take her friends in it, if she wanted."

Oden also was interested in the arts. And again, at all functions of the arts organizations, he encountered Esther everywhere he turned. Intrigued, he quietly became an avid Esther-watcher.

Oden and Esther were among the founders of an arts movement in Altus. Oden reminisced about that. "We were out here on the prairie where there had just been Indians and jackrabbits. What we wanted to do was bring civilization—music, the arts, performances.

So we organized the Short Grass Arts and Humanities Council in 1970. Part of that involved bringing musicals, performances, and the kind of activities sponsored by the National Endowment for the Humanities and the National Endowment for the Arts.

"Esther was a big part of that kind of activity. That was late in her life. She previously had twenty or thirty years of other kinds of cultural support.

"All of us knew that we could call on her and she would buy tickets, and bring her friends, to support the Community Concert Series—a half dozen concerts every year. She would come and bring her friends to the junior and senior high school musicals, the dramatic and musical performances at the junior college. Every semester."

And the more Oden was around her, the more he became aware that she had even more extensive interests.

With her expertise in teaching, she served as an auditor for the Oklahoma Education Association and visited schools around the region in that capacity. She was active in the Oklahoma Arts Institute, headquartered at Quartz Mountain, where nationally known actors, writers, playwrights, directors, poets, photographers, film producers, set designers, cinematographers, and artists came year-round to teach. As a volunteer, Esther operated the institute's store. Although headliners at the institute included such attractions as actors Richard "John Boy" Thomas, Jane Alexander, and Cathy Burns, and writers such as Shelby Heron and Larry McMurtry, the fascination for Esther was the young people attending—annually the most artistically gifted and hardworking students in the state.

Oden also learned that Esther attended summer courses at the University of Oklahoma on space education and served on advisory panels to set up space education curricula for public schools.

"What she did, she probably had at least fifteen or twenty circles of acquaintances," Oden explained. "She wasn't a woman who lived within one field of acquaintance."

Oden sensed those other circles of acquaintance: Fellow football fans who attended games with her at OU. Bird-watchers and professional ornithologists such as the author and painter George M. Sutton, who called her to discuss migrations and bird populations. Retired teachers. Theatrical people. Musicians.

"She had all those circles of friends who made her identity very diversified, and her interests very diversified," Oden summed up. "Therefore she was always energized, carrying out those connections of hers. That kept her so pervasive."

Occasionally Oden caught glimpses of the way Esther dovetailed these activities.

"One time I was at a meeting at about four o'clock on a Sunday in January. And Esther said, 'I've got to go. The birds are coming in.' I didn't know—still don't know—what she was talking about. But I knew she was a bird-watcher. She probably went up to Quartz Mountain, because she went there a lot. Who the other people were that she was meeting, I don't know."

In time, Oden observed subtle differences in Esther's mannerisms with different groups. Among Methodist women, she did the things Methodist women were expected to do. At a concert, she might show a certain flair, such as utilizing the theatergoer's trick of wearing a coat like a cape, to facilitate removal after seating.

"She had a theatrical bent to her. She had a role that fitted all those spheres of acquaintances. She was able to function and adapt to the social norms of a variety of groups. And that's why so many people knew and appreciated her. They thought she was like them."

Although Sunderland considered it inconceivable that some controversy in one of Esther's groups might have led to her murder, anything was possible. He asked if she had held office in any of those groups. Oden said she had not.

"I think I know why. She felt her diversity would be damaged if she focused in on one single sphere of activity. It would deprive her of the variety in her life. I've watched them try to nominate her for chairs of church and other groups. She wouldn't take a chair. And the reason she wouldn't, she wanted to be self-determinate. Chairing something would have been more a burden than a joy to her.

"She was fiercely independent, a free spirit. She was a lively, interesting woman all the time I knew her."

Oden said that in his view Esther was living a useful, meaningful life that most women, especially older women, might envy. He could not imagine anyone killing her.

He said that on first learning of her murder, he had found it impossible to maintain his professional objectivity.

"I don't know when I've been as angry."

8 ■ ■ ■

RICHARD GOSS THOROUGHLY DISLIKED the word *suspect* as used by attorneys, journalists, and far too many police officers.

"When you first begin an investigation, *everybody* is a suspect," Goss insisted. In his view, a good investigator entered a case with that philosophy, focusing first on the victim and family, and methodically working his way into the community in concentric circles, clearing suspects as he went.

The removal of Terry Rhine and the party guests from suspicion had widened the field. With a population of nine hundred, Granite contained more than four hundred males. The next logical step was to clear all others known to be out on the night Esther was murdered.

So while television and print journalists kept phones ringing at OSBI headquarters in Oklahoma City, demanding to know if any "suspects" had been found, the six OSBI agents in Granite fanned out to clear more suspects, in Goss's broader sense of the word.

All portions of the investigation involving a pressing time element had now been completed. The agents were free to double back, tie up loose ends, and speculate on motive.

Esther's relatives and close friends were escorted into the house, one by one, for careful searches.

Aside from the billfold, nothing seemed to be missing.

Those who knew Esther's habits said she seldom carried more than forty or fifty dollars in cash. They had noticed that she used credit cards for larger purchases. An alert had been issued on the stolen credit cards, on the off chance that the killer might try to use them.

The completed autopsy report arrived. It defined the murder weapon in greater detail: six inches long, three-quarters of an inch wide near the haft, considerably narrower toward the tip, sharp on one side, blunt on the other. For Goss, those measurements became an obsession. He made a drawing from the medical examiner's description. The agents sat around his sketch and brainstormed.

The blade plainly was too narrow for an ordinary hunting knife. Guesses varied widely: A scissors blade? A narrow, sharpened file? Something off a farm implement?

Goss pinned the drawing to the door of the conference room. As the agents came and went on assignments they often stopped and stood for a while, studying it.

FBI criminal profiling was still in its infancy. Many veteran investigators remained dubious of its worth. But Goss felt he should take advantage of whatever contributions the profilers might offer. He filled out the long, elaborate questionnaire designed by the FBI

Behavioral Science Unit and sent it to the profilers at Quantico, along with color photographs of the crime scene.

The OSBI lab report arrived. Hard evidence was scant but potentially significant: four hairs and a red fiber, along with B-antigen in the sperm.

The agents held long sessions in the back room, discussing what they knew, what they yet needed to know, and the probable motive behind the crime.

Was it rape and robbery?

Or was it robbery and rape?

The evidence left plenty of room for conjecture. The murder did not seem well planned. The assailant apparently had taken nothing into the house except, possibly, the as-yet-unfound murder weapon.

The abrasions around Esther's nose and mouth indicated that a throw pillow on the opposite bed may have been used to smother her. That also seemed spur-of-the-moment, utilizing materials at hand.

The fact that the house was undisturbed also appeared to have meaning. Either the killer was familiar with the interior of the house or else he had been provided with a good description of the layout, enabling him to circle through the living room to the hall and on in a horseshoe circuit to Esther's bedroom, all in the dark, without knocking a single article of furniture out of place.

Was it someone Esther knew?

Had she admitted the killer into her house?

Wearing a nightgown?

Again the agents went out and interviewed neighbors. They found consensus on one point: aside from family, Esther never entertained late-night visitors, such as a boyfriend.

The agents tended to believe them. In this small town, people knew each other's habits. Any slipping around was done elsewhere, not in one's own home.

The cuts on Esther's thumbs indicated that she had fought her killer. Everyone who knew her agreed that she was wiry, strong, and active. Chances were good the killer would be marked.

One night as Goss sat looking at the drawing he had made, a revelation came.

"A fish-fillet knife," he said aloud.

The next day he went to a hardware store and purchased a fish-fillet knife. The blade matched his drawing almost exactly.

Sunderland followed through on Terry Rhine's tip. He found that on the night of Esther's murder, Rhine's drinking buddy Steve Barton had played video games at his mother's house. Barton had stayed there with several friends until about 11:30 P.M. His mother then drove him home. He remained at home with his wife and grandmother the rest of the night.

One more name on the "suspect" list was cleared.

Esther's niece Betty Monday—Viola's daughter—remembered that Esther once had said she was afraid of a certain young man. The remark was so unusual—Esther expressing fear of anyone—that Betty remembered.

The young man was a member of one of the town's most respected families. Earlier in life, while residing elsewhere, he became a classic victim of drugs, burning out his brain in a manner symptomatic of the heavy use of speed and LSD.

After extensive treatment, he had returned to Granite. He lived alone and worked at the quarry.

Somewhere along the way he had become an intensely evangelical Christian. In his fervor, he often turned aggressive. Sometimes, coming on strong, he would seize a person's hand and not let go. For the uninitiated, the experience could be frightening. Perhaps taken by surprise, and for once not in control of the situation, Esther had become alarmed.

Sunderland knew the young man. On one memorable occasion, on a street in Altus, he himself had received the evangelical treatment. He believed the young man to be harmless. But the lead had to be checked out.

Sunderland ascertained the man's whereabouts on the night of Esther's murder. His name was eliminated from the list.

Other tips were coming in. Several residents were concerned about a retarded youth who hung out at the pool hall and often rode up and down Main Street on his bicycle, passing frequently in front of Esther's house.

Sunderland was aware that retarded persons are almost invariably of a gentle nature and are rarely connected with violence. But the youth was checked out.

Further tips revealed an amazing number of people out drinking and doing dope on the streets of Granite on the night of Esther's murder.

Each was interviewed at length.

The list kept growing.

On Friday, two days after Daisy's discovery of the body, Goss and Sunderland drove the twelve miles to the county seat at Mangum to interview the two youths who had wrecked their pickup southwest of town on the night of the murder.

They parked on the tree-shaded courthouse square and walked into the sheriff's office fully anticipating yet another dry run and the elimination of two more "suspects." Preliminary calls to the Sheriff's Office and to the Mangum Police Department had indicated nothing in the record of either young man that suggested a tendency toward violence. But after deputies were dispatched to bring the youths in for interviews, Sunderland and Goss sat talking with Sheriff Rogers.

"We thought for a while we might be able to send one of those boys up for the assault robbery of his eighty-five-year-old grandmother," Rogers said. "As it turned out, we just didn't find enough evidence to make a case."

Sunderland and Goss exchanged glances. This was the first crime encountered in the investigation even remotely similar to Esther's murder. Goss wondered aloud why they were just now hearing about the earlier case.

"There wasn't enough to file charges against him," Rogers explained. "Some of the family thought he did it. But we didn't have much, and the rest of the family wouldn't go forward with it."

Rogers said that although the case had been dropped, his investigators still believed that the twenty-one-year-old youth, David Wayne Sadler, could have been the culprit.

Sunderland and Goss pressed for details. Rogers described the crime: On an evening in July—nine months before—Sadler's grandmother, Mrs. Louise Hughes, had been struck from behind as she walked from her kitchen toward the front of her house. She did not see her assailant. She was knocked unconscious. Severely injured, she was hospitalized. She never recovered her health, and was placed in a convalescent home. She died there a few months later.

Five hundred dollars that Mrs. Hughes kept in a purse at the bottom of a trunk in her bedroom was missing.

As far as the sheriff's investigators could determine, only family members knew of the hidden money.

One family member was vocal in her belief that it was David Wayne who struck his grandmother and took the money. But no convincing evidence was found to support her contention.

Sadler's police record was brief. Five years ago, at sixteen, he had been referred to county juvenile authorities on a theft charge. He had been supervised for three months on deferred prosecution. During those three months, he maintained the required contacts, and the charge was dropped. Two years later, at eighteen, he had forfeited a fifteen-dollar bond on a charge of careless driving. Three years after that, he paid a twenty-dollar fine for public intoxication. And in March, only a month before Esther's murder, he had been fined one hundred dollars plus fifty-one dollars in court costs in adjoining Jackson County on a charge of public intoxication.

When the sheriff's deputies arrived with Sadler a few minutes later, he did not seem impressive on first glance. He was five-nine, but so thin he seemed smaller. Sunderland estimated his weight as one hundred and thirty-five pounds. His fine brown hair was trimmed short, almost in a crew cut. His most arresting feature was his eyes—intensely blue, and totally devoid of emotion.

Those cold eyes seemed to look right through a person.

Sadler's calm demeanor won the immediate attention of both Sunderland and Goss. Their experience with criminals suggested that Sadler might be a rare bird.

During his career, dealing with thousands of criminals, Sunderland had developed a theory about killers. He had found that the majority are the most trustworthy in the prison population. Most had killed in the heat of passion, usually in family situations. In all probability, they would never kill again. As warden, Sunderland always picked this type as his personal trusties. They were not thieves. They would not steal, for their best hope of early parole lay in a clean record. They never caused trouble.

But Sunderland had found that there was another type of killer— the rare ones, of a different personality—cold and emotionless.

Those cold, cold eyes that stared right through you.

Sunderland had always remained alert for this type, for they were trouble. In his experience, he had found that they most likely would kill again. Instinctively, that was exactly where he put Sadler, right in that category.

Goss was leader in the interview. No tape recorder was used. Sunderland sat to one side and took notes.

Goss introduced himself and Sunderland. "We're here to interview you concerning the murder and rape of Esther K. Steele in Granite on the night of April fourteenth," Goss said. "We need to establish your whereabouts and your activities on that night."

Sadler did not appear dismayed in the slightest that he was being questioned in a rape and murder. He remained calm, in full possession of himself. That struck both Sunderland and Goss as significant.

Goss told him that he had the right not to answer questions and, if he wished, he could have his attorney present.

"I'll answer your questions," Sadler said.

Goss read aloud the OSBI's version of the Miranda statement. It is slightly longer and more complete than the one used by most police agencies. Sadler signed it, signifying that he fully understood the waiving of his rights to remain silent and to have his attorney present.

"We need to know where you went, what you did that evening," Goss said. "Let's start at the beginning. How did you come to be out drinking that night?"

Sadler answered in short, terse sentences. "Bugs called me about six. He asked if I wanted to go drink some beer. I said okay. So I went down to his house. Then we walked over to his uncle's house."

Goss interrupted to establish that "Bugs" was the nickname of Phillip Pat Adams, Sadler's companion on that evening. Goss also established that Sadler was living with his paternal grandmother, Hazel Sadler, that Bugs was living with his mother and stepfather, and that the uncle they went to visit was John Schoolcraft.

"How long did you stay at Mr. Schoolcraft's house?"

"About an hour."

"What did you do next?"

"We asked to borrow his pickup."

"What time did you leave Mr. Schoolcraft's house?"

"About eight thirty."

"Where did you go?"

"We went to the Gulf station and got four quarts of beer."

Sadler's answers came in a relaxed manner. He never went beyond the minimal reply to each question.

"Where did you go next?"

"We drove out west of town, parked, and drank the beer."

"How long did that take?"

"About an hour."

"What did you do after you finished the beer?"

"We came back into town and went by Danny Harper's house. But Danny said he'd partied the night before. He didn't want to come with us."

"What did you do then?"

"We went and got more beer."

"How much this time?"

"A six-pack."

"Where did you go next?"

"Bugs asked me if I wanted to go to Blair and see Rick McGregor. I said okay."

Blair is a small town about sixteen miles southeast of Mangum.

"What time did you arrive there?" Goss asked.

"About ten thirty."

"What happened in Blair?"

"Missy came out and told us Rick wasn't home."

"So what did you do then?"

"We got more beer."

"How much this time?"

"A twelve-pack."

"Where did you go to drink the beer?"

"We just drove around a while. Then we started home. That was when we wrecked the pickup."

"In your driving around, did you go through Granite?"

"I was drunk. I don't remember. You'll have to ask Bugs. He was driving."

After concluding the interview, Goss and Sunderland escorted Sadler to his paternal grandmother's house to retrieve the clothing he said he had been wearing that night. But the jeans and T-shirt had been washed. If any bloodstains had existed, they now were gone.

On the way back to the sheriff's office, Goss and Sunderland discussed their mutually strong reaction to Sadler and his emotionless demeanor under the pressure of being questioned in a murder investigation.

They both felt they probably had found their man.

But as yet, that was just a hunch.

They had obtained no indication that Sadler was involved in any way with the murder.

■ ■ ■

Phillip Pat "Bugs" Adams was Sadler's opposite in almost every respect. He was short, balding, and chubby, weighing more than two hundred pounds. In sharp contrast to Sadler's calm manner, Bugs was nervous from the moment the deputies brought him in. And unlike Sadler, Bugs was talkative. He spoke with the glib manner of one long accustomed to talking his way out of scrapes.

Goss and Sunderland noticed scratches on his left cheek. They asked about them.

"When I was throwed out of the truck, I landed in some brush," Bugs explained.

At twenty-seven, he was six years older than Sadler. His police record was longer, but no more serious. At twenty he had paid a fifteen-dollar fine for reckless driving. In the following year he was fined twenty dollars for a violation defined on the police form as "trespassing/window peeping (drunk)." In the next year he was fined thirty-seven dollars for careless driving, speeding, and driving left of the center line.

His heaviest offense came at twenty-three, when he posted and forfeited a two-hundred-dollar bond for driving under the influence. At twenty-six he paid a fifty-dollar fine and spent three days in jail on a charge of public intoxication.

Goss read him his rights. Bugs signed the Miranda statement. Again Goss was leader in the interview while Sunderland sat to one side and took notes.

Responding to questions, Bugs told essentially the same story concerning the early hours of the evening, of phoning Sadler, of going to John Schoolcraft's house, of borrowing the pickup, and of buying and drinking the first four quarts of beer.

But from this point his account contained slight variations.

When Goss asked what they did after returning to Mangum and buying more beer, Bugs said they drove *back* out into the country and drank it.

"Where in the country?" Goss asked.

"I don't know," Bugs said. "I don't remember."

But Bugs provided more detail than Sadler. He said that after driving to Blair to visit Rick McGregor, and learning that McGregor was not home, they bought a twelve-pack and drank it while on the way to Granite to visit another friend, Johnny Monroe.

"And did you see Johnny Monroe?" Goss asked.

"No. His mother came to the door and said he wasn't home."

"What did you do then?"

"We started back to Mangum. That was when we wrecked the truck."

Bugs said he was drunk and did not remember much about the rest of the night.

Yes, he had known Esther Steele. He had lived in Granite. She had been his teacher in the fifth grade. Yes, he had gotten along with her.

After concluding the interview and releasing Bugs, Goss and Sunderland discussed the slight inconsistencies in the two versions. Again, they had obtained nothing connecting either Sadler or Adams with the murder. But they felt that something was not quite right.

And they also felt that, if the two were guilty, Bugs Adams would be the one to break.

9

ESTHER'S BODY WAS RELEASED BY THE
state medical examiner on Friday. At last
O.C. was freed to make the funeral arrangements. He scheduled services for Saturday
afternoon at First United Methodist Church.

Emotionally exhausted, he endured the
formalities of the day in a daze. He responded
to the steady stream of friends offering condo-
lences. Afterward he could remember little of
what was said.

The church was jammed beyond capacity.
The sanctuary, the fellowship area, and the
foyer were filled to standing room only.
Others stood in the doorway and just outside
the church.

O.C. was vaguely aware that OSBI agents

also attended, to keep watch for anyone who did not seem to fit in. The agents had explained that FBI criminal behavior researchers, in their extensive interviews with killers, had ascertained that twenty-seven percent of killers do indeed return to the scene, some to relive the thrill of the murder, some to try to determine the progress of the police investigation. Some admittedly returned for both reasons.

Bill Mease directed the services. After the pallbearers loaded Esther's casket into the hearse, the long funeral procession traveled east along graveled streets, passing Terry Rhine's house as it approached Main Street.

Rhine stood in his front yard watching, naked to the waist, a live snake draped around his shoulders.

Lost in his grief, O.C. did not notice. But others did. Many interpreted Rhine's display as a calculated gesture of disrespect, not only for Esther but also for the community.

The procession took Esther on her last trip down Main Street and to the cemetery south of town. After a brief service, surrounded by relatives and friends, Esther's body was lowered into her grave.

The day was ending. The long rays of the setting sun kindled the mountains in sharp relief. It was the hour and season when, ordinarily, Esther would have been driving out to await the arrival of birds at a grain field, a patch of woods, or at water's edge.

The view from Esther's grave is fitting. Quartz Mountain, where she spent much of her time teaching and studying nature and enjoying the performing arts, lies just to the southeast. Headquarters Mountain and Granite, where she spent most of her life, form the northern horizon. The broad valley of the North Fork of the Red River provides a panorama to the east. In late April, when all is lush and green and alive, the landscape defies description. But Captain Randolph B. Marcy, the first Anglo to explore the North Fork, made a bold attempt. Near this spot, at the western end of the Wichita chain, he wrote in his journal:

> The beautiful and majestic scenery throughout the whole
> extent of that portion of the chain we have traversed, with

the charming glades lying between them, clothed with a lux-
uriant sward up to the very base of the almost perpendicular
and rugged sides, with the many springs of delicious water
bursting forth from solid walls of granite and bounding along
over the debris at the base, forcibly reminds me of my own
native hills, and the idea of leaving these for the desert
plains gives rise to an involuntary feeling of melancholy similar to that I have experienced on leaving home.

Marcy must have been powerfully homesick. Only diligent
search would find much resemblance between the Wichitas and his
native Massachusetts. But clearly Marcy—along with Esther and
thousands of others through the thousands of years of human habi-
tation here—saw something in this land that touched him deeply.

Few places on the map of North America remained blank in the
mid–nineteenth century, but this region was among them. On
maps, the upper reaches of the Red River inevitably bore an evasive
notation: *Comancheria*. Few Anglos had dared to travel into that
blank space.

So in 1852 Marcy was dispatched by the U.S. Army to find and to
map the headwaters of the Red River. Earlier expeditions given the
same assignment had failed, either from following the wrong stream
or from wandering into Mexican captivity.

Marcy led his seventy-man party up the Red River to a point calculated by his quartermaster to be on the hundredth meridian. Six
miles farther west, the river split into two streams roughly the same
size.

Marcy chose to follow the one on the right, the North Fork.

His pace was leisurely. He had been ordered not only to map the
river but also to collect specimens of soil, flora, and fauna. His
detailed journal indicates that the jaunt was lighthearted, rewarding,
and enjoyable. Virtually unavailable today except to scholars, his
journal contains a wealth of fascinating local lore.

Marcy was the first to write of the plight of Cynthia Ann Parker, whose frontier story conveys all the pathos of Greek tragedy. Marcy entered into his journal an account he later forwarded to the U.S. Secretary of War:

> There is at this time a white woman among the Middle Comanches, by the name of Parker, who, with her brother, was captured while they were young children from their father's house in the western part of Texas. This woman has adopted all the habits and peculiarities of the Comanches, has an Indian husband and children, and cannot be persuaded to leave them. The brother of the woman, who had been ransomed by a trader and brought home to his relatives, was sent back by his mother for the purpose of endeavoring to prevail upon his sister to leave the Indians, and return to her family, but he stated to me that on his arrival she refused to listen to the proposition, saying that her husband, children, and all that she held most dear, were with the Indians, and there she should remain.

The children Cynthia Ann would not bear to leave were her two sons, Pecos and Quanah Parker.

It was Quanah who later became the last great chief of the Comanches and, even later, the close friend of George Briggs.

Eight years after Marcy's report, Cynthia Ann and her baby daughter, Prairie Flower, were captured by Texas Rangers on the Pease River, just south of the Red. She was returned to her white family in Texas. There she resisted "civilized" ways, pined away, and died.

George Briggs once had helped Quanah obtain a daguerreotype made of Cynthia Ann shortly after her capture by the Rangers. When the old chief received the picture, he wept.

Marcy also wrote of his own adventures. While stalking antelope using a "deer call," imitating a wounded fawn, he heard a noise to his left and belatedly saw a large panther charging him full-tilt. He barely brought up his gun in time. The panther, one of four killed on the expedition, measured eight feet from its nose to the tip of its tail.

Marcy also described the lighter moments in camp. At Quartz Mountain, one of the Indian guides captured two bear cubs. Their antics kept the expedition highly amused.

Neither Marcy nor his men had any inkling of the uproar their expedition had caused in the East. Through false rumors, he and his command had been reported massacred by Comanches. A memorial service had been conducted for Marcy in his home town of Greenwich, Massachusetts. Among those attending was his more prominent cousin, William L. Marcy, governor of New York.

Newspaper editors throughout the East were berating President Millard Fillmore and the War Department for sending such a small party of explorers into a region known to be ruled by hostile Comanches.

Blissfully unaware of the false report, Marcy continued on up the North Fork, past the site that was to become Esther's grave, past Headquarters Mountain, past Comanche Springs.

The only glimpses of Comanches Marcy and his men obtained were of small hunting parties at a distance.

Marcy and his second-in-command—and future son-in-law— Captain George B. McClellan, mapped the North Fork to its source on the High Plains far to the west. They then turned south and found the source of Prairie Dog Town Fork and Palo Duro Canyon. Forewarned by friendly Indians, they carried sufficient water to cross the extensive gypsum beds and brackish water on their homeward trip down Prairie Dog Town Fork.

The first reports of their arrival back in the land of the living seemed miraculous and created yet another sensation in the East.

Their seventy-seven-day Red River Expedition was considered a success. But in truth, most of the information they obtained had been available elsewhere. Pedro Vial, a Frenchman in the employ of the Spanish, had mapped the sources of the Red River in detail sixty-five years earlier. His map lay unnoticed in the Spanish archives at Santa Fe.

The Spanish were eminently familiar with the river. Comanche chief Quanah Parker told George Briggs that Spanish trade caravans had traveled along the North Fork, on their way from Santa Fe to Louisiana, since long before anyone now alive could remember.

But the effects of Marcy's Red River Expedition were far-reaching.

In his sightings, McClellan had placed the hundredth meridian at least fifty miles too far to the east. When the meridian later was restored closer to its proper place, upstream from the two forks of the river, a vital question arose: Which was the main stream, and thus the boundary between Texas and U.S. territory? The North Fork? Or the South Fork?

The Texas legislature moved into the cartographic vacuum in 1860 by designating the North Fork as the Texas boundary, thus claiming all land between the two forks, an area the size of Delaware and twice the size of Rhode Island.

The U.S. government objected. The matter was taken before the U.S. Supreme Court. The land remained in limbo for the next thirty-five years, delaying the region's frontier experience until the end of the nineteenth century.

That long historical delay profoundly affected the life of everyone in the region, even down to the present.

10 ■   ■   ■

By the fifth day after Esther's
murder, only Goss and Sunderland remained
on the case. The other agents had been summoned elsewhere to investigate newer crimes.
Granite residents were beginning to wonder if
Esther's murder would ever be solved.

Dozens, if not scores, of leads still demanded attention. Many "suspects" yet
needed to be cleared.

Most of the drudgery that remained was
what Sunderland thought of as plain garbage,
the type of material that always came up in
such investigations. Tips ranged from the eso-
teric to the possible. None could be ignored.

A woman called with an anonymous report

that a strange vehicle had been seen near Esther's house on the night of the murder. She supplied the license number and a description of the driver.

Sunderland followed the tip to a community near the Prairie Dog Town Fork of the Red River, on the border of Texas.

There he ascertained that the owner of the vehicle matched the description given in the tip.

For a time, Sunderland thought he might be onto a hot track. The subject's wife confirmed that her husband was away from home. She hinted that he had been acting strange lately. But interviews with in-laws and associates of the suspect raised doubt.

After considerable digging, Sunderland arrived at an unmistakable conclusion: The man and his wife were in the midst of a stormy divorce. She had phoned in the anonymous tip to put some heat on him.

The wife's small measure of revenge put two hundred miles on Sunderland's car and cost him most of a day.

Among the lingering questions demanding attention were the inconsistencies in the stories told by David Wayne Sadler and Phillip Pat "Bugs" Adams.

Sunderland interviewed Elsie Brooks, mother of Johnny Monroe, the Granite youth Adams claimed he and Sadler drove to Granite to see on the night Esther was murdered. Johnny Monroe's mother confirmed the visit.

"Bugs was so drunk that when I opened the door, he just fell into the house," she said. "I told them Johnny wasn't home, and they left."

"What time of night was that?" Sunderland asked.

She thought for a moment. "About midnight. Maybe a little before."

She said she knew Bugs well. But she was not acquainted with Sadler.

"I stood in the front door and watched them leave. Bugs was so drunk the other one had to help him into the truck."

"Who was driving?" Sunderland asked.

"Bugs."

She said she continued to watch them as they sat in the truck for several minutes. Then they drove off.

She volunteered that she was not happy that Bugs was now running around with her son Johnny. She told of an occasion, six years before, when Bugs tried to climb naked into her daughter's bedroom. She said she had been alerted by her daughter's screams and had chased Bugs away with a shotgun, firing over his head to speed him on his way.

Bugs had left most of his clothing behind that night.

"We need to talk to Johnny," Sunderland said. "Where would we find him?"

"He's gone to Dallas."

"When did he leave?"

"Last Wednesday. That same night."

Sunderland's interest in Johnny Monroe took a sizable leap.

Could Johnny have encountered Sadler and Adams while they were in Granite, learned of the murder, and left because he was scared? Could he be involved in some way?

Or was his departure on the night of Esther's murder simply a matter of unfortunate timing?

"We need to talk to him," Sunderland said again. "Get him back here."

"I don't know how to reach him. I don't know where he's staying."

"Find out," Sunderland said. "Get him back here."

Sunderland and Goss continued to work their way through the list of people coming forward with information. Among them was Pearl Johnson.

They interviewed her in her apartment at the rear of the old
Kozy Theater. Back during the Depression, when the theater was in
its prime, a former owner had built comfortable living facilities
behind the screen for his family. The apartment remained quite liv-
able, even though it faced the alley and the theater itself had long
been closed.

Pearl Johnson told an intriguing story.

"On the night Esther was killed, I was watching television. My little dog started barking. I heard a noise. I looked out my kitchen window to see what was going on. A pickup was pulled up near to the
building."

She explained that H.K., her teacup poodle, had been injured
early in life in a car door accident. He was one-eyed and partially
blind. Perhaps for that reason, his hearing seemed especially keen.

Again Goss asked the questions, while Sunderland made notes.

"How close to the building?" Goss asked.

"Eight, maybe ten feet away."

"Exactly where was it parked?"

"Just to the north of the building."

Sunderland and Goss looked out the kitchen window to the spot
where the truck had stopped. The theater and apartment extend
deep into the alley. So does the old hardware building on the corner,
four doors to the north. The three buildings in between are shorter,
leaving a recessed area. Pearl Johnson said the pickup parked in that
recess, next to the building.

"What kind of truck was it?" Goss asked.

"A red-and-white Ford with a bed-wide toolbox immediately
behind the cab. I'm fairly sure I recognized it."

She explained that she commuted to Mangum, where she
worked at Love's, a combination convenience store and service station.

"John Schoolcraft brings that pickup in almost every day for a few
gallons of gas."

Sunderland and Goss glanced at each other. Pearl Johnson's

information placed Bugs Adams and Sadler prowling downtown Granite in their borrowed pickup.

"About what time was that?" Goss asked.

"I didn't look at my watch. But it was between twelve and twelve fifteen. I know, because the program I'd been watching had gone off at midnight."

Goss and Sunderland silently assessed the time sequence.

Apparently Adams and Sadler had driven downtown after leaving Johnny Monroe's home.

Goss asked Pearl Johnson to go back to the beginning and describe the exact sequence of events.

"I first heard the pickup motor," she said. "Then the driver killed the motor. The truck sat out there for a while. Then they drove off."

"How long did it sit there?"

"About ten minutes. Then they started the motor and drove off south. I looked out the living room window and got a good look at the truck when it went under the streetlight."

"Could you see how many persons were in the truck?"

"Two."

"Male or female?"

"I can't say for sure. Their faces were in shadow. But from the way they were sitting—well apart—and the shape of their heads, I believe they were both male."

She said she continued to watch as the truck reached the end of the alley, turned east for a half block, then made a left and disappeared to the north.

Goss and Sunderland took special note of the direction.

When last seen by Pearl Johnson, the truck was headed toward Esther Steele's house, three and a half blocks away.

And that was within the time frame of the murder.

Goss asked Pearl Johnson if she knew John Schoolcraft's nephew, Phillip Pat "Bugs" Adams.

"I've known him since he was that high," she said, placing one hand with its palm down at her waist. "He and my son David are about the same age. When Bugs was little, he spent more time in my house than he did in his own."

She said that as Bugs grew older, she began to miss money from her billfold.

"Not much," she said. "Maybe fifteen or twenty dollars at a time."

She stressed that the thief could have been any one of David's other friends running in and out of the house. But she suspected Bugs. For this reason, and others, she had insisted that David cool his friendship with Bugs.

She said one of the figures in the pickup might have been Bugs. But she could not make positive identification.

Goss and Sunderland's interest in Adams and Sadler now took precedence over other, less promising areas of the investigation. They drove to Mangum to interview John Schoolcraft.

From the start, Schoolcraft's version of the early portion of that evening differed from the stories told by Bugs and Sadler.

Schoolcraft insisted that he had not given Bugs permission to use the pickup.

"I had to leave the house for a while. When I came back, it was gone. I looked all over town for it."

"What time did you leave the house?" Goss asked.

"About eight thirty."

"What time did you return?"

"About nine. And it was gone."

"Where was it parked?"

"Out back. Behind the house. With the keys in it."

"Do you normally leave the keys in it?"

"I usually do."

Schoolcraft said his nephew and Sadler had come to his house a short time earlier and stayed about thirty minutes.

"At that time, had they been drinking?"

"No sir. I don't think they was."

Schoolcraft explained that he had been concerned about the

truck because it belonged to Kelly Bowen, his boss, who allowed him to use it as if it were his own. He said he had hunted for the truck all night but did not find it until the next morning when a brother-in-law came to tell him that Bugs and Sadler had wrecked the truck and were in the hospital.

Schoolcraft said he met the truck as it was towed into town.

"Do you remember how your nephew was dressed that evening?" Goss asked.

"I would say blue jeans and a T-shirt."

"And Sadler?"

"Blue jeans. And a kind of reddish sweatshirt."

Goss and Sunderland badly needed to find that sweatshirt. The single fiber found caught in Esther's fingernail had been red.

Goss and Sunderland told Schoolcraft they probably would be talking to him again.

Correctional officer Mitchell Dwayne Murley told Sunderland that he had noticed the young man in green coveralls staggering along the east side of Main Street in Granite at about 3:40, or maybe 3:45 A.M., while on his way to work in kitchen security at the reformatory.

"I first thought he was just drunk," Murley said. "But then I wondered if he had been injured. I stopped, rolled down my window, and asked if he needed any help. He said he'd been in an accident and needed the police."

Murley knew the type of information Sunderland needed. Sunderland let him talk uninterrupted.

"I asked him if he was hurt, and he said he was, somewhere in his ribs. I asked him if he thought the ribs were broken. He said no. I told him to go up the street and sit down in front of the police station, and that I would go find the police."

Murley said he drove around several minutes, searching for the duty officer. Unsuccessful, he returned to the police station, put the young man into his car, and drove to the Conoco station to use the pay phone. He called the police emergency number and reached Duty Officer McCormack. He returned to the police station and sat in his car with the young man until McCormack arrived.

Sunderland wanted to be certain of one point. "You said he had on green coveralls?"

"Green coveralls and tennis shoes. No hat. No coat. And it was *cold* that morning. He smelled like a brewery. I asked him if he'd been drinking. He said, 'Yes, a little bit.' "

Police officer Alan McCormack told Sunderland that he met Murley and his passenger in front of the police station. The passenger said he had been in a wreck and that his friend was still out there, injured. McCormack took charge of the young man, allowing Murley to go on to work.

"I asked him where the accident was. He just pointed to the southwest. I put him in the car and drove down to Highway Nine. I stopped there and asked him if he could be more specific. He just pointed southwest again."

Driving west on the highway, McCormack asked the young man his name.

"I believe he said it was Haygood," McCormack told Sunderland. "It was something-good. I think it was Haygood."

McCormack said the young man did not talk much. When he did, his speech was slurred.

"I thought he was just too drunk to talk. I kept after him, asking him if he remembered any landmarks around where the accident occurred. He said it was somewhere around a cemetery. He remembered walking around a cemetery. I asked him if it was the City Cemetery or the Lutheran Cemetery. He pointed southwest, so I figured it was the Lutheran Cemetery. I asked him if there was anything else he remembered. He said it was on a dirt road near a curve. The only two places I know with a dirt road and a curve are near Benny Graumann's or Fred Lippert's house."

McCormack said he drove to the curve near Benny Graumann's

place and did not find the wreck. He drove on toward Fred Lippert's house. There he found a red-and-white Ford pickup overturned in the ditch. Another man was lying in the ditch facedown.

The full moon was still two hours high. The night was so cold that the ground was white with frost. McCormack said he was especially concerned about the injured man lying in the ditch, exposed to the cold.

"When I first got there, it appeared to me he wasn't breathing. I shook him to see if he was alive. He rose up, and I said, 'Are you all right?' And he said yes."

McCormack said he used his radio to call the Mangum Police Department, who notified the Oklahoma Highway Patrol in Altus. Ambulances were dispatched.

"How was this first man dressed?" Sunderland asked.

"Green coveralls. Tennis shoes."

"Was he injured?"

"He had a bruise and some blood near his left eye. I didn't notice anything else."

"And the man in the ditch?"

"He had blood and scratches on his face. I didn't move him to look further. I knew he might have a spinal injury. When the medics came, they strapped him to a board and turned him over. I did notice blood on the legs of his jeans."

The wreck fell under the jurisdiction of the Highway Patrol. McCormack had no reason to suspect that the two young men had been involved in a crime. He did not investigate further.

Charles Lynn Hayden confirmed to Sunderland that he had been an attendant in the first ambulance to reach the scene.

He said that when he arrived, Bugs Adams was lying facedown in the ditch. Sadler was about twenty feet away, sitting on the ground, his head in his hands. Officer McCormack was in his police unit, talking on the radio.

Hayden said he noticed blood on Sadler's hands.

"Probably a fourth of the area at the back of Sadler's hands was smeared with dried blood. Adams had a cut on his forehead. And there was blood on his face."

Hayden said he and the emergency team immobilized Adams on a board and loaded him into an ambulance.

Sadler was ambulatory. But on the trip to the Mangum City Hospital, he complained that his ankle hurt.

"We took his shoes off and palpated the ankle, and compared them to each other to see if there was any deformity."

"What type of shoes was Sadler wearing?" Sunderland asked.

"Just tennis shoes."

"Do you remember what type clothing he had on?"

"He was wearing green coveralls."

"You say you took his tennis shoes off. Did you have to take his socks off?"

"He didn't have any socks on," Hayden said.

Douglas McCormack gave Sunderland and Goss the best description of the wreck scene. McCormack was a maintenance man and janitor at Granite High School. He also served as a certified emergency medical technician with the Granite Ambulance Service. Police officer Alan McCormack was his brother.

Douglas McCormack said Adams seemed to be the most seriously injured and received his immediate attention.

"Adams was laying facedown in the bar ditch in front of the pickup," McCormack said. "We did our primary and secondary assessment, which is simply to see if the patient is breathing and maintaining the airway and stopping bleeding and such. I applied traction to the head, and another EMT applied a cervical collar around the neck to stabilize it. We then arranged ourselves so we could log roll him over on a long spine board. Two or three other EMTs checked the extremities and such before we rolled him over, to make sure there wasn't anything broken. We then secured him to the spine board and loaded him."

McCormack said that Sadler was sitting up through the early part of the ride to the hospital.

"I looked at him and saw that he was going sour on us. He was getting pale. I asked him if he wanted to lie down, and he said yes, he would."

Sadler rode the rest of the way lying on a stretcher.

Hayden said that when the ambulance reached the hospital, and the patients were carried into the emergency room, the medical people removed the jeans from Bugs Adams.

"I noticed quite a bit of dried blood on his upper legs. But there were no punctures or injuries. That struck me as odd. I wondered how he got the blood, with no punctures."

"Where exactly was the dried blood?" Sunderland asked.

"It was between his knee and his hip, in the front area."

McCormack said most of the blood was on his left leg.

"Did you see any cut or abrasion at all that would have caused any bleeding in that area?"

"No. I didn't," McCormack said.

From other medical personnel—both with the ambulance service and at the hospital—Sunderland and Goss learned more details about events after the wreck.

Janean Mulford, the registered nurse on duty in the emergency room, remembered that Sadler was "acting crazy" and talking incoherently at the time of his admission. He vomited a dark mass the consistency of coffee grounds. For a time the medical personnel thought the vomited matter might be blood, the product of internal injuries. But on examination the dark mass proved to be snuff that Sadler had swallowed sometime during the night.

Sunderland went back out to talk with Elsie Brooks.

"When Pat Adams and David Wayne Sadler came by your house that night, what were they wearing?"

"Bugs had on jeans and a T-shirt."

"And Sadler?"

Elsie Brooks did not hesitate. "Blue jeans and a red pullover with a hood."

"Have you contacted Johnny?"

Elsie Brooks shook her head negatively. "I can't find him. I don't know where he's staying."

Sunderland was how half convinced that Johnny Monroe participated in Esther's murder, or else knew something about it, and had fled town.

"Find him and get him back here," he said. "If you don't, we'll get an arrest warrant, go get him, and bring him back."

From the string of interviews, Sunderland and Goss developed certain circumstantial evidence:

At some time during the night Esther was murdered, Sadler had changed clothes.

Two independent witnesses—John Schoolcraft and Elsie Brooks—had seen him in a reddish pullover through the early part of the evening.

Everyone who saw him *after* the wreck—Mulford, the McCormack brothers, all the medical personnel—said he was wearing green coveralls.

At the wreck scene, and at the hospital, observers had noticed dried blood on Bugs, mostly on his upper legs, under his jeans. No one could remember any injury to account for the bleeding there.

And as yet, no satisfactory explanation had been given as to what Adams and Sadler were doing on the back road where they wrecked the truck.

Bugs had lived in Granite and Mangum all of his life. He surely knew that in going from Granite to Mangum, the only two ways to cross Elm Fork of the Red River were either via the bridge on Highway 6 south of Granite or on Highway 283 to the north of Mangum.

The road Bugs chose was taking him into a dead end in the river bottom, with no bridge to cross. He seemed to have been avoiding highways, where he might be seen.

Again Goss and Sunderland discussed what they knew, what they yet needed to know.

Other facets of the investigation were winding down. This one was growing hotter the deeper they went into it. They decided that the next logical step in the investigation should be thorough background checks on both Sadler and Adams.

11   ∎ ∎ ∎

THE DETAILED REVELATIONS CONCERNING Granite's clandestine nightlife left most of the town's residents in dismay, if not in shock.

Reports of murder, drugs, robbery, and rape were common on the nightly news. But Granite still retained a vision of itself as a place apart, to a large degree untouched by the ills of contemporary society. Prior to Esther's murder, few residents had seen any hints that the town was not as immune as they believed.

Dr. Lenaburg remembers his first inkling. It came while he was attending a medical convention about two months before Esther's death.

"One program listed a session on doctors and drugs. I wasn't interested. I didn't think we had a drug problem in Greer County. Then I learned that two of the doctors on the panel who'd had trouble with drugs were from Mangum."

Recognition of the changes in Granite came slowly. A disproportionate segment of Granite's population is elderly. Those older residents still tend to see the Norman Rockwell–style town that once existed.

Typical is Ernest Craig, who at eighty-seven vividly remembers the Granite he knew in the thirties and forties, when Main Street served a large rural population.

Craig and his wife, Altabelle, owned and operated Granite Variety, next door to the Kozy. Stocky and energetic, Craig resembles an aging Jimmy Cagney with a spicy blending of George Burns. As he talks, his eyes take on the glaze of the accomplished raconteur who sees in his mind the scene he is describing. He especially remembers the Saturdays, when everybody came into town to buy supplies.

"Why, you could hardly drive down Main Street! Cars double-parked on both sides! The stores full of people! The sidewalks full! That's hard to believe now. So many empty buildings. Young people here just don't know how it was."

He shakes his head, marveling at his own memories. "Oh, boy, we used to have it down there! We'd open the door at six thirty, seven in the morning, and we'd stay in that store until midnight or one o'clock the next morning. That was work!"

Ernest looks out at Main Street. "It's sure different now."

He talks of the pattern of life in those days, the pleasantness of it all. The older rural people would come into town early on Saturday to do their shopping and to sell their butter, eggs, and cream. The young adults and teenagers would stay home until late afternoon to feed the livestock and milk the cows before dressing and coming in for dates and their own social life, centered around a late movie at the Kozy.

Craig remembers the basic honesty of that life. Once on a busy Saturday he gave a farmer ten dollars too much in making change. In the middle of the night he was awakened by a knock at his front door. The farmer had discovered the error and driven back to town to return the money. Such honesty would not keep until Monday. The farmer was concerned that Craig might have noticed and would "think hard" of him until he spoke up.

The additional influx of young people and their cars on Saturday evenings added to the traffic jam on Main Street. But the problem of double-parking was easily solved through a common courtesy: keys were left in ignitions. If a car was in someone's way, it could be moved. Occasionally a car owner would emerge from a late movie at the Kozy, hunt for his car, and find it a block or more up the street, perhaps moved a half dozen times to new parking places.

Craig could not remember a car ever being stolen, or even taken for a joyride. A fundamental decency in those days prevented such behavior. Not everyone was a saint, but even the drunks usually made it to church on Sunday.

Ernest and Altabelle Craig closed the doors of their variety store for the last time in 1977. She died in September of 1980.

Craig speaks of her with sadness. "She didn't make it six weeks after she found out she had cancer."

After a moment he smiles. "Remember how she used to call everybody 'kid'?"

He remembers Altabelle as a woman of great humor and warmth. She was forty-four when her first and only child, Ernest Wayne, was born. Today Ernest Wayne is a commercial artist with the *Daily Oklahoman* in Oklahoma City. He comes to visit the elder Ernest every other weekend.

"His wife got up and left him about two years ago. I have a grandson, twenty-one. He doesn't have anything to do with me or his dad."

Ernest shakes his head in a gesture of puzzlement and a hint of pain. "You know young people today. That's just the way things are now, it looks like."

■ ■ ■

Doris Broiles Post also remembers the Norman Rockwell–type town of her girlhood back in the thirties. After living away most of her life, she possesses a sharper recognition of changes.

Doris and her husband, the actor William D. Post, retired to Granite in the late eighties. Doris stresses that the move came after much thought.

"We'd had the best of New York for forty years. It was a wonderful, good place to be. We hated to leave it, because we had to leave friends and a life that was rewarding to us. However, we were getting older. Bill had had a few strokes. I had had four eye operations. The city had become a little bit—I'm not going to use the word *frightening*—but scary. When you're older and in New York City, you are more at the prey of people. So we began to look for a place where we might be, quote-unquote, safe."

They considered Switzerland, the south of England, other places.

"Out of looking around the whole world, everywhere, for a small village where we could find a cozy house and take better care of ourselves, somehow or other this kept coming to mind. We decided to try it."

Doris grew up here. After high school she went to New York to obtain a degree from Columbia University. Upon graduation, she moved to Finch College as registrar, and later taught music and English at the Dwight School in Manhattan, eventually becoming dean of the College Preparatory School.

Bill, a New Jersey native, attended Phillips Exeter Academy before receiving his degree in literature and philosophy at Yale. He then studied at the American Laboratory Theatre under the fabled team of Maria Ouspenskaya and Richard Boleslavski.

He moved to Hollywood for roles in *The House on 92nd Street*, *Call Northside 777*, *The Moon Is Down*, and other films. But he vastly preferred the stage, and returned to Broadway. Through the years he played roles in productions from Shakespeare (*Richard II* and *Richard III*, for example) to O'Neill's *Ah, Wilderness!* and

Shaw's *Caesar and Cleopatra*. In television, he performed long runs
on the serials "Edge of Night," "Days of Our Lives," "All My
Children," "Another World," "As the World Turns," and "The
Guiding Light." He also appeared in commercials for corporate
clients such as Coca-Cola and Oldsmobile.

And for twenty-five years he was head of the Drama Department
at Finch College in Manhattan.

The Posts' move from Manhattan's East Seventies to a small
Oklahoma town required drastic adjustment. Bill is a member of the
Yale Club and the Players Club. In New York the Posts enjoyed
extensive acquaintance in musical, theatrical, and artistic circles.
Their social life was active.

Granite is, in a word, quieter.

Doris saw many changes in her hometown, and not all for the
good. She believed she understood one reason the town woke up to
its drug situation so belatedly.

"You remember that when you and I were growing up here,
everyone lived in the front part of the house. Your parents, my parents, everyone. They looked out the front windows, and they saw
what was happening. They helped to keep an eye on the children.
Now everyone lives in the back of the house, around the television
set. No one keeps an eye on the children."

The rape and murder of Esther, and the revelations of rampant
drugs—so reminiscent of the worst of New York—came as a shock
to the Posts.

Doris voiced her appreciation for Esther's effort to make them
feel welcome when they came to Granite. "She took us to the meetings of retired teachers, introduced us, and went out of her way to
do all she could. We really valued her as a person."

Doris still recognizes surviving facets of the town she knew in her
girlhood. She recalled the warmth of the last holiday season.

"We went to the Christmas tree lighting. This town never looked
more beautiful! The Christmas tree in the center of Main Street was
a big, lush one. The tree on the mountain, the star, lovely! All the
children were there, the junior and senior choirs."

The tree on the mountain is formed by lights strung on the heights at the head of Main Street. One year the *Guinness Book of World Records* listed it as the largest "tree" in the world. Airline pilots point out the sight to travelers.

Doris expressed special appreciation for the participation of the children in the festivities.

"Our generation may be the last of the old guard, who were brought up to respect their elders, to do for their country, to love, to do, for others. But there seems to be a little bit of that moving here now."

Among those who are making the effort to recapture the old values of the town as it used to be, she especially commends Jan Wingo Locklear, publisher of the *Granite Enterprise*, and her work on the revival of the chamber of commerce and the cleanup and refurbishing along Main Street.

Jan Wingo Locklear and her husband, David, were reared in Granite. After living elsewhere for a while they made a carefully considered decision to return—Jan to revive the weekly *Enterprise*, David to work in his family's roofing business.

Jan is honey blond, tall, and so vigorous one tends to forget she has battled allergies and rheumatoid arthritis from childhood. There is a pixie quality about her—serious one moment, filled with humor the next. She speaks with quiet intensity of their decision to return to Granite.

"First of all, it was home. We knew it was a good place to grow up, a good place to raise our children. We knew the schools were good. And my kids love it! They didn't even miss the bigger towns. That was strange, because I really thought they would. I was the one who cried over what I miss. The kids climb the mountains, keep busy. They love it."

Jan and David have three children and two grandchildren.

Jan sees herself as carrying on a family tradition. Her father, Bill Wingo, published the *Granite Enterprise* for twenty-seven years.

Her grandfather was also a newspaperman. Wingos have been pub-
lishing weekly newspapers for more than a hundred years.

Through editorials, Jan instigated rebirth of the Granite
Chamber of Commerce, long defunct, and served as chamber president. Her newspaper suggested and supported a cleanup of residential areas and the Main Street renovation.

David takes time from his roofing work to serve as managing editor, and he writes much of the copy.

Jan's father set type on a clattering Linotype machine and
printed the newspaper on an old Washington flatbed press. Today
Jan and David set type by computer and take page-ready layouts to a
nearby town for printing.

Jan's editorial policy differs markedly from her father's in only
one way. Bill Wingo never printed anything he felt detrimental to
the community, such as crime news. Jan prints a weekly police blot-
ter, along with a list of countywide indictments obtained from the
district attorney.

Some readers have protested, but Jan remains adamant. Her policy was formulated after considerable thought. She believes that in
Granite, where everyone knows everybody, public exposure helps to
deter crime.

Esther's murder and the revelations of Granite's ongoing drug activity were of deep concern to William A. Manning, who owns and
operates a ranch north of town with his wife, Joyce.

Bill has seen firsthand what drugs can do to a country and to
good people.

Bill grew up in South America. His father was an American engi-
neer, and his mother was Colombian. Bill first visited Granite in the
spring of 1947, the guest of his roommate at the University of
Oklahoma. He had known Esther since that first visit. Joyce had
known Esther all her life.

Joyce grew up in the Lake Creek community north of town, one
of the McCurdys, a large family. She left to serve as an army nurse

in World War II. She met Bill at the university, and they were married in Lake Creek Baptist Church in 1947.

Some in Granite said the marriage of two people of such different backgrounds would never work. Today Bill and Joyce have four children, all grown, and eleven grandchildren.

Their return to Granite was the realization of a longtime dream. To make it possible, Bill took early retirement as professor emeritus of Inter-American Studies at San Jose State University, and Joyce ended her career as a head operating room nurse.

Bill is tall and fastidiously thin. He retains courtly Latin manners and an unbounded interest in people and the world around him. Joyce, known for her unflappable nature and quiet wit, puts their return to Granite in philosophical perspective.

"Maybe we're like elephants. When we get old, maybe we find our way back home."

Bill was reared on a South American ranch and loves cattle. He and Joyce bought a spread on Lake Creek and named it the Northern Cross Ranch. Joyce's medical skills are now put to use in the birthing and rearing of Santa Gertrudis calves.

In this region of vanishing fences, Bill has created a marvel—a white rail lane leading from the road to his house. The fence quickly establishes the parklike atmosphere of the ranch. The house is low, long, modern, and comfortable. In the front pasture, Bill's Arabian saddle horse grazes amidst cattle and a flock of white ducks.

In green pastures across the creek, the Manning cattle graze. Headquarters and Quartz mountains form the southern horizon. The sense of peace and tranquillity is overwhelming.

Bill and Joyce express unbounded contentment that they no longer must battle the overpopulated chaos and pressures of life in northern California, the heat of international seminars, university politics, and the burdens of academia. Today Joyce spends much time fishing in the creek. Bill's first degree was in petroleum geology; he has revived his engineering skills by building a bridge over the creek so his land would not be divided by heavy rains.

Bill's long involvement in inter-American studies has given him a feel for trends. Today his concerns are deeply rooted. On visits to his native country he has witnessed the effects of a drug culture running amuck—governmental corruption, political assassinations, paralyzing fear, economic chaos, anarchy.

He battled bureaucracy for years to bring the rest of his family out of Colombia. He knows that what happened in Colombia can happen here. In Los Angeles, Miami, and other places, he sees insidious signs. He is disturbed that so little is being done and that no one seems to recognize the extent of the danger. He is deeply troubled, because here on his Northern Cross Ranch he has found happiness.

On this he is most emphatic.

"It is like I have died and gone to heaven. It is like paradise. Every morning I wake up, look at my wife, the land, the mountains, my cattle, and I am at peace."

12   ■   ■   ■

SUNDERLAND'S THREAT TO BRING JOHNNY
Monroe back to Granite under an arrest warrant produced results. Monroe returned voluntarily.

He told Sunderland and Goss that on the
night of Esther's murder he was out drinking
with a friend. He said he did not see Adams
and Sadler that night, nor did he know that
they were in town looking for him. Monroe's
friend confirmed his story, as did various people who had seen them at different locations
throughout the night.

Sunderland and Goss emerged from
the interviews convinced that Monroe was
telling the truth and that his departure for

Dallas on the night Esther was murdered was only a coinci-
dence.

Monroe was the last to be interviewed among those known to be
out running around that night. All phases of that aspect of the investigation were now completed.

Sunderland and Goss turned their full attention to assembling
profiles of David Wayne Sadler and Phillip Pat "Bugs" Adams.

Shortly before Bugs Adams was born on December 31, 1959, his parents were divorced.

He never saw his father.

He attended school in Granite until the seventh grade. His former classmates expressed their opinions that Esther Steele had been
"hard on him" because she did not feel he was doing work anywhere
near his potential.

He later attended school in Mangum. His mother remarried
when he was fifteen—about the time he dropped out of school in
the eighth grade. Family members said he did not "get along" with
his stepfather.

His employment record was extensive but varied. Most recent
was a five-month stretch as an attendant at the Kerr-McGee Service
Station in Mangum, pumping gas, changing oil, and fixing flats. He
had been released because of a lack of work.

He was currently unemployed.

His most stable accomplishment was his nine years of service in
the Oklahoma National Guard. He had attended weekly drills and
summer training with but few lapses. He had made sergeant but lost
a stripe for drunkenness and missing a week of summer camp.
During his first two years in the guard he trained and worked as a
mechanic. Through the last seven years he had served in artillery.

He had worked full-time five months of the previous year at the
armory, doing general maintenance. Earlier, he had been employed
more than a year with the Sanitation Department at Mountain
View, fifty miles to the east. For eighteen months he had worked as

a painter for a firm in Oklahoma City. At various times he had worked as a carpenter's helper. His former employers consistently termed him a good, trusted worker.

His contemporaries said he had been using alcohol and drugs since the age of twelve, and that since the age of fifteen he had been a heavy user of marijuana, crank, cocaine, amphetamines, and alcohol.

Only one aspect seemed to separate Bugs Adams from Sadler.

Almost everything Sunderland and Goss learned about Bugs supported a terse summation they heard several times from former classmates: "Bugs is just a big ol' dumb boy."

Of the two, Sadler appeared to be the more intelligent. His IQ had been pegged at 104 two years before his graduation from Mangum High School. In his senior year his classroom grades averaged a borderline 69, rescued by the 98 he received in athletics.

He had not been a standout in sports, but he was remembered as a hardworking, dependable player, especially in baseball and football. He had doubled in football as defensive back and wide receiver. Former teammates recalled that he had been nicknamed "Wolfman" because he then wore his hair shoulder-length and scraggly.

His school records revealed that throughout the years his teachers consistently had labeled him "a loner" and "a dreamer."

Several teachers recorded their opinion that he was considerably more intelligent than his grades indicated, that he simply did not apply himself.

He had been born in Mangum on July 18, 1965, the oldest of three children. His sister Paula was eighteen, three years younger. His sister Katrina was twelve.

According to Mangum authorities, David Wayne's father, Jerry Wayne Sadler, had been a heavy abuser of alcohol in the years prior to his death. He was killed in a car wreck when David Wayne was thirteen.

Family members said David Wayne was profoundly affected by

his father's death. His schoolwork took a sharp downturn from that date. One school counselor noted that the family was not close and that David Wayne more or less fended for himself.

In the seventh and eighth grades he was placed in a Special Education class because of his deficiency in reading. Afterward he was shifted to a vocational program.

In the three years since high school, his employment had been sporadic. A week at a service station. Four months of temporary work at Mangum Livestock Company. He had hauled hay and worked part of one summer at a youth camp at Quartz Mountain State Park. He had never held a long-term job of any description, even though his short-term employers called his work "satisfactory."

His mother, Linda Sadler, was currently unemployed. David Wayne was living with his paternal grandmother, Hazel Sadler.

He had served with the National Guard three years and was assigned to a cannon crew. He had attended drills and summer training regularly, and this apparently accounted for the bulk of his income. His only recorded trouble in the guard stemmed from drunkenness and fighting.

Former associates said he had been drinking since the age of thirteen and that he had been severely addicted to speed for a two-year period when he was about fifteen or sixteen. He still used speed occasionally, along with marijuana and cocaine.

But his major weakness was beer. In recent years, he had been averaging a case a week.

Some of his acquaintances said Sadler often "went crazy" when drinking. They said he would urge others to hit him and would "bang his head against walls."

Sunderland and Goss returned for another interview with John Schoolcraft.

"Did you have a knife, or anything resembling a knife, in the pickup?" Goss asked.

Schoolcraft nodded. "I kept a fish knife on my dash."

"Could we see it?" Goss asked.

"I don't have it," Schoolcraft said. "I hunted for it all over after the wreck. I went out to the lot where they towed the truck and searched the cab good. I couldn't find it."

"Could you describe it for us?"

"It was just a regular fishing knife with a wooden handle. The blade was six, maybe seven, inches long, and about an inch wide. I always kept it in its scabbard, resting on the dash."

"How long had you had it?"

Schoolcraft thought for a moment. "About fifteen years."

"You sharpen it a lot?"

Schoolcraft nodded. "I kept it good and sharp."

"Was the blade worn down to where it was kind of narrow?"

Again Schoolcraft nodded. "It was a lot narrower than when it was new."

"You miss anything else out of the truck?"

"My coveralls. I kept an old pair of green coveralls behind the seat to use in cold weather or when I had dirty work to do. They was missing. I looked all over for them. I couldn't find them anywhere."

The preliminary profile of Esther's killer arrived from the FBI Behavioral Sciences Unit at Quantico:

> The subject will probably be a white male, in his late teens or early twenties. On the night of the assault, there was heavy drinking involved. Some form of alcohol. Subject recently had a major confrontation with a female in his life. Girl friend. Wife. Or mother. Or he was experiencing financial troubles, in which he targeted the victim for money. The victim and the perpetrator knew each other. Postcrime behavior: probably very heavy drinking. Probably has minor record of simple offenses, such as breaking and entering.

Criminal profiling was just coming into common use. Early in the program, one of the participants, Special Agent Robert K. Ressler, observed that no one actually knew much about the minds of serial killers. On his own, Ressler set out to interview convicted serial killers. Others joined him. After the first three dozen interviews, the profilers found that almost every killer had certain experiences in common. Later interviews confirmed these initial observations.

Virtually every serial killer interviewed was born to a dominating, cold, emotionless mother, from whom he was estranged. The father was weak-willed or missing. In most instances there was abuse, either from the family or from others. And in almost every case, from an early age the killer nurtured a fantasy, usually one of getting even. He would be known as a loner, a daydreamer. He invariably remained so quiet that later few people would remember him, even those who had been around him every day. His early crimes would be minor but significant. Setting fires. Torturing animals. Bullying younger children.

Eventually, the subject began living out his fantasies, and killed. But the reality never measured up to the fantasy. So he killed again and again, trying to get it right.

In his writings, Ressler stresses that these circumstances do not necessarily produce a serial killer. But he notes that serial killers seem to grow up in those circumstances.

Both Sadler and Adams came from broken homes. Both seemed to feel the absence of a father. Sadler had been pegged as a "loner," a "daydreamer," by teachers long before Ressler and his associates made their observations.

The age bracket of the FBI's criminal profile on Esther's probable killer seemed to fit Sadler better than Adams. All of Sadler's former associates seemed to think he was a young man on the edge. Many admitted they had been afraid of him, afraid of what he might do.

But Bugs was the one who had been acquainted with Esther. Bugs knew his way around Granite. He had been driving. He was older and, from both accounts, the leader in the night's activities.

Sunderland and Goss wondered: Were the FBI profilers picking up clues from both, blending two profiles into one?

"I want to try something," Goss said to Sunderland. "Let's do a visual investigative analysis."

Goss felt that the investigation had become too complex to track mentally. With the myriad times and places gleaned from various witnesses, he felt that he and Sunderland might not be seeing some essential correlations.

The visual investigative analysis (VIA) he proposed is a spin-off of the business community's project evaluation review (PER). In a PER, business managers chart the interrelationships and dependencies of all activities in a project.

In the investigative field, the VIA procedure is the same. Times and locations are drawn on a chart. The parallels provide a graphic picture of the sequence of events.

Working from their elaborate notes, Goss and Sunderland time tracked Adams and Sadler, both from their own accounts and from the reports of witnesses who saw them at certain times and places. Drive distances were calculated. Estimates were projected for the time required to consume each purchase of beer.

Esther's activities were added to the chart—her arrival home from church, the probable time she went to bed.

The accounts given by Sadler and Adams had differed by an hour or more on the exact time they left Mangum. Other times and locations they offered also had differed.

But when the time track of independent witnesses was added to the chart, and drive times figured, a close correlation emerged. The chart also showed correlation between Esther's time track and the one for Sadler and Adams.

From every indication, Esther had been killed between midnight and 2:00 A.M. Daisy Brown left her in the driveway at 10:30 or 10:45. Correctional Officer Harry Ellis noticed her house dark shortly after midnight. This matched the estimate provided by the medical examiner as to the time of death.

The track of Sadler and Adams, as defined by independent witnesses, showed a two-hour gap in the time frame of Esther's death. Pearl Johnson had placed them downtown shortly after midnight, headed in the direction of Esther Steele's house. The next independent witness—Correctional Officer Murley—found Sadler staggering along Main Street about 3:40 A.M. Even allowing Sadler an hour and a half to walk the four and a half miles into town from the wreck, two full hours remained unexplained in the accounts given by Sadler and Adams.

When put down on paper, that two-hour gap seemed to jump right off the chart.

After completing the graphic analysis, Goss and Sunderland were thoroughly convinced that Esther had been killed by either Sadler or Adams—or perhaps by both. Yet they had no proof.

The bare hard evidence consisted of only four hairs, a tiny red fiber, and the B-antigen in the sperm.

Attempts to link that evidence to Sadler and Adams would be difficult, at best. Defense attorneys can be depended upon to go to great lengths to convince jurors that hair comparison is not the same as a fingerprint. Without corroborating evidence, hair comparison will seldom convict.

And they had no such corroborating evidence. They did not have the murder weapon. They did not have the shirt that possibly might match the red fiber. The value of the B-antigen found in the sperm was questionable, because Esther was a B-antigen secretor. The defense could argue that the B-antigen could be Esther's own.

Yet the circumstantial evidence was strong. Schoolcraft could testify that the knife had been in the truck. Now it was missing. Witnesses could place Sadler and Adams near the crime scene in the proper time frame. Sadler had changed clothes within that time frame. Medical technicians could testify that blood patterns they saw on Adams and Sadler did not match the wounds they received in the wreck. And Adams would have to explain his apparent flight away from highways into the river bottom.

Goss and Sunderland again reviewed their evidence, and discussed it at length. They agreed that they needed more. Much more.

But they also agreed that, at this point, they were unlikely to find further evidence, no matter how hard they worked. The murder weapon, Sadler's red pullover, and Esther's billfold probably would never be found. And most likely, no additional witnesses existed.

Any new information would have to come from Sadler and/or Adams.

"Let's just take a run at one of them," Goss suggested, "and really hit him hard."

They felt that Bugs Adams would be the best candidate. Before obtaining the arrest warrants, they checked on the whereabouts of Sadler and Adams.

The Mangum National Guard unit had gone off to summer training at Fort Sill.

Bugs Adams was in camp.

Sadler was AWOL.

13 . . .

At Fort Sill, the Criminal Investigation Division provided Sunderland and Goss with a small room for the interrogation of Bugs Adams. Two civilian-clothed CID officers went out to bring him in from the artillery range.

He arrived wearing fatigues, wet with perspiration. He searched the faces of Goss and Sunderland apprehensively. As he spoke to them, he seemed nervous and scared.

The interrogation room was army-neat and uncluttered. As soon as Bugs was seated, Goss informed him in firm tones that he was under arrest for the murder of Esther K. Steele.

"We'd like to ask you a few questions,"

Goss went on. "But you have the right to remain silent and to have your attorney present. Do you want a lawyer?"

Bugs had talked his way out of jams all of his life. He did not hesitate. "I'll answer the questions."

Goss read the Miranda statement aloud. Bugs said he understood it. He signed the form. Goss and Sunderland signed as witnesses to his signature. They then fell into their good-cop, bad-cop roles.

"We know you killed her," Goss said in a stern, no-nonsense manner. "Why don't you tell us about it?"

Bugs shook his head. He had expected more questions about where he had been that night and how much beer he drank.

Not this.

"Bugs, we know you were there," Goss said, his voice rising in volume. "We have witnesses."

Over the next few minutes Goss's questions became ever more hard-edged and scathing. The tempo gradually rose until he was screaming and shouting questions at Bugs. Then, as if his anger had reached the breaking point and he simply could not take any more, Goss abruptly left the room, leaving Sunderland and Bugs alone.

Sunderland patted Bugs on the shoulder and sat down beside him. "Now, Bugs, we know you killed her," he said. "And I know it's bothering you. I can tell by the way you act. Why not talk about this? Get it off your chest? I can't promise you anything. But if you'll cooperate, I'll certainly tell the DA that you did."

To Sunderland's total surprise, Bugs burst out crying.

Sunderland had expected Bugs to break eventually, but not this soon.

"We done it," Bugs said, sobbing, his head lowered. "We killed her. I didn't do it. Wayne's the one that went in. I waited in the pickup. I wanted to tell you guys before. But I was afraid."

Bugs could not stop crying. Goss returned to the room and sat quietly.

Bugs seemed relieved to tell his story. He spoke between sobs. "I couldn't sleep. It was bothering me. I've lied to a lot of people."

Gently, Sunderland took him back through his movements that night, beginning with the start of the drinking in Mangum.

Through the early portion, Bugs told essentially the same version that he had given in his first interview a month earlier.

But from the moment in Granite when he and Sadler learned that Johnny Monroe was not home, his story became far more detailed—and different.

For the most part, Sunderland and Goss allowed Bugs to talk without interruption.

Bugs had regained some of his composure. "After we left Elsie's house, we parked there at the wooden bridge and drank the rest of the beer," he said. "We'd spent all our money on the beer. We talked about where we was going to get some more money at. And Wayne asked me if I knew any old ladies we could rob."

Bugs said that discussion continued as they drove downtown.

"We went to Pearl Johnson's house. I got out there and took a leak. We got back in and drove off from there, and was going down the street, and I told Wayne I knew where an old lady was. While we was going down the street, I pointed out the house."

"Whose house?" Sunderland asked.

"Mrs. Steele's."

Again Bugs started sobbing. An interval passed before he could resume. Sunderland told him to relax and to take his time.

He said that at the corner beyond Esther Steele's house, he parked.

"Wayne grabbed the knife off the dash and got out of the truck."

"What kind of knife?" Sunderland asked.

"A fillet knife."

Goss could not suppress a sharp intake of breath. He had guessed the type of knife. But Schoolcraft had insisted on calling it "just a regular fish knife."

"Wayne got out in front of the car lights and took off his shoes and put his socks over his hands," Bugs said. "Then he left the truck."

"In what direction?"

"Toward the sidewalk."

"Then what did you do?"

"I drove around for a while. Circled the block. I kept coming back there, looking for him. Then I saw him coming out of the rock ditch."

"How long did you drive around, from the time you left him, until the time you saw him again?"

Bugs again was crying so hard he had trouble answering. "I don't know. A long time."

"Try to estimate."

"I don't know. It was quite a while."

"When he came back to the truck, what did he say?"

"He didn't say anything. He didn't talk about it."

"How did he look?"

"He was shaky. He showed me a billfold and gave me ten dollars out of it. Then we took off."

"What happened to the knife and billfold?"

"We went out into the country a little way. Wayne told me, 'Stop here so I can get rid of this stuff.' Wayne got out of the pickup and went out into the dark. When he came back, he was naked from the waist up. He got some old coveralls out of the truck and put them on."

Beyond that Bugs would not, or could not, go despite continued questioning.

He insisted that he thought Sadler had merely stolen the money. He said he did not know about the murder until the following day.

"I heard about it at the bowling alley," he said. "And when I got home, it was on the news."

"Why didn't you go to the police?" Sunderland asked.

Bugs answered without hesitation. "I was afraid of what Wayne would do to me if I told."

Sunderland and Goss concluded the interview and put Bugs in their car for the sixty-mile trip to the Greer County Jail in Mangum.

Bugs alluded to the murder only once on the road.

"I sure do feel better since I've got that off my chest," he said.

Then he went to sleep. He slept most of the way to Mangum.

Some detectives claim that sleep is a better indication of guilt than a polygraph test. They say that if a guilty man and an innocent man are placed in a jail cell, they can come back a short time later and determine which is guilty.

The innocent man will be climbing the walls, screaming his innocence. The charges and the situation are new to him. He cannot rest.

The guilty man will be asleep.

After many days of worrying, and many sleepless nights, arrest for the guilty often brings a strong sense of relief.

Before their trip to Fort Sill to arrest Bugs, Goss and Sunderland had discovered that Sadler had left town with a carnival. By telephone, Sunderland had tracked the carnival to Woodward, a town one hundred and thirty miles to the north.

This information and the arrest warrant had been turned over to OSBI agent Donnie Crane in Woodward.

On their return to Mangum with Bugs, Sunderland and Goss learned that Crane had already made the arrest. Sadler had offered no resistance, and he was being held in the Woodward County Jail.

Sunderland and Goss left Mangum immediately. They arrived at the Sheriff's Office in Woodward a few minutes before 9:00 P.M.

For their interview with Sadler, they were provided with a tiny room just off the lobbylike entrance to the sheriff's offices.

Sadler arrived from jail sleepy-eyed, but calm and collected.

Sadler, Sunderland, and Goss took seats at a small table in the little room, with Goss and Sadler facing, and Sunderland slightly to one side, taking notes.

"I just woke up," Sadler told them. "I've been asleep since this afternoon when they put me in jail."

"You are under arrest for the murder and rape of Esther K. Steele," Goss told him. "We would like to ask you some questions. But you have the right to remain silent and to have your lawyer present."

Sadler gave Goss his see-through stare and did not answer.

"This form says you have been read your rights and that you understand them. If there's anything you don't understand, please ask and we will explain it."

Goss read the Miranda form aloud. Sadler signed it. Goss and Sunderland witnessed his signature.

"Do you want a lawyer?" Goss asked again.

"I'll answer your questions," Sadler said.

Goss began the tough-cop game that had worked so well on Adams. "I'll tell you up front. Pat Adams is also in custody. He has given us a complete statement. He names you as the one who committed the murder. So you might as well tell us about it."

Sadler did not seem fazed. But he hesitated.

"I think I want a lawyer," he said.

Goss was not especially surprised. He had not expected to get Sadler's cooperation. From the start Sadler had shown himself to be a cool individual. The confession from Bugs had been a breakthrough. Goss did not want to jeopardize the case by risking a Miranda violation.

"Then we can't talk with you further," he said.

Goss and Sunderland rose to leave the room. They were tired after their sixteen-hour day and the two-hundred-mile drive from Fort Sill to Mangum and then to Woodward. A coffee urn stood behind the dispatcher's desk in the lobby. They started walking toward it, intending to drink a cup of coffee while they asked the dispatcher to help them find a motel room for the remainder of the night. They planned to get a few hours of sleep before taking Sadler back to Mangum the next morning.

But as Sunderland walked out the door of the small room, he glanced back at Sadler, who still appeared sleepy. "You want a cup of coffee?" he asked.

Sadler nodded affirmatively. Sunderland followed Goss across the lobby to the coffee urn. They drew three cups. Sunderland took one back to Sadler.

Sunderland and Goss left him alone in the small room, drinking coffee.

They took their own cups to the dispatcher's desk and were making motel reservations when Sadler pushed open the door to the little room, stuck his head out, and called across the lobby.

"Could I talk to you guys?"

Only a few minutes had elapsed. As Sunderland walked back toward Sadler with Goss, he recognized the potential legal jeopardy of resuming the interrogation. Under the Miranda rule, police officers must terminate questioning once a subject says he wants a lawyer. The individual in custody has the option of instigating further talk, if he so chooses. However, the courts have ruled that there must be a definite break.

As far as Sunderland was aware, that exact interval had never been defined.

Was four or five minutes enough?

Sunderland felt that he and Goss should take care not to endanger the case. Even before sitting down, he reminded Sadler he had the right to remain silent and to have his lawyer present. Just to be on the safe side, he again read the OSBI Miranda form aloud.

Sadler insisted that he wanted to tell what happened. Goss and Sunderland sat and listened.

Unlike Bugs, Sadler told his story without the slightest hint of emotion. Sunderland took notes. Sadler said that what he had told them in Mangum was all true, except for what happened in Granite.

"We went to Johnny Monroe's house, but he wasn't home. After we left Johnny's house, we drove around for a while. Bugs acted like he didn't want to leave town. We started talking about where we could get some more money for beer. Bugs said he knew where he could get some money."

In a residential area—Sadler said he did not know where—Adams stopped and got out of the truck.

"He took the knife from the dash. He started to walk away. Then he came back to the truck and said, 'Give me your socks.' "

Sadler said he took his socks off and gave them to Bugs and that Bugs again started to walk off, but again came back.

"He said, 'Give me your jacket.' "

Sadler said he gave Adams his hooded red sweatshirt and waited in the truck for a long time.

"When he came back and took the socks off, I saw blood all over his hands."

"Did he say anything when he came back to the truck?" Goss asked.

Sadler nodded. "He said, 'I've been shot. If something happens, you may need to drive the truck.' "

Sadler said Bugs gave him fifteen dollars from a billfold and they drove away from Granite.

"Outside of town, Bugs stopped the truck and got out. He took a brick or rock from the back of the truck, wrapped it in the sweatshirt with the knife and billfold, and threw them into a creek."

Goss pressed for details. "Did Adams say anything else to you when he got back into the truck?"

"He said, 'I killed her, man. I killed her.' "

Sadler said he and Bugs had seen each other only once or twice in the month since. On those occasions they told each other to stay calm. But Sadler added that he had thought about going to the police.

Both Goss and Sunderland were struck by Sadler's cold manner in telling his story. Bugs Adams had cried like a baby. But never a tear from Sadler.

The next morning, Goss and Sunderland drove Sadler back to Mangum and the Greer County Jail. In a sense, they were back to square one.

They had obtained two full confessions. But the two versions

were contradictory. They had no evidence to prove which version—
if either—was true.

They had only four hairs, some antigens that did not point to
anyone, and a red fiber.

More would be needed for convictions.

14 ■ ■ ■

THE ARRESTS OF BUGS ADAMS AND
Wayne Sadler brought a wave of blessed relief
to Granite. The long nightmare had ended.
Tensions eased. Some of the elderly residents
moved back into their own homes for the first
time since Esther's murder.

Yet there was surprise bordering on disbelief.

Everyone remembered Bugs.

"He was always hanging around," said one
former schoolmate. "He'd follow people all
day if they'd let him. Sometimes you had to
throw rocks at him just to get rid of him."

"He had a speech impediment of some
kind when he was in the lower grades," an-

other remembered. "He drooled. Slobbered. Some of the kids started calling him 'Bug Juice.' I know other explanations came out later. But I always thought that was where he got the nickname 'Bugs.' "

"I can't visualize Bugs doing something like that," said yet another. "I don't think he'd have the nerve, unless somebody led him into it. I remember him as a taker, not a giver, when it came to violence. If anyone wanted to beat up on somebody, they went out and hunted up Bugs, and beat up on him. He was always a loud-mouth. But he couldn't fight worth a damn."

Memories were revived. Former classmates recalled that Esther often had trouble with Bugs when he was in her homeroom.

"She was kind of hard on him," said a former classmate. "She felt he wasn't doing what he was capable of doing."

One clash between the two was recalled. One day Esther whipped Bugs after she caught him in a minor theft. Bugs shouted back at her and created quite an uproar.

"I remember the incident," said Jan Wingo Locklear. "I was in the upper grades, maybe a senior, and I was working in the school office that day. I don't remember details. I only remember that the whole school was talking about it."

One classmate remembered that Bugs stood up to Esther on that occasion and shouted, "I'll kill you! I'll kill you!"

"I don't remember that," said another. "But it sounds like some-thing Bugs would do. He was always shooting off his mouth."

In Mangum, the shock was just as profound. Those who remem-bered Sadler could not believe he would be involved in a rape and murder. True, he had always been an odd kid, dreamy, never quite connecting with those around him. Stories persisted about his drink-ing and drugs. But in class he had always been quiet and withdrawn. He had never shown the aggression one would associate with rape and murder.

Among those who found the accusation difficult to believe was Sadler's former football coach, Mike Smith, who was now teaching and coaching at Clarendon in the Texas Panhandle. Smith remembered Sadler vividly. He immediately rejected the theory that Sadler was filled with rage, barely under control.

"I never have seen that rage," Smith said. "If he had it, I think I would have seen it on the football field. But I never saw it. I saw the opposite. I saw a kid that was starved for affection.

"I don't believe David Wayne did it. I just know that David Wayne is the kind of kid that if anyone showed him any respect, he'd do anything. And you could lead him anywhere. I don't think he'd harm anybody."

Coach Smith believed people often misread Sadler's failure to show emotion.

"He wasn't used to showing emotion. The kid had it. He just couldn't show it. He wasn't a bad kid. He was just by himself. He didn't fit in real well with anybody, and he was sort of a loner."

Smith said Sadler earned the high marks he received in sports.

"He sort of found something to hang onto in football. He didn't get to play much, but he was a kid that was always there. And when we got beat in the second game of the playoffs—as far as Mangum had ever gone in the state playoffs—he was just totally torn up. Crying. I still remember to this day. I went into the shower and he was just sobbing. I felt sorry for him, because it really meant something to him."

Smith said he believed there was a time when David Wayne could have been rescued and his life turned around.

"All the kid ever needed was some love. The whole thing just makes me sick."

On the morning after the arrests, the defendants were taken before associate district judge David E. Brooks and formally charged with first degree murder, first degree rape, and first degree burglary.

Bond was denied.

Judge Brooks appointed attorney Ron Wallace of Oklahoma City to represent Adams, and attorney David Cummins of nearby Hollis to represent Sadler.

District attorney H. Russell Wright, who had come to Esther's house from Elk City after her body was found, fulfilled his promise of that night and announced to the press and television that he would seek the death penalty for both Sadler and Adams.

Yet, in truth, the state's case against them remained slim. Each confession damaged the weight of the other. Hair comparison was not conclusive evidence. And the red pullover that possibly matched the fiber found in Esther's fingernail was still missing.

Goss and Sunderland obtained search warrants and escorted Adams and Sadler to Mangum City Hospital. There blood was drawn to determine if either was a B-antigen secretor.

With the two seated in an examining room at the hospital, Goss knelt before them and had each pull hair samples and place them in a small bindle. He sealed and labeled each bindle and put them in an office envelope, which he sealed and initialed.

The blood and hair samples were dispatched immediately to Mary Long at the OSBI lab in Oklahoma City.

Sunderland and Goss then took Adams and Sadler, one at a time, back to the road where they had wrecked the pickup truck for day-long searches in an effort to pinpoint where Esther's billfold, Sadler's socks and sweatshirt, and the murder weapon had been dumped.

O.C. drove out to help with the search. There he saw Sadler for the first time. Police officers from Granite and surrounding communities were spread out along the road, examining every square foot.

Sadler was standing in the wind beside a car.

From first glimpse, O.C. was convinced of Sadler's guilt. In his view, Sadler was a scary-looking individual—skeleton thin, dirty, emaciated, hollow-eyed, grubby. O.C. felt Sadler appeared about as far down as a person can go. He held himself back from walking closer, not trusting himself at the moment to keep his anger in check. But he studied Sadler long enough to become convinced that his earlier theory of the murder was correct.

"That skinny, dopey-looking little guy could not have handled Esther by himself," O.C. later told friends. "*Both* of them must have gone into the house."

Sadler pointed out where he thought the evidence had been dumped. But an all-day search ended futilely.

The next morning, Adams was brought to the scene. He said he remembered Sadler kicking dirt to cover the evidence, but he also insisted he heard Sadler walking through "weeds or water." The areas he pointed out were searched.

The ditch was mowed to facilitate the hunt. A road grader was brought in and the ditch scraped bare. A brush hog cleared the right-of-way and a strip along the adjoining field.

Three days were spent in the search. But the red sweatshirt, socks, billfold, and slim-bladed knife were not found.

Goss and Sunderland's disappointment was eased by an encouraging report from Oklahoma City: Mary Long had determined that the hair samples from Sadler were "microscopically consistent" with the four "unknowns" from Esther's bedding.

Adams's blood was type A. Like Esther, he was a B-antigen secretor. Sadler's blood type was O. He was an H-antigen secretor.

The antigen results did not necessarily link either to the sperm. There was no way to determine if the B-antigen in the sperm came from Bugs or from Esther. But in the days that followed, the possibility arose for a more exact test.

At the time, DNA fingerprinting had not yet been introduced into Oklahoma courts. Recently a Florida conviction had paved the way for its acceptance elsewhere. Already the new technique was being hailed in criminology literature as the greatest boon to prosecutors since fingerprints.

At a convention of district attorneys in Oklahoma City, a representative of Lifecodes, Inc., was included on the program. He explained to prosecutors that his New York firm was now making the technique available to law enforcement agencies.

After his talk, Mary Long, Richard Goss, and Jerry Sunderland met with him. They made arrangements for Lifecodes to receive swabbings of sperm taken from Esther Steele's body and blood samples from Adams and Sadler.

If the DNA matched either, the prosecutors could then move forward with the first case to use the technique in the state of Oklahoma or the Southwest.

In late June—two full months after the murder—Esther's house at last was released to the family. O.C. and Flora Mae, accompanied by their close friends Raymond and Lucille Massey, drove to the house to take possession.

O.C. was not surprised to find all wooden and metal surfaces stained dark with fingerprint powder. The house looked violated. O.C. wondered if soap, water, and paint would ever make it seem right again.

He walked on down the hall, into Esther's bedroom. There he made a traumatic discovery. The blood-soaked mattress was still on the bed. Esther's lifeblood was still streaked down the wall, onto the floor.

O.C. knew he should have anticipated what he might find. But somehow, without really thinking about it, he had assumed that by now someone would have cleaned the room.

It was one of his worst moments yet.

He made himself study the stains and decide what to do about them. He concluded that their removal would be impossible; he would have to replace that entire section of wall.

In July, an event that at first appeared unrelated drastically altered the course of the legal proceedings against Bugs Adams and Wayne Sadler.

District Attorney H. Russell Wright, who had visited the murder scene on the night after the body was found, and who had promised to seek the death penalty for Sadler and Adams, found himself on the wrong side of the jail bars. The FBI, ending a long undercover investigation, arrested Wright and formally charged him with dealing in drugs.

In the wake of the shock that swept through the state's legal system, an obligatory game of musical chairs began.

The governor appointed Assistant District Attorney Stephen Coit to replace Wright as DA. Coit, in one of his first official acts, rehired David Cummins, a former assistant district attorney who had resumed private practice during Wright's tenure. Because Cummins previously had been court-appointed as Sadler's defense attorney, the court now was required to appoint new defense counsel for Sadler.

And because Cummins had been Sadler's defense attorney but was now a prosecutor, the DA's office was required to distance itself and turn the case over to a special prosecutor.

Charles V. Williams of Watonga accepted the appointment as special prosecutor with mixed feelings. A cursory first reading of the files revealed that hard evidence against the defendants was scant. The case would have to be won in the courtroom. That was the kind of challenge Williams relished. He liked the role of putting bad guys away. And not many capital murder cases came along in southwest Oklahoma.

But he also saw complications.

He would be entering the case late. Already the preliminary hearings had been delayed because of the Wright drug indictment. In appointing Williams, the presiding judge indicated he would not look with favor on futher motions for delay.

Mangum was more than a hundred miles from Williams's home in Watonga. Preparation for the preliminary hearings and trial would require many hours of travel back and forth.

Moreover, all of this work would come on top of his regular duties as assistant district attorney in Blaine County. In effect he would be holding down two full-time jobs a hundred miles apart. He did not welcome spending that much time away from his family.

Yet he wanted to try this case. He was close to retirement. A victory in a tough capital case such as this would fit nicely as a cap to his career.

He was under no illusions as to why he had been appointed. He had worked hard to earn his reputation as a conscientious, hard-driving prosecutor. He had shown himself to be especially effective in working with juries.

This skill was no accident. In the Plains states, as in many other sections of the country, there still exists the lingering tradition of the spellbinding courtroom orator. This colorful heritage, dating back to Abraham Lincoln and beyond, tends to infuse an element of drama into the proceedings. Juries expect it. Williams had cultivated that professional role. At six-two, he took care to keep his weight below two hundred pounds for a trim appearance. His thick, silver-gray hair, fashionably cut, was enhanced by a small, well-trimmed mustache. He was painstaking with his well-fitted suits and tasteful ties, lent added flair by diamond rings and stickpin.

He knew these Oklahoma juries. He had been born and reared in Tulsa. He had received his law degree there. After five years in North Carolina, conducting investigations for the insurance industry, he had returned to Oklahoma in 1974 to serve six years in the DA's office at Elk City.

Then, with spectacular bad timing, he entered private practice in 1980. He was building his clientele when the oil bust came, sending the Oklahoma economy reeling into the pits. He joined the DA's staff in Blaine County in 1987.

His first concern in the Sadler-Adams case rested with the timing of the court docket. Like an athlete in training, a prosecutor must pace himself. If he waits too long to prepare, he finds himself rushed in the final stages. If he prepares too soon, he forgets his case amid the press of other work.

For several months Williams devoted most of his daylight hours to his duties in Blaine County and worked after hours on the Sadler-Adams case, familiarizing himself with the bulky files forwarded to him from the Greer County DA's office.

From the beginning there was a strong likelihood that the cases would be split and that he would serve as special prosecutor in two separate trials.

Normally, the testimony of each defendant could be used to help convict the other. But with each defendant telling a different version, the worth of that testimony would be thrown into question.

Day by day, the case seemed to grow more complicated.

Attorney Ron Wallace of Oklahoma City, appointed to defend Bugs Adams, interviewed his client at length. Bugs was scared—and talking. Wallace came away convinced that Bugs was telling the truth, or at least a reasonable version thereof.

Wallace felt that in his experience he had developed an instinct about people. He simply did not believe that Bugs Adams was the type to commit murder and rape. Although Bugs was six years older than Sadler, Wallace felt that Bugs had been the follower, and not the leader, in the night's activities.

"Oh, I believe Pat'll lie," Wallace conceded. "I believe he was involved in it. But I don't believe he was actually the one who raped that woman. Honestly I don't.

"In my opinion, you'd almost have to hold his arm with a knife to get him to do something like that. I'd say he just didn't have the heart to do it."

Wallace was familiar with life in a small town. He had grown up in Wright City, a town about the size of Granite, in the southeast part of the state. After receiving degrees from the University of Oklahoma and from Oklahoma City Law School, he entered practice in Oklahoma City in 1981.

A year prior to this murder he had tried a manslaughter case before Judge Brooks. Apparently Judge Brooks was impressed, and remembered. When Brooks could not find an attorney in the Mangum area who did not know Esther Steele or her family, Wallace received the call to defend Bugs Adams.

As Wallace prepared for the preliminary hearings, he became even more convinced that Bugs was not the murderer. When the other attorneys in the case sought polygraph tests to determine which defendant was lying, Wallace did not object.

He felt certain that Bugs would pass.

Richard Hovis of Hobart, now representing David Wayne Sadler, became equally convinced that *his* client was telling an approximate version of the truth.

He felt that Goss and Sunderland had misread Sadler from the beginning.

"The only reason they thought Sadler was the mean one was because he didn't break down and cry. But he's an inward type of person. I don't believe you can label anyone a killer just because they don't readily show their emotions. Since they got to Adams first, and made him break down first, I think they wanted to believe him."

And as he delved deeper into the case, Hovis grew uncomfortable with the OSBI investigation.

"I think Goss—particularly Goss—violated some main principles of police investigation," he concluded. "I think he let his personal feelings get involved, and I think he neglected certain facts, got carried away in a couple of really important areas, particularly the semen test. I think he got it in his head that Sadler did it, and kind of worked the case around that."

Hovis believed the evidence cast doubt on the version told by Bugs Adams.

"Frankly, I'm convinced that Adams raped her for sure. And Adams might have also killed her. I think the facts support that Adams was there. According to the OSBI semen tests, I don't think Sadler could have raped her."

Hovis felt qualified to comment on the lab findings. Before entering Tulsa University Law School, he taught high school biology for four years—two in Annapolis, Maryland, and two in Tulsa.

A native of Tulsa, and a graduate of Oklahoma State University, he had served as public defender in Tulsa, as legal aid in Muskogee, and on the staff of the district attorney in Muskogee before entering private practice in Hobart in 1982.

He agreed with the other attorneys that the discrepancies in the stories told by the defendants should be resolved. He approved the polygraph tests.

On August 4, Sunderland and Goss drove first Adams, then Sadler, to Woodward for the polygraph tests, administered by an OSBI operator.

Bugs Adams passed.

Sadler flunked.

On the drive back to Mangum, riding in the front seat, Sadler made an odd statement.

"Maybe I *was* the one that went into the house," he said.

He spoke almost as if talking to himself. But both Sunderland, driving, and Goss, in the backseat, heard the remark.

Although the statement became a part of the peripheral record, and perhaps influenced the handling of the case, it could not be used as evidence, for it could not be extracted from the context of the polygraph tests—a subject that could not be mentioned before a jury.

Hovis remained unconvinced that Sadler was the one who was lying. He voiced doubt about the way the polygraph tests had been conducted.

"I was up there for the tests, and they wouldn't let me be present. Sadler's not smart enough to make up the things he told me. Sadler said he overheard them talking, saying things like, 'Well, he passed it, now what do we do?' or something to that effect. It was like they didn't know where to proceed from there. The OSBI was in it so deep they kind of committed themselves. They'd already accepted Adams's version, and they knew the polygraph legally was immaterial. So I felt they lied about that."

O.C. was determined not to miss one word of the legal proceedings. When the preliminary hearings opened in September, he asked to be notified before each session.

Sandwiched among other courthouse business, the hearings in effect were dress rehearsals for a trial. Witnesses were summoned to give the court essentially the same information they had told Sunderland and Goss.

The interior of the Greer County Courthouse tends to be gloomy and claustrophobic. Built in 1908—the year after statehood—the courthouse predates adequate air-conditioning and central heating by a half century. Years ago it was possible to look up from the ground floor to the rotunda, high overhead, lending the building an aura of openness and spaciousness. Now the third floor has been condemned as unsafe and is walled off. The rotunda openings have been boarded over. The lower two floors have been refurbished with dark paneling, and the ceilings lowered, making the interior close and oppressive.

One afternoon O.C. and Flora Mae sat through a lengthy hearing. The courtroom was cold. O.C. was tired, and he felt ill. When Judge Brooks declared a brief recess, most of those in the courtroom filed out during the break to smoke in the outside lobby.

"Let's just stay in here," O.C. said to Flora Mae. "I don't want to breathe that smoke."

But as the courtroom emptied, O.C. and Flora Mae found themselves alone with Adams and Sadler.

The two defendants were seated only a few feet away. No guard was in the courtroom. Neither was handcuffed.

O.C. was not at all comfortable with the situation.

"Let's go on out of here," he said to Flora Mae.

They rose to leave.

As they reached the aisle and started walking out, Sadler snickered and said something. He laughed, and then both Sadler and Adams laughed, looking at O.C. and his wife.

O.C. did not hear what Sadler said. But there was no mistaking the tone. O.C. walked out into the lobby, furious.

He told someone in the lobby what had happened. "I believe if I'd had a gun right then, I think I'd have shot that son of a bitch," he said. "It made me that mad. Him to be laughing at us, after what he did. You know that would make anybody mad."

O.C.'s remark was overheard.

The repercussions were immediate.

O.C. was labeled "a potentially dangerous person." A deputy sheriff was assigned to keep watch over him throughout the remainder of the hearings and the trial.

A few days later a deputy sheriff asked O.C. to come by the jail after a hearing. He said he wanted to talk.

O.C. had known the deputy for many years—clear back to the deputy's childhood. So after the deputy returned Adams to his cell, O.C. and Flora Mae walked over to the jail.

The deputy met them in the lobby. He began by saying he was well acquainted with Adams and his family, and was convinced that Adams was innocent.

"O.C., he's a good man," the deputy said. "I'm sure he didn't do nothing. Why, O.C., I'd trust that ol' boy—"

O.C. lost his temper. "God damn, Bill!" he said. "I come over here, and you start telling me crap like that? Why would you be telling *me* something like that? You can go straight to hell. I'm not going to listen to crap like that."

O.C. and Flora Mae turned and walked out.

"It made me madder'n hell," O.C. said. "That's just stupid! Of course he's a stupid kind of guy. He just carries a gun on his hip. They get used to that. And that's all he's going to do all his life.

"That was one of the worst things in the whole deal. Him trying to tell me something like that! About somebody like that!"

15 ■ ■ ■

TERRY RHINE EMERGED SCOT-FREE FROM
the investigation into Esther's death. But
interviews conducted by the OSBI agents
had uncovered evidence that Rhine's drug
dealing and the sleazy nightlife that revolved
around him were reaching even the school-
children. There was not yet enough evidence
for an indictment. But clearly something had
to be done.

Police Chief Williams had submitted
his resignation just prior to Esther's murder.
The appointment of his successor had not
worked out to everyone's satisfaction. The
Granite City Council met in a series of executive sessions to determine what action

to take to destroy the growing threat of drugs in the community.

The council's solution was as simple as a favorite plot of the old
B-westerns once screened at the Kozy: a hired gun was needed to
come in and clean up the town. And the council had a candidate in
mind.

At six-two and two hundred twenty-five pounds, Charles Jones
looked the part. He was personable, handsome, and imposing—right
out of central casting.

Moreover, he had grown up in Granite. Esther Steele had been
one of his teachers. He still remembered the bird-watching, the
nature field trips. And he possessed ample professional qualifications
for the role.

After high school he had served in the air force during the
Vietnam War. On his return, he had worked as a policeman in
Granite a short time before joining the Police Department in nearby
Sayre. After earning a degree in law enforcement at Northwestern
Oklahoma State University, he had served thirteen years with the
Oklahoma Highway Patrol. An injury to his back had resulted in his
retirement from the patrol.

The City Council offered him the job.

At first, Jones was reluctant. He felt he had seen enough of police
work, and he was working toward a career change. He was in the
process of completing requirements for a master's degree in counseling, and had expected to return to Granite as a case manager at
the reformatory. He was looking forward to this, for he knew that
casework could be rewarding. Case managers counsel convicts
and families. With the proper effort, sometimes a convict's prison
time could be put to productive use. Jones knew that drugs were
at the core of most inmates' troubles. Therefore he had focused
on drug counseling. He firmly believed that he could make a strong
contribution at the reformatory and launch his career in a new
direction.

But he was acquainted with the situation in Granite. Terry Rhine had been operating out of Granite for years and thought no one had the backbone to stop him. Rhine's main weapon was intimidation, and he was good at it. He was a scary fellow. Everyone around him was afraid of him.

The more Jones considered the council's offer, the more he warmed to the idea. He was certain that Rhine was at the center of Granite's retail drug trade and that he was selling to school-aged children. Putting Terry Rhine away would be a definite contribution to the community.

But he foresaw difficulties. In executive session, he told the council he would accept the job only on his own terms. He would not play favorites. He would arrest anyone breaking the law.

"I know the job will be short-term," he warned the council, "because I'll make a lot of people mad."

Every member of the council assured Jones that he or she would back him one hundred percent if he enforced the law and cleaned up the town.

Jones accepted the job. His first days in office brought immediate changes. Many of Granite's drivers had developed sloppy habits. Jones and his small force started handing out warnings, then tickets. Teenagers were corralled. Drunks were arrested.

As Jones had predicted, community reaction was heated. Citizens put pressure on members of the council to tell Jones to ease up. But members of the council kept their word. They continued to support him.

The controversy created an effective diversion from the attention Jones and his men were giving Terry Rhine.

Working quietly, Jones put together a special drug force, coordinating with elements of the Mangum Police Department, the Greer County Sheriff's Office, Assistant District Attorney Mathew Salter, probation officer Paul Wayne Morris, and various officers from nearby towns.

An elaborate undercover watch was kept on Rhine's activities. Every time Rhine rode his motorcycle out of Granite, the direction was noted and phone calls were made. Where he went and what he did were observed by officers in surrounding towns.

After several months, the pattern of Rhine's life left no doubt: he was dealing heavily out of his house in Granite, right next door to the post office.

On November 18, at about 8:00 P.M., Jones led the raid on Rhine's residence.

Rhine was known to be on a trip to Altus. His wife, Susan Carol, answered the door and was served with the search warrant.

Inside, the officers and a drug-sniffing dog borrowed from the Elk City Police Department found a smorgasbord of drugs ranging from marijuana to LSD. The house also contained lab equipment for the manufacture of amphetamine.

It was the first drug bust in Granite's history, and the largest yet conducted in that part of Oklahoma.

The LSD was in the form of "Plutos"—images of the Disney cartoon character printed on LSD-permeated blotting paper. The method was right out of the sixties and, Jones observed, especially designed to appeal to children.

The search also turned up illegal weapons and a twenty-five-foot python, along with a number of baby chickens.

"Terry had a self-feeder-type operation for the snake," Jones marveled. "He had baby chicks in there at the bottom of the cage. When the snake got hungry, he'd just go down and get himself one. Pythons won't eat anything dead, you know. They have to kill it."

The raid was still in progress when Rhine rode up on his motorcycle. He did not resist arrest.

The python was taken to a pet shop in Altus. Rhine was taken to the Greer County Jail.

With Rhine once again behind bars, several persons knowledgeable about his activities felt free to talk.

One was his wife, Susan Carol. At first she, too, was charged in the drug bust. But she soon convinced authorities that she was a victim, not a perpetrator. She said she had been wanting to leave Rhine for some time, but had been afraid to try.

Information from Susan Carol and others led to Rhine's indictment in the death of James Edward Hill, a black whose body had been found dumped in a ravine at Quartz Mountain the previous September.

Specifications of the murder charge alleged that Rhine had laced Hill's dope with rattlesnake venom.

The autopsy report noted that when injected directly into a vein, rattlesnake venom produces sweeping effects in the cardiac, vascular, and nervous systems. Three or more toxic reactions occur simultaneously. The exact cause of death might be considered a race among pulmonary edema, cardiac arrest, vascular collapse, and renal failure.

Rhine's claim to membership in Hell's Angels was soon confirmed. A contingent of motorcyclists swarmed into Mangum, saddlebags loaded with cash, prepared to bail Rhine out of jail. Heading the group was a bona fide, long-haired, chopper-riding lawyer.

But bond was denied. Rhine remained in jail.

Bugs Adams and David Wayne Sadler continued to tell different versions of their activities on the night of Esther's murder. A common defense was impossible. District Judge Charles L. Goodwin divided the case into separate trials.

Judge Goodwin also appointed Stephen D. Beam of Weatherford to join Richard Hovis in preparing Sadler's defense. Beam had tried a murder case before Judge Goodwin in the previous year. Apparently the judge had been impressed, and with good reason.

Only five years out of law school, Beam already had earned widespread reputation as an outstanding trial lawyer. Like Prosecutor Williams, he had cultivated the tradition of courtroom oratory. He was six feet four, and thin. He wore a closely trimmed black beard to match a thick thatch of black hair. The effect was Lincolnesque. He habitually spoke—even in ordinary conversation—with the diction and precision of one who had spent time perfecting the art.

He was well attuned to the psychology of Oklahoma juries. Although a native of the Texas Panhandle, he had grown up mostly in Oklahoma. His father had been in the construction business, and his family had moved around a lot. He entered private practice in Weatherford the year he graduated from the University of Oklahoma Law School.

From the first, Beam felt at a disadvantage because he had not had the opportunity to cross-examine the state's witnesses and get a feel for them during the preliminary hearings. He had only transcripts to use in preparation. And time was tight. He was appointed on December 28. The Bugs Adams trial was set to begin in early February. Sadler's trial was docketed for February 22.

Beam did not have time to make his customary search for potential conflicts. He was deeply immersed in familiarizing himself with the case before he learned that Esther Steele was the aunt of his friend and client Jean Wycoff—O.C.'s daughter—who was engaged in real estate in Weatherford.

When Beam learned this, he immediately considered withdrawing from the case.

"It was Jean's husband who told me that the murder victim was Jean's aunt. And I thought, 'Oh, my God!' Because I knew Jean, and I knew him, and was friends with both of them, as well as representing them."

Beam went to Jean. The meeting was traumatic for him. Wycoff told him that Esther Steele had been her favorite aunt. She told him what a wonderful person Esther was.

Beam told Jean that if the case would affect their personal or professional relationship, he would withdraw.

She said she understood his position, and that his representing Sadler would not cause a problem in their relationship.

"And it didn't," Beam said later. "Up until the trial, I didn't discuss it with her. We never said a word about it. And she was there at the trial every day. She took her daughters out of school, and they sat through part of the trial. It was an uncomfortable situation."

■ ■ ■

In the wake of the successful raid on Terry Rhine's house, Police Chief Jones mounted other, smaller, drug busts.

At 2:00 A.M. on a morning in January, he led city and county officers in a raid at the home of a member of one of the community's most well known and respected families.

A quantity of marijuana and other drugs was confiscated. The young husband and father was jailed on charges of unlawful delivery and possession.

"We were his first buyer," Jones said. "He was just getting started. We put him out of business fast."

Jan Wingo Locklear was faced with a tough decision. Previously, the *Granite Enterprise* had headlined each drug bust on page 1. From the first she had given Jones full editorial support.

But the new perpetrator was one of her in-laws.

The temptation was strong to back off on her journalistic standards, at least to the extent of waffling. With a weekly, an editor has more time to agonize over such decisions. She remembered that her father, throughout his long career, had declined to run crime news, feeling it bad publicity for the community his newspaper was obligated to support.

Had he been right?

Jan remembers that week as the toughest of her life.

Ultimately her journalistic standards won. She ran the story on page 1.

No frills. But there it was.

"I really didn't have a choice," Jan said. "My husband's family knew I didn't have a choice. They supported me all the way."

But Jones and his strict law enforcement were drawing increased criticism from the public. Some thought Jones was taking his role as hired gun a bit too seriously. Along with the narcotics arrests were others for driving under the influence, public intoxication, transporting an open container, disobeying stop signs, speeding, unauthorized burning of trash, improper display of auto tags, letting a dog run loose, and so forth.

Arrests averaged as high as seventy a month—in a community of only nine hundred residents. Many of those nine hundred were dependent on Social Security and Medicare. Warning citations averaged about fifty a month, mostly for such vehicular infractions as speeding, failure to yield right-of-way, improper backing, failure to keep right, improper left turn, and faulty headlights.

This in Granite, where three moving vehicles on the same block might be considered congested traffic, and where for decades motorists had made up their own rules.

Most residents were eager to see Granite returned to a law-abiding community. But now some were beginning to wonder: At what price?

Through late December and early January, Adams and Sadler were like two bullfrogs balanced on a lily pad. The death penalty loomed as a chillingly real possibility for both. But at any moment either could jump for the safety of a plea bargain and dump the other.

In the third week of January, with his trial less than two weeks away, Bugs Adams jumped. He swapped his testimony against Sadler for a life term.

His attorney, Ron Wallace, rejected any suggestion that the plea bargain was the result of elaborate defense strategy.

"Bugs didn't want to die," Wallace said. "It was that simple."

His fear of a possible death sentence was valid. By his own admission, Bugs was the one who singled out Esther Steele as the victim. He, not Sadler, had been her student. He, not Sadler, had been given the opportunity to turn his life around during the many hours he sat in Esther's schoolroom.

One of Esther's teaching colleagues aptly expressed a community sentiment that probably would have been reflected in the jury box: "Esther tried to teach him something. And he killed her for it."

After hours of talking with him, Wallace remained convinced that Bugs was not the one who went into the house and killed and raped Esther Steele.

"But according to law, it didn't make any difference," Wallace pointed out. "He was already in the course of a felony, which was the burglary. Under the law, that's enough for the death penalty."

Wallace worked out the plea bargain agreement with District Attorney Stephen Coit and Assistant District Attorney Mathew Salter. But on January 21, District Judge Goodwin rejected the agreement.

Judge Goodwin said that as he read it, the deal was conditional— Bugs's testimony against Sadler in exchange for dismissal of the rape and burglary charges, and recommendation of a life sentence. The judge said he could not accept the agreement on those terms.

The attorneys went away and drafted a revision. The new wording merely called for Bugs to testify "truthfully" in the prosecution of Sadler.

In his consideration of the new version, Judge Goodwin questioned Bugs at length on whether he understood exactly what was happening.

Bugs insisted that he did.

Judge Goodwin persisted. "Do you understand that by entering a plea of guilty to this offense of murder in the first degree, the court has but one alternative, which is to sentence you to life imprisonment?"

Bugs was nervous but subdued. "Yes, sir," he said.

"That is the sole sentence. There is no minimum sentence or maximum. That is the *only* sentence the court may grant in this case. Do you understand that?"

"Yes, sir," Bugs said.

Judge Goodwin asked him to tell, in his own words, precisely what happened that night.

An abbreviated version spurted out of Bugs without breath or punctuation. "We was out drinking beer and we ran out of money for the beer and went to Granite—"

"Now, who is 'we'?" Judge Goodwin interrupted.

"Me and Wayne Sadler. And when we were over at Granite I went by Johnny Monroe's house to see if Johnny was there and Johnny wasn't there. I went to Pearl's, Pearl Johnson's, and we sat there and drank a glass of beer, and Wayne asked me if I knew any old women, and I said yes. Then we went to Mrs. Steele's house and I dropped him off at the corner and he grabbed the knife off of the dash and he got out of the pickup, and I took off and went around the block, and when I picked him up he was shaking. And from there we had a wreck. Then the next day when I went bowling I heard it at the bowling alley. Then I heard it on the news. Then the OSBI guys talked to me and I was scared to tell them, and when I went to Lawton they asked me there and that's when I told them. That's when I got arrested."

Wallace questioned Bugs for the benefit of the court, drawing out more detail.

"Did Mr. Sadler ask if you knew any old women for a particular reason?"

"Yes."

"What was that reason?"

"To get some money. To burglarize the place."

Bugs told the judge about accepting the ten dollars. Judge Goodwin asked him for a description of the knife.

"The blade of it was eight or ten inches," Bugs said.

Judge Goodwin asked for his estimate of how long he waited for Sadler in the pickup.

"About an hour, an hour and a half."

"And you knew that he took the knife when he went in to burglarize Mrs. Steele's house?"

"Yes, sir. I didn't know exactly what he was going to do with it, though."

Judge Goodwin further questioned Bugs, establishing that he had not been coerced into changing his plea to guilty.

The judge then set March 17 as the date for sentencing. That would be after the start of Sadler's trial, scheduled to begin February 22.

Bugs seemed relieved. He joked with jailers as he was escorted from the courtroom.

For the first time since the night of the murder, he could breathe easier. Even with good time and crowded prisons, he would be spending most of the next two decades behind bars. But the danger was past. He would not be going to death row.

In February a panel of two hundred prospective jurors was summoned into the Greer County Courthouse for the start of the Sadler trial. Special Prosecutor Williams and defense attorneys Hovis and Beam went through them rapidly—and unsuccessfully.

Almost all of the potential jurors either knew Esther Steele or her family, or had formed an opinion.

As the panel dwindled, so did prospects for seating a jury.

The effort ended in a mistrial.

The case was transferred to the town of Arapaho in Custer County, seventy miles to the northeast.

There the trial was set to begin March 31.

In late March, Jerry Sunderland called his wife, Paula, from a motel in the northern part of the state, where he had been sent on OSBI business. He told Paula he would be spending the night there in Enid and would be driving home the next day.

"What time will you be back?" Paula asked.

Sunderland considered the work yet to be done, the distance he would drive before reaching home.

"About two in the afternoon," he said.

They talked of other, domestic, things. The conversation was no different from hundreds of others during their nine years together. But after the call, Sunderland fell to worrying.

Paula had said she was in bed, even though it was early evening. She had sounded even more depressed than usual. Through the last several months her medical condition had continued to worsen. Her headaches were more numerous, more severe. And now, as the result of the old bullet wounds, her intestinal tract was not functioning properly.

Sunderland endured a restless night. The Sadler trial would be opening soon. He would have to be there, spending even more time away from home. Even with the testimony of Bugs Adams, Sadler's trial might be a squeaker. The DNA evidence, which could have been the clincher, had not worked out. The New York firm had reported that the sperm was too deteriorated to test.

Sunderland had no doubt as to Sadler's guilt, but the case against him was not as strong as he had once believed.

The next morning, Sunderland completed his work and drove back to Altus. He arrived home about 2:30 P.M. and found Paula's body.

"She was a real neat person. She'd run the bathtub full of water, got in there, and locked the door. That bathroom was set up with the tub and the stool in a room by itself. And she'd closed the door going in. Then she'd closed the glass shower door, where she wouldn't mess the house up.

"The rest of the house was as neat as a pin."

She had used one of Sunderland's handguns, a .357 magnum.

"I think she knew she was dying," Sunderland said. "At least she thought she was dying. She'd lost a lot of weight. And she did things. She had changed her will. Her will had read that if anything happened to her, the two girls would go to her sister. She made me change that, a month or so before she died.

"She said, 'I want you to have those girls.'

"And I said, 'Okay.'

"And she said, 'I want to change the will.'

"And I said, 'Okay.'

"And she said, 'I don't mean next week, or tomorrow. I mean today.'

"So we changed the will that day. There were things like that. She just got so depressed, depressed, depressed. And I guess she finally reached the point where she couldn't take it anymore.

"She had gotten the girls off to school that morning. She had asked me what time I would be home to make sure the girls wouldn't be the ones to find her when they came home from school.

"Afterward, her doctor came to me and said, 'I can't tell you for certain, but I'm sure some of those fragments were moving in her brain, causing the pain.'

"Nobody knows for sure, because she blew her head off."

Sunderland was excused from participation in David Wayne Sadler's trial for rape and murder.

The trial opened the following week.

16 ■ ■ ■

SPECIAL PROSECUTOR CHARLES WILLIAMS entertained no illusions: bottom line, the state's case rested on the testimony of Bugs Adams—a slender reed—along with four head hairs found in the bedding and a red fiber from a missing sweatshirt. And that was all. The case would have to be won in the trenches, against a formidable opponent. Williams had never before encountered defense attorney Stephen Beam in a case. But he was well aware of the young man's growing reputation.

Yet, as Williams rose to make his opening statement to the jury of eight men, four women, and a female alternate, he felt moder-

ately confident. During the selection process, he had carefully prepared the jurors, educating them as far as the law allowed.

"Can you convict on circumstantial evidence?" he had asked
each. "We don't have an eyewitness to this homicide. In most murder cases you *don't* have witnesses. Manslaughter cases, heat of passion, you usually do. But not murder cases."

He had pointed out that circumstantial evidence is good evidence. He offered an illustration: If a mother put a jar of cookies in a
high cabinet, went to her room to take a nap, and returned to find a
chair pushed up to the counter, the lid off the cookie jar, saw
crumbs leading to her little son's bedroom, and found cookies in his
hand, the evidence would be compelling, even though there had
been no witnesses.

As Williams opened the trial by reading the lengthy formal
charges against Sadler, as the law required him to do, he was still
adjusting to the unusual layout of the Custer County courtroom. It
was different from any in his experience.

The arrangement was circular, like a miniature amphitheater.
The furniture was of light oak, in contrast to the gloomy dark wood
found in most courtrooms. The judge's slightly elevated, curved
bench formed the east side of the courtroom. On the judge's right
sat the court clerk, and on his left, the court reporter. Just beyond
the court reporter, the witness stand also was slightly elevated. After
a break of three or four feet in the circle, the curved defense table
came next, forming the south portion of the circle. There sat
Sadler—nearest to the witness stand—then Hovis and Beam. The
curved prosecutor's table constituted the west side of the circle. On
the north, the jury box completed the circle. Seven jurors sat on the
top row and five on the bottom row. A podium stood beside the jury
box, near the prosecutor's table.

The amphitheater's diameter was of no more than twenty feet,
placing all the trial principals in unusual intimacy.

Williams was pleased to note that the jurors were attentive. This
gave him further reason for hope. Conviction would depend on the

jury's ability to string many seemingly inconsequential facts into a cohesive whole. He had attempted to choose jurors capable of such concentration. He felt he might have succeeded.

In selecting them, he had made personal responsibility his prime criterion. He believed that jurors who demonstrated responsibility in their own lives would be more inclined to accept the responsibility of sending a murderer away for life, or to sentence him to the death chamber.

All but two were high school graduates. Three held college degrees. All were parents. Only one was divorced. All were partners in a two-income marriage.

Earlier, the defense had attempted some humor. The jury had not responded. That indicated to Williams that this jury was taking the job seriously.

He had won yet another reason for hope: Over vigorous objections from the defense, he had received the judge's permission to keep OSBI agent Richard Goss at his side throughout the trial as an advisory witness. The bare-bones prosecution budget did not provide for legal assistance. But Goss was thoroughly familiar with the case and knowledgeable in court procedure. He could make notes, keep track of papers, do research, and advise Williams on details of the case.

Williams finished reading the charges. He paused, signaling to the jurors that one segment of the trial was concluded and that another was about to begin.

Raising his voice against the hum of the air conditioner, he walked back and forth in front of the jury, making eye contact, communicating individually with each juror as he began his opening statement.

"Ladies and gentlemen, our evidence will show that during the evening hours of April 14, 1987, the defendant, David Wayne Sadler, and a codefendant, Phillip Pat Adams, got together in Mangum and started drinking beer . . ."

He went on to trace the erratic meanderings of Adams and Sadler as they drove from town to town drinking beer, searching for friends. He described the arrival of Adams and Sadler in Granite, out of beer and out of money.

"And while in Granite, they decided one way to get money would be to go in the home of an elderly person."

He paused in his pacing and raised his voice, as he always did when he wished to emphasize a point.

"Phillip Pat Adams suggested that they go to the home of Esther K. Steele."

In the jury box, second seat from the left in the back row, juror Alice Brown listened to the unfolding story with growing fascination. Special prosecutor Williams was tall and, with his gray hair and William Powell mustache, quite distinguished looking. He was a superb, mesmerizing speaker. She had just retired from her career as clerical supervisor for the Department of Human Services in nearby Clinton. She was accustomed to evaluating people. She found herself responding to Williams intuitively. As he spoke, he stood relaxed, his thumbs hooked in the pockets of his vest. His suit was impeccable.

She decided that she would place her faith in him. She felt that he was going to do the right thing and that he was going to make the jury do the right thing.

But her husband, Leo Brown, an auctioneer well known in the region, had always said she tended to jump to conclusions. She knew she would have to guard against that.

She glanced across the room to the defendant. He seemed not to be listening. He sat looking at the jury, his face devoid of expression. He appeared heartbreakingly young to be in so much trouble. In his ill-fitting, horrible purplish suit, he looked absolutely pathetic.

Her own five children were grown and away from home. She knew she would have to guard against thinking as a mother when the time came to decide on the verdict.

■ ■ ■

In front of Alice Brown, two seats from the right on the front row, Barney Brown—no relation—concentrated on the words of special prosecutor Williams and tried to ignore an irritating distraction.

For the last several minutes Brown had been under the defendant's expressionless stare. In the circular courtroom, the defense table faced the jury box. Sadler's stare was direct, cold, and unwavering.

Earlier, during jury selection, Brown had tended to feel sorry for Sadler. The young man appeared thin, and was not far removed in age from Brown's own two daughters and his wife's two sons. His daughters were married. Both boys were still in college.

Since his semiretirement from the Case Tractor Company, Brown had been spending more and more time working with a small Baptist church. At first he had been asked to teach Sunday school. Then he was called upon to serve as lay pastor. He enjoyed the work. He always liked to think he looked for the good in people. But under the relentless gaze of David Wayne Sadler, he began to think of Sadler as a dangerous individual. It was a feeling that persisted, and grew.

Brown once had served as jury foreman in a rape trial. He knew what might be required of him during the next few days. He pushed Sadler's stare out of his mind and listened as Williams described Sadler's return to the pickup, the division of the money, and the subsequent wreck southwest of Granite.

Williams told of the discovery of the body, and of the criminal investigation that led to Sadler and Adams.

"Four hairs found in the bedding of Esther K. Steele were microscopically consistent with the hairs of the defendant, David Wayne Sadler," Williams said.

Brown noticed that this was the only hard evidence Williams mentioned.

He found himself wondering if four head hairs were all the solid evidence the state had to offer.

■ ■ ■

On the bench, Associate District Judge Alan D. Markum monitored
the jurors. He also had concluded that this seemed to be an unusually attentive, hardworking group.

He was still mildly amazed to find himself trying this capital case.
Judge Goodwin had been scheduled to preside but had become ill.
On "docket Monday," only forty-eight hours ago, the case was
passed to Judge Markum. He was still absorbing the details of the
case. As Williams talked, Markum studied the seating diagram he
had drawn, matching names of jurors to faces.

Some he knew. Others were of a regional ilk. Custer County was
a part of the old Cheyenne-Arapaho Reservation, opened by a "run"
in 1892. The descendants of those pioneers usually bore a certain
stamp Markum recognized, for he had lived in the region most of his
life. He had grown up in Clinton, only five miles to the south of
Arapaho. He had received his B.A. at Southwestern Oklahoma State
University in Weatherford, fourteen miles to the east.

It was during his second year of law school at the University of
Oklahoma that he first experienced difficulty in keeping up with his
schoolwork. In high school, he had played football and competed in
track. But suddenly it seemed that he lacked stamina. He felt a persistent weakness in his legs.

The Vietnam War and the draft were in progress. Markum
enlisted in the National Guard and went off to summer camp. There
the weakness in his legs grew worse. One day in the field, he found
he simply could not get up from the ground.

His memories of that episode are not pleasant. The noncoms
assumed he was malingering. He was verbally abused, and kicked. A
burly sergeant seized him under the armpits and squeezed. When
the pain failed to drive him to his feet, the sergeant at last understood that something was wrong.

Markum was given lighter duties. But afterward, the symptoms
continued. Markum sought medical help.

The diagnosis, when it came, was devastating: amyotrophic lateral sclerosis, better known as Lou Gehrig's disease, usually fatal within a short time.

Markum had outlived that diagnosis by two decades. Now the doctors frankly admitted they were mystified. They could only offer theories.

Despite the pessimistic early diagnosis, Markum had gone on with his life. After law school, he served five years in the district attorney's office in Clinton. In the early eighties, he entered private practice. He was appointed to the bench by the governor on recommendation of the Bar Association. He was married, and was the father of two children—a son, seventeen, and a daughter, fifteen.

He maneuvered around the courthouse on an electric scooter. He had become so adept in its use that he utilized it in his body language, moving forward to stab out a cigarette, turning to face a speaker in conversation, backing to catch a phone. Perhaps there were even advantages: The singing of his scooter in the hall helped his staff and others to keep track of him.

He had not allowed his illness to interfere with his work. His caseload was heavy, sometimes brutal. He had been instrumental in the campaign to win voter approval for a bond issue to expand and refurbish the courthouse. He had researched and designed his own courtroom, using as a model a design perfected by the American Bar Association.

Told once that he was greatly admired for continuing his work in the face of his difficulties, he laughed.

"There's not much else you *can* do," he said.

"A great deal of what Mr. Williams has said will be uncontradicted," defense attorney Richard Hovis told the jury in his opening statement.

"The critical and very important part of the case will come when Mr. Sadler will be pointing at Mr. Adams, and Mr. Adams will be pointing at Mr. Sadler. Our evidence will show that, in fact, it was

Mr. Adams that went into the house and murdered Mrs. Steele and raped her."

Hovis was not as eloquent a speaker as Williams. His voice was soft, and he often spoke hesitantly.

He said the defense would demonstrate that the four hairs were not conclusive evidence, and that a critical point in the investigation came when the OSBI talked first with Bugs Adams.

"Bugs broke down and cried and gave them a real good scene and confessed, and said Sadler did it. The evidence will show that from that point on the OSBI investigated the case as if Sadler did it."

Hovis paused in front of the jury box and made eye contact with each juror.

"Mr. Williams has indicated there were no eyewitnesses. In fact, we have Bugs Adams and Wayne Sadler. They both saw who got out of the pickup. It will be up to the state to prove to you beyond a reasonable doubt that it was Mr. Sadler who got out and not Mr. Adams. I believe at the end of the evidence you will find they have *not* proved that beyond a reasonable doubt."

Williams called O.C. as his first witness.

The limits were narrow on how much information a member of the victim's family could give. By law, the jury must be guided in its decision solely by the evidence, unaffected by any taint of sympathy for the victim or for the victim's family.

But Williams recognized that this case offered a degree of latitude. The health and strength of the victim might be considered relevant. He would suggest in his closing arguments that only through premeditated use of a knife would this thin, frail defendant be able to rape and murder Esther Steele. Beyond this he could not go.

O.C. was escorted to the stand and sworn. Williams secretly hoped that O.C. would weep at some point in his testimony. Honest tears were the most effective way to present a crime in human terms. In considering their verdict, days from now, members of the jury would not easily dismiss the memory of a grown man crying for his dead sister.

But O.C. felt far removed from tears as he responded to the introductory questions. In fact, he was determined not to weep in public. He had done all that in private. Instead, he felt driven by the anger that had continued to grow throughout this seemingly endless nightmare.

He felt further frustrated by the limitations now imposed upon him. Warned not to offer opinions or personal feelings, he could not say what was in his heart. He wanted to tell the jury about Esther's prevailing high humor and her boundless enthusiasm for life. He wanted to tell how she constantly helped others. He wanted to describe the priceless good she had done in the classroom through her dealings with generations of students. He wanted to tell them of her devotion to church, education, art, nature, and music.

Instead, he was forced to give answers that even to him sounded flat and colorless: He was a self-employed farmer, the brother of Esther Steele. She retired in 1976 after thirty-three years of teaching in Granite public schools.

Only once was he able to give the jury a glimpse into Esther's personality. Williams asked him if he was familiar with Esther's health and physical condition. He said he was, that her health and physical condition had been good.

"Why do you say that?" Williams asked.

"Because she was an outdoor-type person."

"How do you mean, outdoor?"

"She was a nature person," O.C. explained, speaking directly to the jury, hoping that what he was saying would register. "She loved nature in all respects. She was always out observing nature, birds, animals, and so forth."

"Did she in some way try to maintain her physical condition?"

O.C. said she did. "She had a daily routine of exercise in her home, plus all the trails and mountains that she was involved in with her nature study."

"Was she strong for her age?"

O.C. attempted to put all his conviction into his voice. "Yes, sir."

The questions moved to other subjects, and that was all the characterization of Esther he was able to offer. He testified that Esther and defendant Sadler were not married—an absurdity, it had been explained to him, that under law must be entered as evidence in every rape case. He identified Esther's house in an aerial photograph and traced the location of the rock ditch that ran behind the house. He testified that his sister Viola died of congestive heart failure in October, after Esther's death in April.

At last the questions ended.

The defense declined to cross-examine. O.C. was dismissed from the stand and, by special arrangement with the court and the defense, was allowed to join other members of his family seated at the front of the gallery.

O.C. had insisted that family members attend the trial, if at all possible, to show the jury, and the world, that Esther was loved and valued. Most of them were there, at least for portions of the trial.

The exception was Penny Hook, who could not bring herself to attend. She felt that all of this sordidness had nothing to do with her Aunt Esther. She knew O.C. was unhappy with her decision. But she felt strongly about it.

To her mind, Esther had lived on one plane, the defendants on quite another. She could not bear to see her Aunt Esther, and all the good implicit within her, associated with such profound degradation.

17 ▪ ▪ ▪

"ARE YOU READY TO CALL YOUR NEXT witness?" Judge Markum asked.

"Call Phillip Pat Adams," Williams said.

Williams had thoroughly steeped himself in Bugs's confession and in the testimony Bugs had given at plea-bargaining. In general, Bugs had been fairly consistent in his story. But the details had varied wildly with each telling.

Williams retained strong reservations about what Bugs would say—or not say—on the stand. If not handled properly, Bugs might become a loose cannon and do the state's case irreparable harm.

As Bugs walked to the witness stand and was sworn, he bore little resemblance to the scared, weepy character Goss and Sunderland had arrested at Fort Sill. Now all his worries of death row were behind him. He answered the introductory questions from Williams with a cocky grin.

He appeared to be enjoying his new status a bit too obviously. In jails and prisons, murderers are the baddest of the bad. In his new world, Bugs was a celebrity.

"Are you the same Phillip Pat Adams that in Greer County, Oklahoma, pled guilty to the offense of murder in the first degree?" Williams asked.

"Yes, sir," Bugs said in a tone some of the courtroom thought arrogant.

"And you're going to receive a life sentence in this matter, are you not?"

"Yes, sir."

Williams went through his schooling, his work experience, his service in the National Guard. Bugs told of calling Sadler on the night of the murder and suggesting they go out and drink some beer. He told about going over to his uncle John Schoolcraft's house.

"And when you left his house, how did you leave?"

"In a pickup."

"Did he give you permission to drive his pickup?"

"Yes, sir."

"How did you get the keys?"

"Got them from him."

From his front-row seat, O.C. listened carefully. He had never quite managed to hide his total contempt for Bugs. Now he no longer tried. He thought Bugs a perfect example of the mindless, shiftless, worthless ignorance Esther had fought so hard to correct all of her life. Esther had experienced few failures in her life. Bugs Adams was one of them. If Bugs did not kill her, he at least had led the killer to her, driven by deep-seated motives he himself probably did not understand.

■ ■ ■

In the jury box, Bugs and his testimony received mixed reactions.

"He just turned me off!" said juror Alice Brown. "Just automatically! He looked like a *slob*. Of course, I couldn't tell anything about
his personality from looking at him. But he certainly didn't look like
any prize."

Seated to Alice Brown's right, juror Bonnie Steiner, a registered
nurse, also felt an immediate negative reaction.

"I wouldn't have believed him if he'd told me it was raining outside and I heard the thunder. I didn't believe one word he said. I
didn't trust him. He was too old to be going out and getting drunk
every night. He was so worthless! I just thought he was disgusting."

Bonnie Steiner noticed that for the first time since the trial
began, Sadler no longer stared at the jury.

He now sat glaring at Bugs.

In front of Bonnie Steiner, at the end of the front row of the jury
box, juror Otis Ray Martin's initial reaction to Bugs was more chari-
table.

"He looked like he could be the head person in a gang. He looked
like he could have been a responsible guy, if he chose."

But Martin, a compressor mechanic for Delhi Pipeline and the
youngest of the jurors, soon was wondering how much of Bugs's
story he should believe.

"Parts of it sounded real believable. Then parts of it you couldn't
tell whether he could have been lying. You had to forge through it.
But some parts of it, I think he was telling the truth."

"Do you recall seeing anything on the dash of the pickup?" Williams
asked.

"There was a knife on the dash."

"Had you ever seen that knife before?"

Bugs shook his head. "No, sir."

That was the wrong answer. In his confession, Bugs had expressed long familiarity with the knife.

Williams decided not to pursue the erratic answer. To do so would give jurors the impression that he was arguing with his own witness.

"Can you describe the knife to me?"

"It's kind of long. It's in a case and it had a brass end."

Williams walked to the exhibits table. "Now, this is not the knife. But I will hand you what's been marked for identification State's Exhibit Number One and ask you, was it similar to something like this?"

Bugs nodded. "Yes."

"Did you ever have an occasion to actually pull the knife out and see the knife and blade?"

"No, sir."

That, too, was not in keeping with his earlier testimony.

The answer also surprised defense attorney Beam. "Was the answer to that 'no'?" he asked.

"Yes," Williams said.

Williams changed the subject.

"Do you recall the condition of the weather that night? Was it chilly or what?"

"Yes, sir," Bugs said.

"Was it cold?"

"Yes, sir."

"Where did you go when you left John Schoolcraft's house?"

"We went to the Gulf station and bought some beer, and went out in the country."

Bugs said the purchase was four quarts of Coors. He could not remember exactly where they went in the country. He estimated they each finished two quarts of beer in an hour and a half.

"What did you do after you consumed the two quarts and left the country?"

"We threw the bottles out and went and got some more beer."

Bugs said this time they bought a six-pack of Milwaukee's Best. Then they returned to the country, but to a different place. He was not sure exactly where.

"When you got out in the country, what did you do?"

"We sat and talked. I was supposed to be back, have my uncle's pickup back, in an hour. I asked Sadler if he wanted to go to Blair to see Rick McGregor, and he said okay."

Bugs insisted he did not know the distance to Blair, the direction, or how long he drove to get there.

In the front row of the jury box, juror Otis Ray Martin was listening intently. He could not believe that Bugs, who claimed to have been reared in Greer County, could be so ignorant as to distance and direction in his own backyard.

Martin decided that Bugs was picking and choosing, amending his story to the way he wanted to tell it.

Martin also was logging the amount of beer consumed. He noted that by the time they left for Blair, each had swilled three and a half quarts—almost a gallon of beer.

"What did you do when you got to Blair?" Williams asked.

"We stopped and got some more beer," Bugs said.

"Do you recall what size bottles or cans you got?"

"We got cans."

"And was it a six-pack or what?"

"It was a twelve-pack."

Bugs said they then drove to Rick McGregor's house, but were told he was not home. Williams asked what they did then.

"I asked Sadler if he wanted to go to Granite to see John Monroe, and we went to Granite."

"Do you know what time you got to Granite?"

Bugs shook his head. "No, sir."

He told of the visit to Johnny Monroe's house. He said Johnny's mother, Elsie Brooks, told them Johnny was not home. Bugs said they drove down the road to a wooden bridge, parked, and drank more beer. He could not remember if they finished all the beer. But he remembered that they had run out of money while they were in Blair. He said they discussed where they might get some money.

"Sadler asked me if I knew some old ladies. I told him yes."

"Do you know where you were when the defendant asked you if you knew some old ladies?"

"We went to Pearl Johnson's house and I got out and used the bathroom there and got back in and drove off and was going down the street. I told him, yes, I knew where an old lady was. While he was going down the street I pointed out the house."

A deep hush had fallen over the courtroom.

"Pointed out whose house, sir?"

"Mrs. Steele's."

"And did you actually drive in front of her house?"

"Yes, sir."

"And what happened after you pointed out Mrs. Steele's house?"

"I went to the corner and dropped Wayne Sadler off."

Williams walked to the exhibits table and brought back the aerial photograph of Esther Steele's house, identified earlier on the stand by O.C.

"Can you take this pen and mark an X as to where you dropped the defendant off?"

Bugs studied the photograph for a moment, then made an X.

"All right, when you dropped the defendant off, did you see him do anything when he got out of the car?"

Bugs nodded. "I seen him grab the knife off the dash."

"Did you see him do anything else?"

"That's when I saw him put his socks on his hands."

"Can you tell the jury how he put his socks on his hands?"

Bugs glanced at the jury box. "Outside the door, in front of the headlights."

"Do you know what color socks he had?"

"White."

Williams wanted this scene and the socks firmly implanted in the minds of the jury. "Did you actually *see* him take them off of his feet?"

"Yes, sir."

Williams bore down for even greater emphasis. "Did he actually put one sock on one hand, and the other sock on the other hand?"

Again Bugs nodded. "Yes, sir."

Williams paused. "Do you recall what type of clothing he had up here about his chest at that time?"

"The only thing he had was the jacket. Orange jacket."

"What happened then, after he got out of the car, took his shoes off, took his socks and put them on each hand, and took the knife from the dash? What happened then?"

"He started walking off. And then's when I took off."

"Which direction did he start walking off?"

"Toward the sidewalk."

"And you say you took off. What did you do, sir?"

"Went riding around."

Williams felt Bugs might not be speaking loudly enough for all of the jury to hear. "Sir?"

Bugs repeated his answer. "Went riding around."

"Had you made arrangements with him to pick him up?"

"Well, I told him I would pick him up at the same spot that I dropped him off at."

"Did you actually see him at the same spot you dropped him off at?"

"No, sir."

"Did you see him at another spot?"

"Yes, sir."

"Do you recall how long you had been driving around before you picked him up at this other spot?"

"Quite a while."

"How far was this other spot from Mrs. Steele's home?"

"The same distance."

"Which direction from Mrs. Steele's home?"

"Coming out of the ditch."

Williams asked Bugs to draw a square on the photograph to show where he had picked up Sadler.

"Are you familiar with a canal that runs behind Mrs. Steele's home?"

"Yes, sir."

Bugs said he had played in the rock ditch as a child. He said it was easy to walk in, and that concealment in it was possible. He said he saw Sadler emerge from the rock ditch and return to the pickup.

"When he returned, and got in your pickup, did he have anything with him that he didn't have when he left?"

"Well, I seen a bulge in his pocket."

"Did you later find out what this bulge was?"

"Yes, sir."

"What was it, sir?"

"It was a billfold."

"And where were you when you saw the billfold?"

"Out in the country, where we had the wreck at. Before we had the wreck."

"All right. You started driving?"

"Yes."

"Did he say anything when he got in the pickup?"

"No, sir."

"How did he act when he got in the pickup?"

"Kind of shaky."

"Did you see the knife when he got in the pickup?"

"No, sir."

"Did he have on the same orange-colored top when he got in the pickup?"

"Yes, sir."

"Did he have the same stockings on his hands?"

"I didn't recognize it."

"In the billfold, did you happen to see any money?"

"Yes, sir."

"Was any money shared with you?"

"Yes, sir."

"How much money was shared with you?"

"Ten dollars."

Bugs described the route he drove out of Granite into the coun-try, heading back toward Mangum.

"Were you taking the main route back to Mangum?"

"No, sir."

"Any particular reason why you weren't taking the main route?"

"Not really."

Every member of the jury was studying Bugs intently. Thus far, he had given them plenty to speculate upon.

He had "seen a bulge" in Sadler's pocket—in the dark. He at least knew a burglary had been committed. But he claimed they did not discuss it. He could not explain why they left the highway for the back roads.

Bugs told of stopping the pickup so Sadler could throw out a bundle.

"I stopped the pickup, and Wayne was wrapping it up. I don't know what he put in there. He got out and went in the ditch. I heard weeds or water, and he came back and got in front of the headlights and showed me the billfold."

Bugs said that when Sadler returned, he was bare-chested.

"He grabbed some coveralls from the back of the seat."

"Whose coveralls were those?"

"My uncle's."

Williams was not content to stop with the single answer. Again he wanted members of the jury to envision the scene. The green coveralls might be the single most valuable piece of circumstantial evidence.

"Did you see him put the coveralls on?"

"Yes, sir."

"Was he standing outside when he put the coveralls on, or inside the pickup when he put the coveralls on?"

"Standing outside."

"Then what happened, sir?"

"He got back in the pickup and we went down the road. I guess I fell asleep or something at the wheel, and that's when we had the wreck."

Bugs described the way the pickup turned over, dumping him into the ditch. He admitted that he would consider himself and Sadler drunk.

He said he later spent the ten dollars that Sadler gave him.

"At that time, did you know Esther Steele had been killed?"

"No, sir."

"What did you think had happened?"

"I thought she wasn't there, and he went in there and found the billfold and come back."

"Is what you're telling this court and this jury today the truth?"

"Yes, sir."

"Did you later on have remorse and feel sorry that Esther Steele was killed?"

"Yes, sir."

"Do you still have remorse and feel sorry?"

Bugs was now more subdued. He answered quietly. "Yes, sir."

Hovis opened his cross-examination of Bugs Adams in a scathing, disbelieving tone. "You're trying to tell this jury that you pleaded guilty to life imprisonment for sitting there drinking beer, and driving up in front of a house, and some guy gets out and kills somebody, and you pled guilty because of that? Is that what you're trying to tell everybody?"

All of his life Bugs had defended himself verbally. This was nothing new. He answered easily. "Yes, sir."

But Hovis was not through. "Wouldn't it be more correct to say you pled guilty to life imprisonment, and you pled guilty to first degree murder, because you were worried and you were concerned that sooner or later it would come out that you, in fact, went in and killed Mrs. Steele?"

Bugs shook his head emphatically. "No, sir."

Bugs insisted he had received no deal from the DA in exchange for the testimony he now was giving against Sadler. Again Hovis adopted an incredulous tone.

"When you pled guilty, it was with the clear understanding that you would receive life in prison. Is that not correct?"

"Yes, sir."

"So you *did* have a deal with the DA's office, didn't you?"

Bugs saw a loophole. "My lawyer had the deal. I didn't."

"Your lawyer's not the one going to prison, is he?"

"I know that."

"So *you* had a deal, didn't you?"

"Yes, sir."

"Specifically what did the district attorney's office tell you you must do in order to receive this sentence of life imprisonment?"

"They ain't talked to me," Bugs clarified. "They talked to my lawyer, and my lawyer told me."

"It was your understanding that you must testify against Wayne Sadler. Isn't that correct?"

"Yes, sir."

"It is your understanding that you must state that he was the one that went in and killed Mrs. Steele. Isn't that correct?"

"Yes, sir."

At this point it was obvious to everyone that Hovis was seriously undercutting the testimony of Bugs Adams. The question was how much.

Juror Barney Brown had been maintaining a running assessment of the story Bugs was telling.

"I felt like there were things he was confused on. I think he was so drunk that there was a lot he didn't know. There were things he said that just didn't fit together. I felt he was just trying to save his own hide."

Juror Otis Ray Martin felt he understood exactly why Bugs accepted a life term in exchange for testifying against Sadler. "He was scared, afraid he was going to get a death sentence."

But Martin also thought he read another motive into Bugs's claim of remorse. On that point, Bugs had sounded sincere. Martin believed Bugs truly might have started feeling guilty.

Hovis drew an admission from Bugs that, at two hundred and one pounds, he considered himself bigger and stronger than Sadler.

"Mrs. Steele was a teacher of yours at one time?" Hovis asked.

"Yes."

"What type of teacher was she?"

"She was a good teacher."

"Was she fairly strict?"

"No, sir."

That answer struck O.C. and the Granite contingent in the courtroom as patently false. Esther had been strict on herself and on her students.

"Did you like Mrs. Steele?" Hovis asked.

"Yes, sir."

"When you and Wayne were drinking beer almost every day, how much would you drink?"

Bugs shrugged, then grinned. "Oh, maybe a case or two. Something like that."

"A case or two?"

"Yes."

"How does beer affect you?"

"It depends on how much I drink."

"Do you sometimes get kind of crazy?"

"No, sir."

Hovis walked away, then turned and asked the next question as if it had just occurred to him. "Why do they call you Bugs?"

Again Bugs grinned. "Well, a long time ago I ate a bug off a wall."

Hovis reacted as if he wanted to make sure he had heard correctly. "Your statement was that a long time ago you ate a bug off the wall?"

Bugs nodded. "Yeah."

"Had you been drinking at that time?"

"Yes, sir."

"You didn't consider that a crazy act?"

"No, sir."

"That's perfectly normal?"

"Well, a lot of people *survive* off of bugs," Bugs insisted.

Hovis asked if he had ever been convicted of any felonies. Bugs admitted he once pled guilty to driving under the influence. He said he had borrowed his uncle's pickup on several other occasions.

Hovis asked if he had seen the knife before. Bugs said yes. Hovis pointed out the inconsistency of that answer with the one he had given only a few minutes before, when Williams asked him the same question.

Bugs answered with the aplomb of a man accustomed to resolving his own inconsistencies. He said that in his testimony a few minutes before, he had meant that he had not seen the knife out of its scabbard that night. But he had seen it at other times, when his uncle whittled.

He insisted that as far as he knew, Sadler found the coveralls behind the seat because he just happened to look back there.

Again Hovis asked a question as if it had just occurred to him. "Have you ever had any kind of a sexual problem? Such as liking to peek in windows of girls or older women?"

Williams knew exactly where Hovis was heading. But the window peeping incident on Bugs's record had been a misdemeanor, inadmissible as evidence.

"Objection," Williams said. "Irrelevant."

"Your Honor, we are talking about the crime of rape," Hovis insisted. "I don't see how that could be irrelevant. Raping an older woman."

Judge Markum also knew where Adams was headed. "I don't believe that is within the statutory code," he told Hovis. "I will sustain the objection."

Williams was irritated—and a bit frustrated.

In broaching the Peeping Tom incident, Hovis had managed a maneuver as old as jurisprudence. By asking an improper question, knowing that an objection would be made and sustained, Hovis nevertheless had managed to plant a possible sexual deviation in the minds of the jurors. The implication was that if Bugs were a Peeping Tom, he might be a sex deviate, and if a sex deviate, maybe the rapist, and thus the killer in this case, not Sadler.

"You mentioned the canal or ditch behind Mrs. Steele's house," Hovis said. "Had you been in that ditch before?"

"Yes," Bugs said.

"Wayne Sadler, as far as you know, had never even been in that ditch. Isn't that right?"

"Yes, sir."

"How did he know enough to go into the ditch and conceal himself, when that was his first time in the area?"

"Objection," Williams said. "That's not within his knowledge how Mr. Sadler knew."

"Sustained," ruled Judge Markum.

But again, with his question, Hovis had raised a valid point for the jurors to ponder.

He phrased the question in a more acceptable form. "You're trying to tell this jury that Wayne, who had never been in that area to your knowledge, just happened to go behind the house, and happened to find this ditch where he could conceal himself. Is that what you're trying to tell this jury?"

Bugs shook his head doggedly. "No, sir."

"What are you trying to tell them?"

Bugs could only fall back on his earlier testimony. "I saw him coming out of the ditch."

Hovis questioned Bugs at length on his inconsistencies about the disposal of evidence—if it was buried, as he had once told the detectives, or thrown into water, as he also had claimed.

Bugs said he did not see Sadler do it. He just heard the sounds of Sadler walking either through water or weeds.

Abruptly Hovis returned to the Peeping Tom incident.

"Mr. Adams, have you ever been convicted of a crime involving moral turpitude?"

"Objection!" Williams said.

Judge Markum halted the proceedings and asked that the jurors be escorted from the courtroom.

Juror Bonnie Steiner, for one, was beginning to dread each return to the undersized jury room, only ten by twelve, and crowded with a large conference table, twelve chairs, and a coffee maker and stand. The arrangement might have been comfortable and pleasant for three or four people. But seated at the table, the jurors were jammed knee to knee, and there was no place left to stand. The adjoining, closetlike bathroom served both sexes. When anyone used it, the other jurors waited outside in the hall.

Several of the jurors smoked. The small room lacked sufficient ventilation to handle the overload.

"It was just awful," Steiner said.

With the jury out, Williams, Beam, and Hovis debated whether the Peeping Tom incident could be admitted as evidence.

Court had now been in session almost eight hours. Tempers flared.

Williams argued that the incident was irrelevant and inadmissible. "Peeping Tom is a misdemeanor," he pointed out.

"Even if it's not a conviction, I think if we show he goes around peeping in windows at older women, that's relevant," Hovis countered.

"Are you going to ask him if he has a penis because rape is involved?" Williams shot back.

Judge Markum intervened. He upheld Williams's objection and admonished Hovis for mentioning the Peeping Tom incident in front of the jury.

"I want to caution you right now," Judge Markum told Hovis. "We aren't going to have that kind of a trial."

Judge Markum voiced his concern about running on into the night. He invited a response from the attorneys.

Both defense and prosecution said they preferred to go on.

Judge Markum agreed, with reservations. "Let's just monitor how the jury is looking. Whether they're staying with us, and attentive, or whether they're starting to wander. I'll monitor that."

The jury returned. Hovis resumed his cross-examination.

"Mr. Adams, you stated a while ago that you liked Mrs. Steele as a teacher?"

"Yes."

"If that is the case, why was it that you picked her house for Mr. Sadler to go into?"

"Because it was close."

"It was just the closest house you could find?"

"Yes."

Bugs said that when Sadler returned to the truck, he was wearing the hooded sweatshirt. Bugs insisted that he did not see any blood.

Hovis again began at the beginning, when Adams and Sadler first set out on their beer-drinking spree. This time he concentrated on times and distances—when and where they bought beer, how much time they spent drinking it, how far they traveled from place to place.

Bugs became ever more vague in his answers.

"How long did it take you to drive from Blair to Granite?"

"I don't know."

"Did you take the highway, or dirt roads, or what?"

"Highway."

"About how far is it from Blair to Granite?"

"I really don't know."

"When you first arrived in Granite, what is the first thing you did?"

"Went to Johnny Monroe's house."

"And how long did you stay there?"

"I stayed there . . . I don't know how long I stayed there."

"Ten minutes? Fifteen minutes? Thirty?"

"I imagine about fifteen, twenty."

"Then what did you do?"

"Then I went and backed out, and we sat on the bridge."

"Where is the bridge located?"

"It's about a block and a half down the road."

"Block and a half from Granite?"

"I don't know for sure. It's pretty close."

What did he and Sadler talk about?

Bugs could not remember.

He did not know how far he drove from Granite before they had the wreck.

"Could it have been five miles?" Hovis asked.

"I don't know."

"Do you have any judgment or estimate of how far a mile is?"

"No, sir."

"So you're telling this jury you don't know whether you drove five miles or whether you drove a quarter of a mile? You don't have any idea how far you drove?"

"No, sir."

"You're just saying to all of my questions, you don't know. Is that right?"

"Yes, sir."

"From the time Wayne came out of the ditch and you picked him up until the time you had the wreck, can you give your best estimate of how long that was?"

"I don't know."

"You don't know whether it was ten minutes or an hour?"

"I didn't have a watch."

"Well, you can estimate time, can't you?"

"No, sir. I'm not good at that."

"You know the difference between ten minutes and two hours, don't you?"

"Yes, sir."

"Objection," Williams said. "This is argumentative."

Hovis turned to Judge Markum. "Judge, he's very precise and definite on questions from the special prosecutor. And now he doesn't know anything."

"I think you made your point, Counsel," Judge Markum told Hovis. "Objection sustained."

As Bugs was dismissed from the stand, subject to recall, Williams felt both relief and concern. Considering the limitations of Bugs Adams, his testimony had gone about as well as could be expected. But Williams knew that the state's case had been seriously damaged. Bugs—the backbone of the prosecution—was not a believable witness.

Williams could only hope that when jurors began deliberations they would remember—and believe—the key portions. Until then, he must present a vast array of testimony, much of it seemingly insignificant, in support of the version of the murder offered by Bugs Adams.

18   ∎   ∎   ∎

THE TRIAL CONTINUED ON INTO THE EVE-
ning. For a time, the courtroom seemed
isolated from the rest of the world. On the
witness stand, Dr. Lenaburg described the
call from Daisy Brown, his hurried trip to
Esther's home, and what he found.

"She was supine. On her back. Her gown
was ripped to the waist. Blood was all over
everything. I felt her pulse, and knew she was
dead. Rigor had started in the right arm. She
was cold. I saw the blood, and felt it was murder."

Dr. Lenaburg described the wounds.

From a manila envelope, Williams extracted a large color photograph. "Is this

photograph a true and correct representation as to how you recall
Esther Steele on April fifteenth?"

Dr. Lenaburg examined the photograph. "Yes."

"May it please the court," Williams said. "I would offer State's Four
in evidence at this time, and ask the jury to view the photograph."

As Williams expected, Beam objected. "Your Honor, whatever probative value that photograph has is greatly outweighed by the prejudicial value in front of the jury. We don't contest that she's dead."

"We also object to it being a color photograph, Your Honor,"
Hovis added. "It is prejudicial and inflaming."

On the bench, Judge Markum knew he had arrived at a crucial
point. He had been determined from the first to handle this trial
conservatively and not allow anything to occur that conceivably
could cause the case to be overturned or remanded. He wanted to
consider this ruling carefully.

Again he asked the bailiff to escort the jurors from the courtroom. He summoned the attorneys to the bench.

"How are you going to use the photograph?" he asked Williams.
"Is the doctor going to point?"

Williams explained that both Dr. Lenaburg and, later, the state
medical examiner would use this photograph, and others, to illus-
trate the fatal injuries. He cited legal precedents for the introduction
of such photographs.

"I don't care what other judges have done," Markum told him.
"I'm going to do what I think is right and appropriate. How is this
going to help the jury learn more?"

Williams explained that the photograph would corroborate medical testimony, show the nature of the wounds.

"Your Honor, we will have no rebuttal as how she died or even
the weapon that was probably, possibly used," Hovis said. "The only
reason we can see for the photograph is to prejudice the jury to see
the elderly woman lying there dead, nude."

"It's a horrible, horrible photo," Beam said.

Judge Markum studied the picture. Beam was right. It was a horrible, horrible picture, and definitely inflammatory. The close-up showed the victim's body on her blood-soaked bed. But it did not depict the crime scene well, nor did it show with any precision the location of the wounds. The view also included the victim's face. That certainly might be interpreted as prejudicial.

To Judge Markum's mind, the key question was whether the photograph would be required to support the medical testimony.

He could not see that it would be.

"I don't believe the medical examiner's testimony will need any corroboration," he told Williams. "At this time, I'm going to sustain the objection to the photograph."

Williams was surprised and disappointed. He had fully expected the photographs to be admitted. He had used similar photographs in other murder trials.

Also, he was a bit confused. The judge had said he was sustaining the objection "at this time."

Williams understood that to mean that Judge Markum was leaving the door open for later use of the photographs and their possible admission.

He did not know how much this ruling had hurt his case. Pros and cons existed either way.

The jurors now knew that the photographs existed. No doubt they would surmise that they were too horrible for them to see. Their imaginations would be at work.

Yet, if he had been allowed to show the photographs to jurors, the graphic image of Esther lying dead in her own blood certainly would have been foremost in their minds during deliberations. Now he would have to find other means to depict the crime.

At the defense table, Beam also was surprised by the ruling. He felt it was a bit of luck for the defense.

The jury returned to the courtroom. Dr. Lenaburg was still on the witness stand. Williams asked him his first impression as to the cause of Esther Steele's death.

"I thought it was gunshot wound, initially."

Williams asked why he thought that.

"Because the wounds of entrance were about the size of a thirty-caliber bullet."

At that point, Williams performed one of those adept legal maneuvers that never appear in trial transcripts, and thus are not reviewed by the appellate courts, yet often greatly influence the outcome of a trial.

Williams was still holding the large photograph and the manila envelope. In one smooth movement, as if to free his hands of clutter, he moved two steps to the nearby defense table and placed the large color photograph of Esther Steele's body squarely in front of David Wayne Sadler, almost under his nose.

As if oblivious to what he had done, Williams turned back to the witness stand and Dr. Lenaburg. He took a pen from his shirt pocket, handed it to Dr. Lenaburg, and asked him to point out the locations of the wounds on Esther Steele's body.

Using Williams as a model, Dr. Lenaburg began a description of the wounds. But the attention of most jurors remained locked on the drama taking place behind Williams.

"Sadler looked down at those pictures with no—I mean no—emotion," said juror Bonnie Steiner, the registered nurse. "How *could* he? With *no* emotion? We talked about it later in the jury room. How *could* he?"

It was a ploy Williams had used successfully in other murder trials. He never knew how a defendant might react. But whatever the defendant did would tend to cast him in a bad light, and probably would be observed by at least a few members of the jury.

Beam's attention was on the witness stand. He did not notice the maneuver or the jury's reaction. Told about it later, and of the jury's reaction, he was aghast.

"If I had seen it, I would have raised holy hell!"

In his cross-examination of Dr. Lenaburg, Beam concentrated on the number of persons in Esther's house after the discovery of the body.

He developed the same theme with the next witness, William H. Greer, the Mangum funeral director who transported Esther's body from Granite to Oklahoma City.

Greer admitted that there had been "quite a crowd" in the house.

Williams had no effective ammunition to counter the points Beam was making. Overburdened, the OSBI had not done hair-and-fiber and fingerprint checks on everyone who had been in the house.

Williams knew that Beam was setting the stage to point out these deficiencies in the investigation. And if Beam was successful, the jurors might well conclude that "reasonable doubt" existed on the four hairs.

Oklahoma Highway Patrol Trooper Kerry Pettingill described his investigation of the wreck. He said that in his expert opinion, Bugs Adams would have failed a Breathalyzer test. He said he did not have occasion to approach or to talk with Sadler at length, and could not evaluate Sadler's degree of sobriety.

He said he noticed some scratches on Adams's face.

In the cross-examination, Hovis asked Pettingill the nature of these scratches.

"Just like from a bush or something like that."

"Could they have been made by something other than a bush?"

"I don't know."

"Did some of them look like scratches that might have been made by fingernails?"

"They didn't appear to be," Pettingill answered. "The reason why I say this is because they weren't wide. They were thin."

Williams felt a degree of satisfaction with that answer. He knew that the defense was setting up for the testimony of Dolly Schoolcraft, who at the preliminary hearings had admitted that when she first saw the scratches on her nephew's face, she had teased him by asking, "What girlfriend scratched you?"

Pettingill's answer might tend to blunt the persistent contention of the defense that it was Bugs, not Sadler, who went into the house and raped and murdered Esther, and thus received fingernail scratches.

From the witness stand, Pearl Johnson told the jurors of the events around her apartment on the night Esther was murdered. She identified State's Exhibit Number 3, the photograph of the pickup Adams was driving, as of the same make and model as the one that had stopped beside her apartment, then disappeared in the direction of Esther Steele's house.

Thus far Beam and Hovis had cross-examined the state's witnesses—even Adams—with a measure of restraint.

But with Pearl Johnson, Beam became much more aggressive.

Williams was pleased to discover that Pearl Johnson was no pushover.

"You could not recognize anyone in that pickup," Beam asked. "Is that your testimony?"

"That's my testimony."

"But you think the two people were male?"

"Yes, sir."

"But you can't tell me for sure they were male, can you?"

"No, sir."

"Ma'am, Mr. Williams showed you State's Exhibit Number Three and you said the pickup you saw looked like this pickup. Is that correct?"

"Yes, sir."

"But you can't tell me for sure that it was this pickup, can you?"

"No."

"In fact, it could have been—if we had pictures of red Ford pickups that are that same model, you couldn't tell me which one it was, could you, if they all had toolboxes in the back? If I showed you, say, a series of pictures of red-and-white Ford pickups with toolboxes in the back, you wouldn't be able to tell me which one you saw that night, would you?"

"Not by picture. I could recognize the pickup."

"But you can't tell from the picture for sure that this is the pickup?"

"Not positive. But pretty well certain. It's the same shape, color of the pickup I saw that night."

Beam tried to trip her up on the time sequence. She remained adamant. Her poodle started barking about midnight. She looked out and saw the pickup. It sat there about ten minutes, then left.

Beam tried the ploy of misstating her testimony. "So it sat there running for ten minutes?"

Pearl Johnson promptly set the matter straight. "No! The motor was killed."

Beam was unable to shake Pearl Johnson's conviction about the truck and its movements.

Again Williams felt encouraged. Pearl Johnson's testimony supported the portion of Bugs's story in which he said he went by Pearl Johnson's apartment and urinated in the alley.

Perhaps this corroboration would help jurors conclude that if Bugs was truthful on that part of his story, he might have been truthful on the rest.

Also, Pearl Johnson's account placed Sadler and Bugs driving toward Esther's house in the proper time frame.

Pearl Johnson could not tell the jurors of her own belief that she herself first had been selected as the victim that night. In his rambling search for beer money, it would have been natural for Bugs to have thought of her apartment, where, she believed, he had stolen small amounts of money in the past.

Her suspicion made sense: With the whole wide world to use for a bathroom, why had Bugs and Sadler driven into the alley outside her window?

If she had gone to bed early, and if her dog had not raised such a racket, she might have been the victim.

She had not mentioned her suspicions to Goss and Sunderland. But her son David had voiced similar thoughts.

"Your guardian angel was really looking after you that night," he had told her.

■ ■ ■

John L. Schoolcraft described his nephew's visit to his house that night.

He constantly referred to his nephew as "Bugs."

"Why is he called Bugs?" Williams asked. "Do you know?"

"Well, it's just a nickname he got a long time ago."

"How long ago was this?"

"Since he was a little tyke."

Jurors noted the glaring discrepancy from the explanation that Bugs Adams had given for his nickname.

Schoolcraft told of returning home a short time later and finding the pickup gone. He described his search for it, and of meeting it when it was towed into town the next morning.

Williams asked if he noticed anything missing when he examined the wrecked truck.

"My knife and my green coveralls."

Schoolcraft described the knife. "A regular fishing knife with a wooden handle."

In cross-examination, Hovis reestablished that Schoolcraft first missed his pickup about 9:00 P.M.

"Were you home at the time?" Hovis asked.

"At the time it was stolen?" Schoolcraft asked.

The word *stolen* had not been used previously. With that phrasing, Schoolcraft labeled as a lie his nephew's claim that he had received permission to use the pickup.

Former Granite Police Chief L. D. Williams was the final witness of the evening. He testified that he had known Esther all of his life and that she was a very active woman.

He told of Dr. Lenaburg's call, and of his arrival at Esther's house. He said he had entered the bedroom, observed the body and "a lot of blood," and called Sheriff Rogers, who in turn called the OSBI.

He described the search for evidence, both on the grounds and in Granite's fifty-two Dumpsters.

In cross-examination, Hovis again concentrated on the number of persons in the house when the police chief arrived.

"Would it be safe to say there were ten or fifteen persons in the house?" Hovis asked.

"I would be safe in saying at least ten to fifteen."

As the former police chief was excused, Judge Markum observed that the hour was late. He declared the court to be in recess until the following morning.

He again admonished the jurors not to discuss the trial with anyone.

Juror Bonnie Steiner was accustomed to twelve-hour shifts at the hospital. But eleven hours as a juror had left her exhausted. She found no difficulty in complying with Judge Markum's directive not to discuss the case, not even with her family.

"After you drive home, and fall into bed for a few hours of sleep, it's time to get ready for the next day. Even if you wanted to, you don't have time to talk about it."

19 ▪ ▪ ▪

SOMEONE HAD TOLD DAISY BROWN THAT
the first day of the trial would be devoted to
jury selection and that she probably would
not be called to testify until at least the second or third day. So she had ignored her sub-
poena for that first day. She could see no
reason to drive the sixty miles to Arapaho just
to sit around useless, when she had many
other things to do.

Her failure to appear created a small furor.
On the second day, and on every day there-
after, the Custer County sheriff sent a car and
deputy for her. Daisy told everyone how ex-
traordinarily nice the people in Arapaho were
to her.

On Wednesday she had sat in the witness room all day while others were called. But on Thursday, the third day of the trial, she was the first called. She followed the clerk into the courtroom and to the witness stand, where she was sworn.

With the hum of the air conditioner, she experienced some difficulty hearing the questions. She asked the lawyers to repeat, and did the best she could.

Once again she told of going to church with Esther that evening, of their arrival home, and of Esther's remark that she might go to Oklahoma City the following day. She told of the call from Esther's sister-in-law, of her decision to go see about Esther, and of her discovery of the body.

She described the way Esther's black alligator purse was lying on the other twin bed.

"Do you know if Esther Steele normally carried money with her?" Williams asked.

"I'm sure she did. I never did know how much or anything, but she did always have a little money with her."

Daisy braced as the tall defense lawyer, Beam, rose to cross-examine her. But she was pleased to discover that he was gentle and courtly. He mostly was interested in the exact times that different things happened, how many people were in the house, how many were in the bedroom, and who leaned over the bed.

Daisy answered his questions the best she could.

Then her part in the trial was behind her. The judge excused her. She left the stand with a feeling of relief.

But after she walked out of the courtroom and into the hall, the full weight of the tension of the last few days suddenly swept over her. Reliving that horrible day had brought a frightening reality to all that had happened.

Daisy felt dizzy and disoriented. She began crying and could not stop.

Esther's sisters—Polly Williams and Lenore Musgrove—came into the hall and helped her to a seat. They told her she had done an excellent job on the stand.

Gradually Daisy regained her composure. But she remained disturbed. In a way she could not explain, her testimony had given Esther's death a devastating sense of finality.

For a time the trial seemed to move faster. After Daisy Brown came Mitchell Dwayne Murley, who described seeing defendant David Wayne Sadler staggering along Granite's Main Street about 3:40 A.M. on the morning after Esther Steele was murdered. Murley's testimony put Sadler in the green coveralls, corroborating the version told by Bugs Adams. Policeman Alan McCormack told of answering Murley's call and transporting Sadler to the scene of the wreck. Ambulance attendant Charles Lynn Hayden described the ambulance run to the hospital with Sadler and Adams.

Hayden said Sadler complained of pain in an ankle. He said he and another attendant took Sadler's tennis shoes off and examined the ankle.

"How was he dressed?" Williams asked.

"He was wearing green coveralls."

"Do you recall whether or not he had any socks on under his tennis shoes?"

"I'm not for sure," Hayden said.

Williams was momentarily taken aback. When interviewed by Goss and Sunderland, and later in the preliminary hearings, Hayden had said that Sadler wore no socks. That testimony was sorely needed to support the claim of Bugs Adams that Sadler had taken off his socks before the murder and that he had thrown them away afterward.

Williams was put in the position of contradicting his own witness. He turned to Hayden's testimony at the preliminary hearings. He read aloud the portion pertaining to the socks.

"Do you remember that, sir?" he asked Hayden.

Hayden shook his head. "No, sir, I don't."

"That is what it says here."

"Okay."

"Was your memory of the particular events that occurred better then than now?"

"Yes, sir," Hayden said. "I have made several ambulance runs since then."

But Hayden said he remembered that dried blood covered about a fourth of the surface of Sadler's hands.

As Hayden left the stand, Williams wondered how much weight the jurors would give to Hayden's lack of a firm grasp on his memory of Sadler's not wearing socks.

Taken alone, Hayden's testimony was not an overwhelming piece of evidence. But it was a key part of the mosaic Williams needed for conviction.

The testimony given by OSBI senior crime scene specialist Bruce Richard Spence was lengthy and, for the most part, boring. There was no way that Spence or Williams could enliven the necessarily detailed chain of evidence testimony concerning the bagging, labeling, and custodial transfer of each item.

Williams sought relief from the legal technicalities by occasionally asking Spence for descriptions of his work. Spence told of photographing the murder scene and the house. He described dusting the house for fingerprints. He said those found were not of sufficient quality for comparison. He added that he had obtained one clear, partial palm print from inside the front door, but was unable to find a match. He told of going to the office of the state medical examiner, where he fingerprinted Esther Steele's body and collected hair and fingernail specimens, blood samples, swabbings, and articles of clothing.

Spence was an experienced witness. He easily sailed through his detailed testimony.

But Beam's first question on cross-examination alerted Williams that something was not quite right.

"Mr. Spence, did you fill out any type of criminalist report or anything like that in conjunction with this case?"

Spence also seemed puzzled by the question. "I have made a report. Yes, sir."

Beam continued with his cross-examination, asking Spence specifically about the fingerprints and the latent palm print.

He established that none had been matched to Sadler.

Beam then turned to the detailed chain of evidence and concentrated on what was left where, who picked up what, who initialed what, and when, seeking any weak link that might raise a doubt that the evidence was properly preserved.

The subject of the report was left hanging.

But with Spence still on the stand, Beam asked Judge Markum for permission to approach the bench. Williams accompanied him.

"Your Honor," Beam said, too low for the jury to hear, "we've never been furnished the crime report or fingerprint report."

Williams was dismayed. If what Beam said was true, the missing reports might be grounds for a mistrial.

And implicit in Beam's claim was the unspoken charge that Williams might have withheld potentially significant evidence.

He knew he had not done so.

He spoke to the judge. "Your Honor, to my knowledge, I furnished them everything."

"We've never seen it," Beam insisted.

Judge Markum raised a hand to cut off the discussion. He again ordered the jury escorted from the courtroom.

While the jury filed out, Williams returned to his table and searched through his records. He returned to the bench with his notes confirming delivery of the missing report.

Judge Markum looked down at Beam. "Your file doesn't reflect you have that one?"

"Your Honor, I was not in the case in October," Beam said. "Mr. Hovis, I believe, was the attorney of record then."

"I don't have it, Judge," Hovis said. "I have looked through my files. I don't have it."

Beam spoke with heat, listing all the motions the defense had made for production, and the dates various judges had acted on each.

"This morning is the first time I have ever heard of the fingerprints or latent palm print," he said. "I have never seen these reports."

Hovis agreed. "Judge, to my knowledge, I never received the reports."

Beam's anger was gathering momentum. "Judge, it's just another item of evidence that we did not have an opportunity to look at or . . ."

Suddenly Williams also was furious. Beam in essence was flatly accusing him of professional misconduct.

"*Which* was the first item of evidence you didn't have an opportunity to look at?" Williams demanded. "You said *another* one."

Judge Markum intervened. "Gentlemen! You better start addressing me."

The judge turned to Spence and, from the bench, questioned him at length on his testimony.

"The fingerprints were simply not good enough to compare with anyone, Your Honor," Spence said again.

Williams was still angry over the implication of impropriety. He requested that his notes on the distribution of files be read into the trial record.

But Judge Markum's mind was on the larger problem of what to do. If the missing reports contained anything at all favorable to the defendant, their disappearance constituted solid grounds for a mistrial.

He pondered Spence's answers to his questions. "By his statement, those prints would have no probative value for anyone," he said.

Beam countered that the defense should have had the opportunity to hire experts to examine the prints. "We are relying totally on a person paid by the state of Oklahoma, and the case is the state of Oklahoma versus David Wayne Sadler."

"Could we take a short break and let me search?" Hovis suggested. "I have four or five files."

Judge Markum agreed. "Let's take a ten-minute adjournment. Then I'm going to have to figure out where we are."

The specter of a mistrial hung over the courtroom during the break. But just before court resumed, the missing reports were found in Hovis's files.

When court reconvened, Beam spoke for the record, saying the files had been located. "I would like to apologize to Mr. Williams, on the record."

Williams felt immense relief. The threat of a mistrial had been lifted. The prosecution was back in business.

"No apology necessary," he said.

When Medical Examiner Fred Jordan was called to the stand, O.C. was determined to endure what was to come, even though he did not know how much more he could take.

Esther's role as victim seemed to be without end. Through no fault of her own, she had landed on a cold slab in Dr. Jordan's morgue. Now she was to be dissected under public scrutiny, stripped of the dignity that had always been so much a part of her.

Answering the introductory questions, Jordan gave the jurors a quick rundown of his education and experience. Again he estimated he had performed at least six thousand autopsies, and perhaps ten thousand.

"Can you tell the jury how Mrs. Steele was dressed when you first viewed her body?" Williams asked.

Dr. Jordan spoke directly to the jury in the way of a veteran witness. "When I received Mrs. Steele's body, she had on a burgundy nightgown which had been torn in the front, the upper part of the chest area, and had some apparent cuts in it. She was received in a body bag, but in a blue fitted sheet, a white fitted mattress pad, and a pillow with kind of a satiny light blue pillow slip."

"Can you tell the jury what you observed?"

"I noted several stab wounds on the external aspect of the body, cuts on her right and left thumbs, and made diagrams and recorded their sizes and locations."

The attention of the entire courtroom was riveted on Dr. Jordan's answers.

"Did you notice any defensive wounds?"

"One might classify the wounds on the thumbs as defensive."

"Can you describe where, using your own hands?"

Dr. Jordan raised his hands, held them out to the jury, and pointed. "On the left hand, there was a cut on the inner aspect of the thumb in that area, the palmar side. And on the right hand, the cut was more on the inside of the thumb toward the first finger."

"Can you tell me how many wounds you saw to her abdomen?"

"The abdomen had one stab wound."

"Where would that have been?"

"It was just to the left of the belly button, and a little bit below."

Williams uncovered a Styrofoam torso he had obtained from a ladies' dress shop—no head, no arms, just torso. He asked Dr. Jordan to step down from the stand and point to the location of the wound in the abdomen.

Dr. Jordan stood slightly to one side so he would not block the view of jurors. "The wound to the abdomen was in about that area there."

"Did you notice any other wounds to the body?"

"There were three stab wounds to the anterior chest and one in the upper back."

"Could you indicate that on the model?"

Dr. Jordan pointed. "One stab wound below the clavicle in this area of the collarbone. Another stab wound in the lower part of the back toward the midline. A stab wound below the breast anterior. There was a stab wound up here in the left shoulder area. And also a stab wound on the left lateral chest."

Williams asked Jordan if he performed an internal examination. Jordan said he did.

"Could you tell the court and jury what you found during this internal examination?"

In the front row of the gallery, Esther's sister Polly saw where the testimony was headed. She was not sure she could keep her composure throughout. But she did not want to cause a commotion by leaving the courtroom.

Besides, she felt driven to hear everything.

She decided that the only way she could endure the next few minutes would be to make herself forget that the doctor was talking about Esther. She would make herself imagine it had been someone else who had suffered so, and whose body had been cut to pieces and examined in such horrible detail.

In the front row of the jury box, juror Otis Ray Martin was surprised by how plainly the medical evidence was being presented.

Who would expect a man of Dr. Jordan's extensive medical background to use terminology like "just to the left of the belly button, and a little bit below"?

Pointing to a large diagram, Dr. Jordan detailed the damage done by each thrust of the knife.

"The top wound, the one on the upper left chest, went rather sharply across the midline toward the right, through the soft tissues, and hit a portion of the right lung. The wound closer to the midline at the lower border of the breast penetrated into the chest cavity. It went in the area of the sixth rib near its junction with what is called the breastbone and perforated or went into the left ventricle of the heart, or part of the pumping chamber of the heart."

"What about this next wound, farther on down?" Williams asked.

"The next wound, the one on the lower part of the chest, went through the space just below the fifth rib, and it injured the left lung and it injured the diaphragm, which is the muscle that separates the chest cavity from the abdominal cavity, and it extended on upward and toward the right, actually causing a cut in the right side of the heart, or the right ventricle, or the right pumping chamber of the heart."

"Now, the wound to the left side. Did that do any damage?"

"The wound to the left side went in just above the seventh rib and it caused a fracture of that rib, and then it lacerated or cut what we call the pleura, or the lining of the lung, of the inner chest cavity on the left-hand side."

"Now, the wound to the back. Did it damage any internal organs?"

"It broke the outside of a rib. It broke the third rib on the back. But it did not extend into the chest cavity."

Again Williams turned to the Styrofoam torso. "Could you use your notes, step down, and use this marker, and show the angle of entry as to each wound?"

Juror Bonnie Steiner found herself growing angry. The medical explicitness of Dr. Jordan's testimony did not bother her. She had worked seven years as an emergency room nurse. She had seen just about everything of a medical nature. But as Dr. Jordan recounted the damage done by each thrust, her experience failed to protect her from emotional involvement.

"This was so *senseless*. In the stomach. In the chest. In the back. I know how *painful* such things can be. That *did* bother me. It made me mad, because it wasn't necessary. They could have taken her money, taken her jewelry, taken her anything. They did not have to do that. They did not have to kill her."

"And the damage to the heart," Williams said. "Would that in and of itself have been fatal?"

"Oh, yes, if you didn't get someone right to surgery. It opened both major pumping chambers of the heart and let it bleed out into the sac in which it sets. Those wounds in and of themselves could have been lethal."

Jordan said the wound below the left breast was the most damaging, because it penetrated the lung, diaphragm, and the right side of the heart. But he declined to say with certainty it caused death.

"I can't pin it down to any one wound, because she had hemorrhage in both sides of her chest and around her heart. I listed the cause of her death as multiple stab wounds."

"Would these wounds have been painful?"

"When I used to do clinical medicine and saw people that had been stabbed, they certainly were complaining about the pain."

Williams paused, giving the jury time to reflect on that.

"In your opinion, after the last stab wound was made, how many minutes would it have taken for her to die?"

"That's a very hard thing to say. She didn't die instantly. There's no way you can pin a biological system down that closely. The lady lived long enough to do some bleeding. Probably five minutes at the minimum."

The courtroom was deathly silent. Dr. Jordan's answer had posed grounds for grim speculation. Did Esther's killer—or killers—remain in the room while she bled to death? Or did they leave her, helpless, to die alone?

"Would these wounds have caused her to become unconscious?" Williams asked.

"Not necessarily. They might have. But there is no direct reason for her to lose consciousness with the stab wounds."

"During your examination of her, did you inspect the vagina?"

"Yes, sir. Mrs. Steele's vagina was bruised. There was an area somewhat larger than an inch severely bruised, and there was a good deal of bruising over the total inside of her vagina."

"And do you know what could have caused this bruise?"

"Any type of a firm object that was forcibly placed inside this lady's vagina."

"And would a mature hard male penis be such an object?"

"It certainly would. Yes."

"Could you tell whether or not the bruise occurred in the vagina before or after death?"

"Before death. A person cannot be bruised in that manner after death."

Jordan described the signs that indicated partial suffocation.

"Could a pillow have caused this suffocation?"

"Certainly."

"Could you tell if she was suffocated to such an extent it rendered her unconscious?"

"There is no way I could tell that."

"Doctor, considering the wounds, and considering the suffocation, do you have any way of telling which came first, the wounds or the suffocation?"

"Not really."

"Doctor, is suffocation agonizing and painful?"

"Suffocation is a scary thing. I have treated patients and watched them die because of an acute asthma attack, or because of congestive heart failure where they're unable to breathe, and chest injury, and it's frightening." He hesitated. "Was your question 'painful'?"

"Yes, sir."

"Painful, I don't know. Frightening, yes."

Williams asked Jordan to identify the photographs of Esther Steele's body made by OSBI specialist Spence at the crime scene, and by Jordan's assistant, Jerry Peters, at the morgue. Jordan pointed to and described the wounds each photograph depicted.

Judge Markum had given no encouragement that he would admit the photographs as evidence. But they nonetheless were serving a purpose. Williams was making the jury thoroughly aware of them and what they contained.

Williams was well aware of a subtle psychology involved: If the photographs *were* withheld from jurors, they would tend to be angry with the court, and with the defense, who were denying them evidence they probably felt they should see. And, at the same time, they would understand that the prosecution was making every effort to get that evidence to them.

In his cross-examination, Beam concentrated on all that Dr. Jordan had *not* been able to determine—the amount of blood lost, the sequence of injuries, the exact cause of death.

He also dwelled on all the testing that was *not* done.

Jordan admitted that he could not say for certain that Esther Steele suffered before her death.

"Could she have been rendered unconscious by the suffocation, and then stabbed?"

"Yes."

"Doctor, if she had been suffocated first, and was not conscious, would these stab wounds have been painful to her?"

"If you're unconscious, you don't feel the pain."

"Would this lady's death fall within your definition of torture?"

"No. Not in my definition."

"In other words, you don't see any evidence that she was bound, or tied up, or anything like that?"

"No. We look for that. I did not see any evidence of binding."

"Do you recall where blood was located on the exterior of the body?"

For the first time in his more than an hour on the stand, Dr. Jordan seemed at a loss for words.

"Oh, gosh, no. In the course of any given week I see so much blood, that's why I have Jerry Peters take the pictures."

Beam persisted. "You have no idea?"

"Oh, goodness, no. Just this morning I . . . well, we won't go into that. No, I can't remember where I see blood. I see too much."

Williams was making notes, assessing damage.

Clearly Beam was building toward further hammering on the limited testing. That was a vulnerable area. To counter this effort,

Williams felt he should concentrate on all that *had* been done and hope the jury would consider it the preponderance of evidence.

But Beam's questions had suggested that Esther Steele might not have suffered before her death. Williams felt he should blunt that scenario. He rose for a brief re-direct examination.

"Doctor, I think you testified on cross-examination that it was possible for her to have been suffocated, or rendered unconscious, and then stabbed. Is that correct, sir?"

"Yes."

"Let's take this one step further. Would it be possible for her to be suffocated, rendered unconscious, raped, and when she woke up, stabbed?"

"Sure," Dr. Jordan said.

20   ■   ■   ■

OSBI FORENSIC CHEMIST ALAN CORNELIUS
told the jury of finding the red cotton fiber.
He described his work at the crime scene. He
traced the lengthy chain of safeguarding that
evidence.

In cross-examination, Beam again concentrated on the number of unauthorized people
at the crime scene.

As Cornelius left the stand, Williams felt
that the lengthy and detailed scientific testimony had taken the jury's attention too far
from Esther Steele.

He felt it time to bring the victim back on
stage.

"Call Richard Goss," he said.

Goss rose from the prosecution table, was sworn, and seated himself on the stand.

After the introductory questions, Williams asked him what he had observed upon his arrival at the crime scene.

For the first time, jurors were given a detailed and graphic description.

"She was in the middle bedroom. And by that I mean the bedroom in the middle portion of the residence. The inside of this bedroom had two twin beds in it. She was lying on her back on the bed to the right as you entered the bedroom."

"How was she clad?"

"She was wearing a maroon-burgundy-colored nightgown that had been ripped down the front."

Goss described the rest of the room as he had found it in the wake of the searches for Esther's billfold and a flashlight—the closet filled with clothes, the door open, a robe hanging on the back of the hall door, two purses on the other bed, along with two articles of clothing, perhaps a sweater and another outerwear garment.

"Where did you see on Mrs. Steele what appeared to be blood?"

"There was blood pretty much smeared all throughout Mrs. Steele's body. The bed, the bedding, was soaked in blood. There was a large area on the wall next to the bed that was also covered in blood."

"Did you notice anything unusual about the bloodlike substance on the wall? Do you have an opinion as to how it got there?"

"The majority of the blood had more or less leaked out of the body and dripped down the wall along the baseboard. There was also a transfer pattern of blood on the wall. It's my opinion that the blood was transferred onto the wall either by Mrs. Steele's hands or the perpetrator who committed this crime."

Using a scale model he had made, Goss explained the layout of the house.

He identified the photographs he had taken of the body at the scene, and the aerial photographs he had made of the house.

Williams asked Judge Markum for permission to approach the

bench. "I think this would be an appropriate time to excuse the jury," he said. "I am going to ask about the defendant's statements."

Again the jurors were sent out of the courtroom.

Judge Markum then began a hearing within the trial, in order to rule on whether Sadler's confession could be presented to the jury.

In lengthy testimony, Goss described his two interviews with Sadler.

On cross-examination, Beam first asked about the Mangum interview. Was a tape recording made? A video recording? Was the interview reproduced in any manner?

Goss said no to each question.

Beam asked if other suspects were interviewed.

"We always get into this suspect part," Goss protested. "Almost everybody is a suspect. We have a lot of names of people that could have possibly been involved. Now, if we interviewed anybody else on April seventeenth, I can't answer that right now. I'm not sure."

Beam asked more questions about the Mangum interview without once mentioning the Woodward confession.

Williams was puzzled. But plainly the time had arrived to make a motion. He asked Judge Markum to rule that Sadler's statement was voluntary.

Before Judge Markum could rule, Beam popped a surprise.

"Judge, if I might have a moment to talk with my client. We would like to call Mr. Sadler to the stand as far as the voluntariness of the statement."

Judge Markum was not sure he had heard Beam correctly. "You're asking me to do what?"

In essence, Beam was proposing a hearing within a hearing, within the trial itself.

"I think that is inappropriate," Williams said.

"I don't think so," Beam said.

While members of the jury lingered in the claustrophobic jury room, wondering what was happening, the attorneys argued at length on whether Sadler legally could be placed on the witness stand for the limited purpose of challenging Goss's testimony.

Responding to further questions, Goss described the interview with Sadler in Woodward. He said Sadler signed the Miranda form voluntarily, and that as soon as he asked for a lawyer, contact was broken, only to be reinitiated by Sadler after five minutes or so.

"Well, let me explain the appearance to me, and you tell me if it's not correct," Hovis said. "It looks to me like you told him to think it over. You stuck around instead of leaving, once he had asked for an attorney. Wouldn't it be correct to say that contact with you had not been entirely broken off, since he was still in the interrogation room and you were still just outside the door?"

"No, sir," Goss insisted. "That would not be a correct statement."

Judge Markum granted Beam's request to place Sadler on the stand for the limited purpose of contesting Goss's testimony. With the jury still out, Sadler was escorted to the stand and sworn.

"Wayne, let's take the first interview first," Hovis began. "On April seventeenth, in Mangum, did Mr. Goss make any statements to you regarding what might happen to you?"

"Yes, sir. He said something about he could see me getting the death penalty for any involvement whatsoever."

"He told you that on April seventeenth?"

"Yes, sir."

Hovis moved on to the May 20 interview in Woodward.

"After you said you wanted an attorney, what happened next?"

Sadler glanced up at the judge. "Well, they told me they can't talk to me no more, but they was going to give me a few minutes to finish my coffee and to think about my decision about wanting an attorney."

"Did Mr. Goss or Mr. Sunderland make any statements regarding anything Mr. Adams had said?"

"They said Phillip Pat Adams done told them everything, that I did it. That's what they told me."

"Were you upset and under pressure at that time?"

"Yes, sir."

"As I understand it, you had just woke up from a sound sleep."

"Yes, sir."

"Were you still a little bit groggy?"

"A little bit."

"That's the reason they gave you the coffee?"

"I believe so, yes."

"Had you had any alcohol or drugs at that time?"

"Not at that time."

"How long had it been since you had any alcohol or drugs?"

"I would say about twenty-four hours."

"Was it alcohol or drugs, or what?"

"Alcohol and drugs."

"What kind of drugs?"

"Speed. Something they call White Crosses. I took four hits."

"How much alcohol did you have?"

"About a twelve-pack."

"After they left the interrogation room, was it your understanding that they were letting you sit back in that room to think it over, and come out and talk to them?"

"Yes, sir."

Sadler said he would estimate the time he was left alone as about five minutes.

"What were your emotions?" Hovis asked. "What were you feeling? What was your mind going through after Mr. Goss told you that Mr. Adams had made statements saying you killed and raped Mrs. Steele?"

"All my thoughts and feelings were going in a hundred different directions at the same time," Sadler said.

In his cross-examination, Williams concentrated on the portions of Sadler's account that differed from Goss's testimony.

"Mr. Sadler, you just got through hearing Mr. Goss testify a few minutes ago, didn't you?"

"Yes, sir."

"Are you telling this court that he's lying?"

"About most of it."

"About most of it? He's lying?"

"Yes, sir."

"An agent of some fifteen years? Teaches constitutional law? Is lying? Is that what you're telling this court?"

"Yes, sir."

Williams moved to specifics. "Isn't it true that basically all he talked to you about in that first interview was the accident?"

"No, sir," Sadler insisted.

"That's not true? You're telling this court during that first interview he said he would see that you get the death penalty?"

Sadler did not notice that his statement had been altered.

"Yes, sir."

"He didn't know who did it at that first interview."

Sadler saw the need for a correction. "He said if I had anything whatsoever to do with it that he would see me get the death penalty."

"Is that a threat?"

"To me, it is."

Williams asked Sadler if he was not treated with respect at all times by the OSBI agents and by the prosecution.

Sadler admitted that this was true.

"You signed both waivers on the seventeenth and on the twentieth voluntarily, didn't you?"

"I didn't sign the one on the twentieth voluntarily," Sadler insisted. "They done had me so confused I didn't have nothing left but to sign, after they told me what Adams said."

"How did they confuse you?"

"My mind was racing a hundred million different ways."

"You didn't answer my question. How did they confuse you?"

Sadler hesitated a moment before answering. "Here they are being nice. They tell me all of this about Adams saying this and that. I told them I wanted a lawyer, and they said, 'Okay. We're going to go outside and give you a couple of minutes to finish drinking your coffee and think about your decision on a lawyer.' And they got me confused plenty."

"You weren't afraid, were you, of them?"

"I trusted Sunderland. I did not trust Officer Goss."

"Why did you trust Sunderland?"

"It was just a look he had in his eyes."

"Did Sunderland go ahead and read you your waiver again, like Mr. Goss said he did?"

"I know they read it to me. But I'm not sure Sunderland read it to me again or not. He probably did."

"What did you tell Sunderland when he read it to you again? You told him you would go ahead and talk with him, didn't you?"

"Yes."

Both the prosecution and defense made extensive arguments and cited legal precedents. But Judge Markum felt the issue rested on three points: Was contact broken? Did the defendant initiate resumption of the interview? Were threats or promises made?

"The law does not say a defendant must be free from all fears and confusion," he observed. "Every person I have ever known that was thrown into jail was fearful."

Nor, he added, could the law exempt a defendant from emotional trauma and confusion.

He said the evidence showed that when Sadler asked for an attorney, he clearly understood that he had the right to break off the interrogation, and that by his own statement, the interrogation was resumed on his initiative.

"The motion to suppress made by the defendant is overruled," Judge Markum said.

Williams felt he had won a significant victory. Sadler's Woodward confession differed from that of Bugs Adams on essential points. But it backed testimony from Bugs that they both were at the scene of the murder and that they both were actively engaged in a felony.

■ ■ ■

The jury returned to the courtroom. Goss repeated the testimony he had given in the hearing. He described the Mangum interview with Sadler and the confession in Woodward.

He told of Sadler's claim that Bugs was the one who went into the house, and that Bugs had borrowed his socks and red pullover.

Goss recounted Sadler's version of the drive into the country, and of Adams's stopping the truck to get rid of the evidence.

"Toward the end of the interview, I again asked him what, if anything, did Adams say when he got back in the truck. Originally he had said that Adams told him, 'I've been shot, and if something happens you may need to drive.' On the second time I asked him the question, he told myself and Mr. Sunderland that Adams said, 'I killed her, man. I killed her.' "

Hovis began his cross-examination of Goss by returning to the number of people in Esther Steele's house immediately after her body was discovered.

"There were several people," Goss admitted. "I would be safe in saying, absolutely, much more than I usually want in a crime scene. There were quite a substantial number."

"Would there be as many as ten or fifteen?"

"I don't believe we quite reached that number."

Hovis asked if fingerprints or hair samples were taken from any of those individuals.

"I don't believe so."

"And hair samples were not taken from any of the other law enforcement personnel, were they?"

"I don't believe so."

"You understand what I'm getting at? I'm not getting at other suspects. I'm getting at possibly excluding some of the unknown hair samples that were later found."

Hovis asked if Goss ever determined who put the Kleenex on the floor beside the bed.

"No, sir, I did not."

"You mentioned that Mr. Adams and Mr. Sadler were suspects at one time in the case. Were there other suspects?"

Again Goss bridled. "Everybody likes the word *suspect.* I don't. Initially everybody could be called a suspect. These were names that had been brought to our attention, either through people that were familiar with the town or through a significant incident that occurred. Two young men living in Mangum, Oklahoma, had had a major traffic accident, one-vehicle accident, just south of town during the same time frame that we determined that the murder could have taken place. So if you want to call them a suspect—they needed to be talked to. We had to inquire as to why they were in Granite that particular evening."

"When did they become a suspect?" Hovis asked. "When you learned the wreck took place? Is that what you're saying?"

Goss hesitated. If he answered that question truthfully, he might trigger a mistrial. Sadler had not been charged, much less convicted, in the assault-robbery of his grandmother. But the discovery of that earlier case was what had focused attention on him.

Goss felt certain that Hovis knew of the earlier case. He phrased his answer carefully.

"Are you asking me, in my opinion, when did I change from just general interviews of this investigation to actually focusing in on Mr. Sadler and Mr. Adams? I can tell you when that occurred."

Hovis retreated. He took the question in another direction.

"What I'm getting at is, there were other what I call suspects. I don't know what else to call them."

He named Steve Barton, Johnny Monroe, and Terry Rhine. He asked if hair samples were taken from each.

Goss confirmed that samples were not taken.

"Was Terry Rhine a suspect?"

"Terry Rhine was interviewed, yes."

"Why was he interviewed?"

"Terry Rhine has a reputation around Granite for being in trouble."

"Are we talking about little trouble or big trouble?"

"Big trouble."

Hovis asked Goss if he and other investigators had not spent more time searching in the areas Adams designated and less time in the spots where Sadler said the evidence was discarded.

"That is not correct," Goss said. "I spent an equal amount of time. It would be pretty much divided by the logistics of the problems that we were dealing with."

Goss was on the witness stand through most of the afternoon. Toward the end of his testimony, he and Williams gave Hovis one last, teasing jolt.

"I think you told Mr. Hovis on cross-examination that you would tell him the moment Sadler and Adams became possible suspects," Williams said. "And he refused to proceed. I will ask you. When did they become possible suspects?"

"When Mr. Sadler's name came up in connection with—"

"Your Honor!" Hovis interrupted.

"Withdraw the question," Williams said.

OSBI criminalist Mary M. Long made an immediate impact on the jury. Tall, good-looking, with long dark hair, she conveyed extraordinary competence from the moment she walked to the witness stand.

"Now she was sharp," said juror Otis Ray Martin. "She really knew her stuff—and made it understandable. She really impressed me."

"I was very, very impressed," said juror Bonnie Steiner, who as a registered nurse perhaps best understood the technicalities of Long's work. "She was well prepared. She presented just her facts. She was a very strong witness."

But Mary Long had worries other than the trial that day. She had driven her own car to Arapaho. A cousin who had grown up in her household was getting married, and Long was on her way to her hometown of Stratford in the Texas Panhandle for the wedding shower. And there were complications. Her father had been a leukemia patient for five years and was very sick. Long was impatient to give her testimony and to get on with her trip.

After establishing her extensive background, Williams asked her to describe her work. She explained that her specialty of forensic serology encompassed testing samples from the human body— blood, semen, saliva, body fluids, and hair. She said she had been with the OSBI for the last eight years and had now testified in more than one hundred and fifty criminal cases.

Williams took her through the chain of evidence. Ordinarily this detailed testimony would have been tedious. But in this instance, the details served a secondary purpose. Jurors were given a firsthand demonstration of Mary Long at work. She gave dates and numbers without hesitation, flawlessly keeping track of the chain of custody for dozens of items.

Only after this background was established did Williams move on to specifics. He asked her what she found in the sheets and blankets from Esther Steele's bed.

Long said she recovered thirty-four hairs from the two blankets and sheet.

Williams asked her to explain how hair comparison was done. Long went to the blackboard, drew illustrations, and offered the jury a ten-minute short course on hair comparison.

"If I find anything in the unknown hair I cannot find in the known hair, I cannot say they're consistent," she concluded.

Williams wanted this underscored. "Do you have to have a certain number of characteristics, like six characters, ten characters, or twelve characters, before you consider them microscopically consistent?"

Long emphasized her reply. "No. They *all* have to be there. *Everything* that I observe in the unknown must be observed in the known, or I can't say that those hairs are consistent."

She said most of the hairs found in the bedding were consistent with samples from Esther Steele.

Williams asked if any were consistent with the samples from David Wayne Sadler.

"From the sheet number sixteen, there were two scalp hairs consistent microscopically with the hairs from Mr. Sadler. From the two blankets and the sheet in the box, one scalp hair was consistent. Also, another scalp hair from number sixteen."

"So that would be a grand total of how many hairs consistent microscopically?"

"Four."

Long said she did not find any hair in the bedding consistent with samples taken from Bugs Adams.

Beam immediately brought Mary Long's qualifications into question. "Mrs. Long, would you tell me what your background is—your training—in hair comparison?"

"I have attended the FBI's microscopy of hairs and fibers class, which was given at their training academy in Quantico, Virginia. Also, I have studied under people at the OSBI for the last eight years."

Beam's next question was asked in a tone of incredulity. "You have attended the *one* training class at the Quantico academy on hair comparison?"

Long did not appear ruffled. "That is the only *formal* training that I've had. However, at the OSBI I've had many, many hair examinations."

"How long did your formal training take?"

"The class that is offered is a two-week class."

"Is it *all* on hair comparison, or on some other things, too?"

"The first week was hair comparison. The second week is other microscopic techniques—on fibers, different trace evidence items."

Beam left that subject for the moment. He asked if hair comparison was considered as accurate as fingerprints.

"The comparison is not done from a central file registry," Long explained. "It is done from one set of knowns at a time."

"You cannot absolutely tell me that those hairs that came off of the bedding are David Sadler's hairs, can you?"

"I cannot say positively they are," Long admitted. "However, they either came from him, or someone else who has the same observable microscopic characteristics."

"And how many people would have the same observable microscopic characteristics?"

Williams had been awaiting that question. He interrupted Long's possible answer. "May we approach the bench, Your Honor?"

He walked with Beam and Hovis to the bench and spoke too low for the jury to hear. "Your Honor, in the case of *State* versus *Brown*, they got into the probability of hair, one out of forty thousand, whatever. I just don't want counsel to go into the hair bit . . ."

"Was it reversed because the state got into it?" Judge Markum asked.

"It was reversed because it was gotten into," Williams told him. "The case was reported in the last *Bar Journal*."

"Judge, I'm not going to foreclose myself to cross-examine this witness," Beam protested.

Judge Markum considered the situation. It was after 6:00 P.M. The jury had been working nine hours, through difficult testimony. Everyone was tired. He and the attorneys needed to review the case that had been reversed. He wanted to consider this matter thoroughly before ruling. He decided to recess for the evening.

So Mary Long was detained overnight on her trip home.

At that point, no one had any reason to suspect that the following day—the concluding day of the trial—would be twice as long, and far more difficult.

21 ▪ ▪ ▪ ▪

THE FINAL DAY STARTED WITH DISARM-
ing routine. Beam continued his cross-examination of Mary Long, staying well clear of the
statistical probability of hair characteristics,
now determined to be a verboten area.

Instead, Beam returned to Long's statement that both Esther Steele and Bugs
Adams were B-antigen secretors and that she
had found B-antigen activity in the semen.

"So could it have been Mr. Adams's semen?" Beam asked.

"I cannot eliminate anyone as being the
semen donor," Long said. She explained that
the B-antigen found with the semen could
have come from Esther Steele.

"So the bottom line, Mrs. Long, is that you

cannot rule out that the semen in Mrs. Steele came from Bugs Adams, can you?"

"No," Long admitted.

"So in these four samples, we've got blood of Phillip Pat Adams, blood of David Wayne Sadler, blood of Mrs. Steele, and the semen from Mrs. Steele. Is that correct?"

"That's correct."

"Now, it's true, is it not, that all four of those items were submitted to Dr. Michael Baird of the Lifecodes Corporation?"

"Yes."

At the prosecutor's table, Williams was stunned.

No one had informed *him* that samples were sent to Lifecodes in New York for DNA testing. And this was *his* case!

"*Why* were the samples sent to Dr. Michael Baird?" Beam continued.

"They were sent because we felt that possibly they could provide us with some information in this case."

"Whose decision was it to send those things off? Was it your decision? Or your supervisor's? Or whose?"

"I believe it was sort of a combination of people who made the decision."

"Is there a report from Dr. Michael Baird?"

"Yes."

Again Williams was taken aback. He had not seen a report from Lifecodes.

"Do you have that report with you?"

"Not with me," Long said. "It's in my car."

Williams felt it was high time he found out what was going on in his own case. "Let me approach the witness a second, please," he said to Judge Markum.

"I would like to approach also," Beam said.

On reaching the bench, Beam lowered his voice. "Your Honor, we've not been furnished this report. I'd like to examine it."

Williams wanted to make his position clear. "Your Honor, I haven't seen it either."

Again the jury was sent from the courtroom. Judge Markum called a break to allow Long to go to her car for the report. At this point, neither Beam, Williams, nor Judge Markum knew how serious the missing report might be.

Beam's questions on the subject had been exploratory. Earlier that morning he had seen Lifecodes mentioned on a long list of production items. Puzzled, he had decided to follow up on it immediately.

Long returned with the report. After it was read by all, Beam asked Judge Markum for permission to continue his questioning of Long, outside of the hearing of the jury, to determine a possible motion for mistrial.

His request was granted.

Responding to questions from Beam, Long described the initial contact with Lifecodes and the forwarding of the material. She said that after the results proved inconclusive, the matter was not pursued further.

"Are you telling me the report just came in, you read it, and that was it? It was a closed chapter right then and there?"

"Yes, really it was, because insufficient male-specific high molecular weight DNA was isolated from the sample to generate results."

"What does that mean?"

"Basically, that means they were not able to make any determinations from the vaginal swabs."

"Was there simply not enough semen, and they wanted more? Or not enough DNA? Or not enough sperm in the samples? Or what would the reason be?"

"Apparently not having enough DNA," Long explained. "There were a lot of sperm cells, but decomposition had taken place. There was not sufficient DNA that they could isolate and work with."

"Were there any additional samples that could have been sent?"

"There were some cervical swabs, but the sperm cells were not intact. So I did not feel those would be good enough quality for them to work with."

"You don't recall having spoken with anyone from Lifecodes

Corporation about obtaining more samples, or running the test again, or why they couldn't test, or anything like that?"

"No."

"Was this the first case you've used them on?"

"We have used them on two cases. I don't recall which one went first, whether it was this one, or the other one."

"So it's safe to say this was at least the first or second time you used Lifecodes Corporation?"

"That's correct."

Beam's baritone voice rolled over the small courtroom amphitheater. "Your Honor, we are four days into a murder trial. They send semen off to be tested some place in New York. There is a forensic report that we are not furnished with until today. We had money for expert witnesses. We could have used some to analyze this report. We could have used it for comparative purposes. We could have been better prepared to cross-examine these witnesses. We could have contacted Lifecodes Corporation. We could have done a myriad of different things."

Beam spread his hands in a gesture of helplessness. "Your Honor, we are put in a bad enough position in these cases. We ought to be furnished every single item of exculpatory evidence, anything that might possibly be relevant. I'm sure they're going to say it didn't test. We ought to be informed there was a no-test. I sympathize with you in that I don't know what to do with the jury, as far as misleading them. I don't want to create any error in this case. The medical examiner is already gone. The people that transported the semen, collected the semen, those people are gone. We can't cross-examine them as to the amount of semen. Maybe we could have had our own DNA fingerprinting done. It really puts us at a big disadvantage. We've got no experts and no ability to contact anybody, or consult with anybody, to do a thing other than to sit here and try to figure out what to do."

Beam paused. "Your Honor, I don't know what else to do but to ask this court for a mistrial. A mistrial ought to be declared, or these charges ought to be dismissed."

At this point Beam felt he had a good shot at a mistrial. He had won mistrials on similar missing reports. In recent months the appellate courts had tended to decide more in favor of the defendant in such instances. And with a thin, circumstantial case such as this, Sadler probably would not be retried.

Williams was well aware of all of this, and he was deeply disturbed. The failure to produce the report clearly was the fault of the prosecution. He rose and once again explained to Judge Markum that he had entered the case late, and that he also had not been furnished with the report. But he also pointed out that the report clearly stated that the tests were inconclusive. Therefore, they could not have helped the defense any more than they had helped the prosecution.

Listening to Williams, Beam again became angry. Williams was claiming he knew nothing about the report. Yet he had OSBI case agent Goss sitting right beside him.

"Your Honor, Mr. Williams can say that he's a special prosecutor and he got in the case late and this and that, but that has absolutely no relevance or no value at all. He's bound by what the district attorney's office did in this case from day one. He can't insulate himself from those problems. We are hamstrung enough in this case. We don't have any money. We've got an indigent client. They've got all the experts. They've got all of the money. They've got all of the witnesses. They have month after month after month to prepare. We get it thrown in our lap, and we have to scramble around and do the best we can. And that's not right. It's not fair. Mrs. Long testified that there were some other partial samples. I would like to know about those. I would like to know from Lifecodes Corporation, could those have been tested? If it had come out favorable to the state, they would have been up there waving that Lifecodes deal right in front of the jury's face and saying, 'Look at this! This test is valid and it points to this man right here!' But it doesn't test, so we bury it, never to be seen or heard from again. Judge, this is a grievous,

grievous problem, and I think it's going to be error not to do something about it. Again, we ask for a mistrial."

Judge Markum was not swayed by Beam's eloquence and fervor.
To his mind, the issue broke down to one essential question: Could
the test results conceivably have helped the defense in any way?

With the jury still out, he questioned Mary Long from the bench
on why the test results were inconclusive.

She said the sperm had deteriorated, and there were no more to
send.

"Judge, that brings up another problem," Beam said. "They have
used up all of the evidence. I don't have a case specifically on sperm.
I do have one on cocaine, that if the state uses up all of the cocaine
in testing, and there is not a sample for the defense to test, they
can't use that as evidence. They're yelling about this sperm, and
they have used it all up."

"I have thrown out a case on that basis," Judge Markum agreed.
"But I don't think the Court of Criminal Appeals rules that way.
They say if it's all used up, that's life. That's the way it is."

"We're not trying to use the sperm as evidence," Williams
pointed out.

"Judge, they are not trying to use it, but they're talking about it,"
Beam countered. "They found sperm right in front of the jury.
They're trying to convict this guy of rape, and now they're saying
they are going to make a statement to the jury, 'Don't consider anything about the sperm whatsoever. Just forget we even mentioned
it.' Judge, that is wrong. That is error."

Judge Markum further questioned Mary Long, this time about
the various types of swabs and the disposition of each.

She said that of the swabs she had left, none contained sperm
that were intact.

Based on Long's answers, Judge Markum could not see that
either the prosecution or the defense had been helped or harmed by
the failure of the tests. He turned back to the attorneys and made
his ruling.

"Well, as to the motion for a mistrial, let me first state that there are certain questions which judges and appellate judges recognize as what is called harmless error. And that is, there may have been a mess-up, but the mess-up isn't significant enough for it to have any effect on the case. That looks to be the situation here. Consequently, the motion for mistrial is overruled."

"Your Honor, this really puts us at a precarious position in front of the jury as far as what to do with this report, and how to handle this," Beam said.

"You've asked her about it, and I think the next appropriate question is, were there any conclusive results received from the report," Judge Markum said. "And her answer will be no. Then whatever else you do, that's left up to you."

"That's what I'm concerned about," Beam said. "How does this play to the jury? How does this look on behalf of my client, now that I've gotten halfway into it? I know those are not problems for the court. Those are my problems. But I'm claiming total surprise this morning."

Judge Markum asked Beam if he wanted a short break to review his strategy.

"No, let's get on with it," Beam said.

And he did. After the jury returned to the courtroom, he began an intense, unrelenting cross-examination of Mary Long, hammering on the theme that she could not be one hundred percent certain that the four hairs found in Esther's bed actually came from Sadler.

He took her back through her Lifecodes testimony, this time in far more detail. Over and over he asked why she had not allowed Lifecodes to determine if DNA could be extracted from the partial sperm she still had in her possession.

Why had she herself made that crucial decision, possibly so damaging to his client?

Beam returned to her testimony about antigens. He suggested that as an older person, Esther might not have secreted much B-antigen, and thus the B-antigen found in her vagina came from Bugs Adams.

He stressed that Long had not found any other type of antigen activity.

"Where did the B-antigen come from? Do you know?"

"That is something I cannot say," Long admitted. "Because first of all, I have to operate under the assumption that at least some of them came from Esther Steele. Beyond that I really don't know."

Beam suggested that Bugs Adams might have been the semen source.

"He could not be eliminated, based on this information," Long admitted.

What about Johnny Monroe?

Long said Monroe was type A, non-secretor, and thus could not be eliminated, either.

What about Steve Barton?

Long said his blood specimen had been contaminated in transport, and that no testing was done.

"Why wasn't another sample obtained from him? Do you know?"

"No. I don't know."

Beam's questions were phrased in such a way that Long seldom could give a positive answer. As the day wore on, her testimony became a litany of such phrases as "I don't know," "I can't say," "I have no way to know," and "That's a possibility."

Was the blood at the crime scene analyzed?

"No," Long said.

"Why not?"

Long explained that Esther Steele's blood would have contaminated that from any other source, and for that reason she elected not to attempt an analysis.

"Ma'am, are you telling me you're assuming that all of the blood on all of the bedclothing belonged to Esther Steele?"

"It either belonged to Esther Steele or had been contaminated with the blood of Esther Steele."

"But you ran no tests to determine that?"

"That's correct."

Beam returned to hair comparison. He introduced textbooks on forensic science and established that her terminology differed in many instances from that of the authors.

Long said she was familiar with the terminology the authors used but did not use it herself.

"Are you familiar with a method of X-ray emissions, spectroscopic analysis of hair?"

"I have read about the method," Long said. "However, we don't employ that at the OSBI."

"Are you familiar with photoluminence techniques for study of human hair?"

"No, I'm really not. I have never dealt with them."

"Are you familiar with the method of analyzing hair known as neutron activation analysis?"

"Yes."

"Do you do that type of thing?"

"No. Again, that is another one that deals with the chemical elements present."

"Are you telling me they're not valid tests?"

"I presume that it's a valid test on the day it's done. But if, say, you did one on my hair one day, and then I went somewhere where there is a lot of smoke or emissions, and then you took hair samples from me and did them again, you might come up with a different reading. Or if I used one shampoo today and a different shampoo tomorrow, or that kind of thing, they can change. That's why they're not routinely used forensically."

"Are you aware that those tests are accepted by courts of law as valid tests for hair?"

"They may very well be. But they're still not routinely employed."

"At least not by the OSBI? You people don't routinely employ them?"

"We don't, and I actually cannot think of anyone who does forensic work who does use that."

One by one, Beam named every person known to have been at the crime scene, and asked Long if hair and blood samples from them had been taken and analyzed.

And with each negative answer, Beam further asked, "Why not?"

He summed up with a tone of exasperation.

"At any time, ma'am, did you receive a list, or try to find out who all had been in the bedroom with Esther Steele, or with the body of Esther Steele, who might have come in contact with the bed-clothes?"

"I never received that information."

"Did you ever try to find out that information?"

"No."

Beam asked her if head hairs deteriorate. Long said she was not aware of any time scale, but that there were head hairs on Egyptian mummies thousands of years old.

Beam cited the four hairs she had found in the bedclothing.

"In fact, they could have been out of the human head and lying on the sheets and bedclothes for months and months, and even years. Is that not correct?"

"It's possible."

"Is it possible to transfer hair from one person to another, or from one item to another, by touching or rubbing against each other, or on clothing?"

"Yes."

"Is it possible, ma'am, that rather than those four head hairs falling out of the donor's head, that they could have been on his clothing, and fallen off his clothing onto the bed?"

"I guess it's possible."

"So if I was wearing a sweater, or an overshirt, and took it off, it would be possible that some of my head hairs could be contained on that sweater or sweatshirt. Correct?"

"Yes, that's correct."

"If someone else then put on that sweater or sweatshirt and began wearing it, my head hairs would be carried by that person on their clothing?"

"Could be. Yes."

"And those hairs could conceivably fall off. Correct?"

"Yes."

Reaction to Beam's vigorous four-and-a-half-hour cross-examination of Mary Long varied among jurors.

"He was very hard on her," juror Barney Brown said. "I was surprised the judge allowed so much of that. It seemed awful long. He just harped and harped. She didn't seem rattled. She was very calm and collected. He was trying to make her make a mistake. But she didn't break."

Juror Alice Brown was not bothered by Mary Long's string of negative answers. She felt they tended to give Long even more credibility. "She was just telling the truth."

Juror Otis Ray Martin also felt Mary Long's testimony was actually strengthened through the relentless cross-examination.

"It seemed like he'd go over a list of questions, then he'd come right back with them again. And she'd give the same answer she did maybe thirty minutes ago. She really impressed me."

"Let me tell you, if you're ever in trouble, you want to get Stephen Beam," juror Bonnie Steiner said. "He's terrific! He really did his homework. He's brilliant! If I ever get into trouble, I know where I'm going. But I did not appreciate what he put Mary Long through. That just made me believe more than ever that she was right."

As a registered nurse, with years of experience, Bonnie Steiner was disturbed by Beam's implication that with only a week of formal training by the FBI, Long was undertrained for her job in hair comparison.

"I know about microscopes and chromosomes and this and that," Steiner said. "I was furious with Beam for trying to run her down. He tried to make the jury believe that in a week she became an expert. This wasn't true! It was in a field of what she already was doing! In a week of concentrated studies, you can . . . I've done this!

I've taken a three-day workshop and learned something entirely new, building on my background. And I've come out feeling good about what I've learned in three days! She had the background for that week of intensive study. I honestly believe she was qualified."

But for some jurors, Beam's cross-examination succeeded in raising a cloud of questions.

"He really put a doubt in the jury's mind that she actually knew what she was doing," Steiner said. "He had them so convinced! They were just snowballed!"

Prosecutor Williams sensed that Beam had swayed some of the jurors. And the scenario Beam proposed for the possible transfer of hair had probably weakened the state's only solid physical evidence linking Sadler to the rape and murder.

Williams felt that his case might have been seriously damaged. How badly, he would not know until the case went to the jury.

After the noon break, Beam recalled Long to the stand. "I'm sure you think it's impossible I skipped something," he said. "But we didn't talk about any of the pubic hair samples."

He asked her about hairs from the bedding that she had redefined.

Long explained that they were "transitional" hair that appears between body and pubic hair, perhaps on the abdomen or legs, and were not "classic" pubic hair, body hair, or head hair.

"At one time did you believe these hairs that we're talking about were, in fact, pubic hairs?"

"I felt they could be, and I wanted to check and see and make sure, because I have seen people in my casework who have pubic hairs that are like this."

"Did you believe those hairs to be pubic hairs, and then later you weren't certain?"

"No. It's just I felt they could be pubic hairs. They still could be. But they are not consistent with the classic pubic hairs of Mr. Sadler or Mr. Adams."

Mary Long spent another hour on the stand. Not until late afternoon was she released to resume her trip home to the Texas Panhandle.

Only one state witness remained. Anthony Hinch, who had spent three days in a cell with Sadler at Greer County Jail, was called to tell his story.

Hinch had written a letter to the District Attorney telling of a jail cell conversation with Sadler. He had convinced Sunderland, Goss, and Williams that he was telling the truth.

But he was not an imposing witness. He was tall, heavyset, with long, stringy hair. His street clothes did not fit. He gave his address as Oklahoma State Reformatory.

Hinch told the jurors that Sadler said he and Adams had gotten drunk and gone to this woman's house, and that Adams was too drunk to go in. But Sadler had said that he remembered going into the house.

"Did he say anything else?" Williams asked.

"He said she got what she deserved."

"Did you ever have a conversation regarding his joining the carnival?"

"He said the OSBI was after him and he wanted to hurry up and get out of town."

"Did you ever have a conversation with him regarding the quality of the case that was filed against him?"

"He said the only way they could convict him is if his partner Adams would testify against him."

"Did he ever say whether or not Adams would testify against him?"

"He said he didn't know."

Williams was well aware that Hinch was not an impressive witness. The basic strength of Hinch's story—that Sadler had bragged about knocking his grandmother in the head and stealing her money—could not be presented to the jury. But it was that detail in Hinch's story that had convinced Sunderland, Goss, and Williams.

How else would Hinch have known about the earlier crime, if Sadler had not told him?

Hinch explained to the jurors how he happened to be in the Greer County Jail. He had been granted leave from the reformatory to go to the bedside of his son, who was undergoing surgery. He had overstayed his leave. Even though he gave himself up, he was charged with escape and held in the Greer County Jail for formal processing.

In his cross-examination, Hovis established that Hinch had been in the reformatory just over a year for receiving stolen property, and that despite the added escape charge, he would be completing his five-year sentence in just four more months.

Hinch claimed he had made no deals in exchange for his testimony. He insisted that he was just a concerned citizen.

His story received mixed reactions among the jury.

"I didn't know whether to believe him or not," said juror Bonnie Steiner. "I was very undecided. It's just a matter of somebody lied or didn't lie. That left a big doubt in my mind. I didn't base anything really on that. It just wasn't a strong point."

Hinch did not seem to make much of an impression on any of the jurors. No one could remember his name even being mentioned during deliberations.

When Williams announced that the state was resting its case, O.C., his family, and the contingent from Granite could hardly believe their ears.

"We kept waiting for the fireworks, but they never came," said Esther's sister Polly. "They didn't have *anything!*"

Beam's devastating cross-examination of Mary Long still hung heavily in the air. Hinch's performance on the stand had been so weak it was almost pathetic. And Bugs Adams's appearance had been almost as bad. O.C. felt certain the case was lost.

"There was nothing to show the jury. No murder weapon, none

of the defendant's clothing with blood, nothing. Goss and Sunderland had built us up quite a lot on this DNA they sent off, and the medical report. So we had been banking a lot on that. We were really let down, and disgusted with what they didn't find, what they couldn't do. We were really worried about what the jury was going to think."

Juror Otis Ray Martin also felt frustrated. The jury had not been allowed to see a single one of the pictures flashed around, alluded to, and shown to various witnesses. Important facts had been introduced in passing, then skipped over, never to be mentioned again.

Martin felt that the jury was not receiving the full story.

"There were a lot of questions I wanted to ask the witnesses. But of course we couldn't do that."

The jurors again were sent out while Judge Markum ruled on a long string of motions.

One by one, Williams offered the state's exhibits. Beam made an eloquent plea against each. Williams won the admission of most, with the exception of the photographs.

Beam argued vehemently against admission of the bedding. He especially cited one sheet so bloody he felt it would be highly prejudicial. "It's covered with blood."

"I don't want it waved in front of the jury," Judge Markum conceded.

Hovis asked if the sheet would be sent back with the jury during deliberations.

"I think not," Judge Markum said. "And I don't think it ought to be unfolded. It can be pointed to in the box or sack. That will be sufficient."

"Is it proper to admit things in evidence and not have them go to the jury?" Beam asked.

"I think the court has discretion," Williams said.

"I do, too," Judge Markum agreed. "You raised the objection about them being inflammatory. I'm simply going to go ahead and properly utilize them as evidence."

Beam persisted. "I'm concerned, Judge, that later on, if the jury sends out a note and says, 'We want to look at the sheets,' and in case Mr. Williams said, 'Let's send them in because they are asking for them.'"

"We will cross that bridge when we get to it, if that occurs," Judge Markum said.

Again Beam asked that the case be dismissed. He cited the lack of strong evidence, and that the only corroboration was the testimony of the former co-defendant, who had not testified in a manner to be believed.

"We've got four hairs, and that's all we've got. Judge, hairs are not proper evidence with which to convict someone on first degree murder."

Judge Markum heard nothing in Beam's argument he had not expected.

"Overruled, with exceptions allowed," he told Beam. "Are you ready to proceed?"

After almost two hours of inactivity in the close confines of the jury room, the jurors felt that the presentation of the case for the defense moved swiftly.

Douglas McCormack, the emergency medical technician, testified that when Bugs Adams's trousers were removed at the hospital, he noticed a patch of smeared, dried blood on his legs.

He said he saw no cut or abrasion that would have caused that type of bleeding.

Johnny Wilson, communications technician with Southwestern Bell Telephone Company, and also an EMT, testified that he did not observe blood on Sadler at the scene of the wreck.

Dolly Schoolcraft said that after the wreck she noticed marks on the left side of her nephew's face.

"Did they look like the type of marks that could have been made by fingernails?" Hovis asked.

"It could have been. We asked him what girlfriend scratched him."

Sadler's paternal grandmother, Hazel Sadler, testified that after her grandson arrived home from the hospital, she did not see blood or semen stains when she washed his clothes.

As Williams rose to cross-examine Hazel Sadler, he sensed that once again the defense had managed to shift the focus of the trial to the defendant and away from the victim.

He felt he should restore the proper perspective.

"Mrs. Sadler, I think you said you're seventy-four?"

"Yes, sir."

"That's one year older than Esther Steele was when she met her death," he observed.

As Williams expected, Hovis was on his feet immediately with an objection.

And as Williams expected, Judge Markum sustained the objection. But Williams felt he had effectively reminded the jury of the victim.

Hazel Sadler said her grandson returned from the hospital wearing his own long-sleeved shirt, and that she washed it the same day.

Williams did not pursue the point. Sadler had been placed in the green coveralls by several witnesses. He did not need to belittle the testimony of the grandmother.

"At that time, where was he living?" Williams asked.

"He was living with me."

That answer tended to blunt testimony from the next witness, Sadler's mother, Linda Sadler, who in a brief appearance said that as far as she knew, her son's departure with the carnival was not a secret.

She said that when the sheriff called and asked about her son's whereabouts, she told him.

■ ■ ■

The defense recalled Bugs Adams. Again the trial ground to a halt.

Jurors were returned to the jury room while the attorneys argued whether the Peeping Tom incident could be introduced as evidence. At last Judge Markum ruled against admission. "Under the system of evidence, you cannot bring up one crime for the purpose of proving another, and that is the whole ball of wax."

Again the jury was returned to the courtroom. But with omission of the Peeping Tom incident, the reappearance of Bugs Adams on the stand was limited to a half dozen questions.

The defense offered only two more character witnesses. Don Sparks, assistant principal and counselor at Mangum High School, said Sadler had been an average-or-below student.

Hovis asked if Sadler was a leader or a follower.

"He was usually a quiet individual, and I would classify him in that direction," Sparks said. "Probably a follower."

Jim Scott, a teacher and counselor at Mangum High School, was a reluctant witness. He said he was acquainted with Esther Steele's family and considered himself a friend.

Hovis asked him what type of person he observed Sadler to be.

"A very quiet, withdrawn, reserved type of student," Scott said.

"Would you say he was a leader or follower?"

"A follower," Scott said.

As Scott left the stand, Beam announced that the defense rested. Only final instructions and closing arguments remained before Sadler's fate would be handed to the jury.

22 ▪ ▪ ▪ ▪

"YOU SHOULD DECIDE THIS CASE ON
the cold, cold facts given by the witnesses,"
Williams told jurors in opening his final argument. "You should not let sympathy or sentiment enter into your deliberations."

Rapidly he summarized the evidence presented by the state's witnesses.

"Mr. Kruska, the brother of the victim, testified she was seventy-three years of age, lived
long, very active, very strong, very sturdy.

"Pat Adams, the co-defendant in this matter, came and testified that on April fourteenth, he and this defendant went out on a
drinking spree."

Again Williams recapped the night, as
Bugs had described it.

He reminded the jurors that Bugs Adams had said that Sadler took the knife from the dash.

"Why did he reach and grab for a knife?" Williams asked. He answered his own question. "He didn't know what was going to happen in that house. He's really not very big and he needed some protection, because he was going into the unknown.

"They then proceeded out into the country and the defendant said, 'Stop here.' Why did he want to stop? He wanted to dispose of the evidence. We might be intoxicated, but we are not *that* drunk. We know what we've done, and we know we have to get rid of the evidence.

"Why did he get rid of that red cotton pullover sweatshirt? It was red, all right. I guarantee you it was red, when he stabbed Esther Steele with the knife six times. He got rid of the knife. He got rid of the red shirt. He got rid of the socks."

Williams stressed that the night was cold, that Sadler returned to the pickup shaking, and that he put on the green coveralls.

"Ladies and gentlemen of the jury, I submit to you from the evidence, the person who put on the green coveralls is the murderer of Esther K. Steele. Who put on those green coveralls? Not Adams. Sadler!"

Williams summarized the testimony of the other state witnesses: Pearl Johnson, who told of the pickup truck's stopping at her apartment and driving off in the direction of Esther Steele's house. Dr. Lenaburg, who discovered that Esther Steele's death was not natural, and who notified the authorities. Former Police Chief L. D. Williams, who determined the death was homicide and sealed off the area. Trooper Kerry Pettingill, who investigated the accident. Charles Lynn Hayden, the ambulance attendant who saw blood on Sadler's hands.

"Where did he get that blood?" Williams asked. "He got that blood from doing this six times."

Williams stabbed the Styrofoam dummy with a pen, counting aloud with each thrust. "One, two, three, four, five, six! That's where he got the blood."

■ ■ ■

In the front row of the jury box, close to Williams and the stabbing, juror Otis Ray Martin felt that the demonstration was excessive.

"The stabbing actions that he did, I don't think they were necessary. He hit that mannequin hard. Of course, it was right in front of us. He could have just showed us where the stab wounds were. I don't think he needed to really hit that mannequin."

Williams continued on through the testimony of other witnesses: Bill Greer, who transported Esther's body to Oklahoma City. Dr. Jordan, who conducted the autopsy.

"Not only was she raped, not only was she slashed and stabbed, she also was partially suffocated."

He recalled the testimony of OSBI agent Alan Cornelius, who testified that he found a red fiber in fingernail clippings taken from Esther Steele's body.

"What type of jacket or shirt did the defendant have? A red pullover sweatshirt. You know how those fibers got there? I think you do."

Williams recounted the testimony of John Schoolcraft, who said his knife was similar to State Exhibit Number One, termed by Dr. Jordan as about the size of the one used on Esther Steele.

"Where is the knife?" Williams asked. "I submit that only one person knows where that knife is. The defendant."

Williams also reminded the jury of the testimony of Mary Long, who found in the bedding four hairs consistent with samples from Sadler.

Williams went back over the testimony of Anthony Hinch, who told of Sadler's bragging about murdering Esther Steele.

"He said she got what she deserved, whatever that means," Williams said. "I don't know what that means."

Williams concluded the first portion of his closing argument on a quiet note.

"Ladies and gentlemen of the jury, this defendant is guilty of murder in the first degree. He is guilty of rape in the first degree. I would ask you when you retire to your jury room to come back with two verdicts. Murder in the first degree, guilty. Rape in the first degree, guilty."

"My closing argument will be fairly brief," Hovis said. "Mainly because I want to emphasize what to me are the very, very important aspects of this case."

Hovis lacked the smooth oratorical style of Williams and Beam, and his voice was not as strong. Although the jury had no difficulty hearing, those in the back of the courtroom often failed to hear his words.

"We had volumes and volumes of testimony, and volumes of reports, and this can be very confusing. It can be confusing enough sometimes to convict an innocent person."

Hovis said that in his opinion one of the most important witnesses was Mary Long.

"She appeared to be a very nice person, very, very good at testifying. But I think you might infer that some of the aspects of the case, she kind of sloughed off, that were pertinent or important to the defendant. Let me be more specific."

He reminded the jury that Sadler was an H-antigen secretor, and that no H-antigen was found in the sperm.

He questioned whether Esther Steele, as an older person, would have the vaginal secretions of a younger woman. He asked that the jurors use common sense, which, he said, dictated that the B-antigen probably came from Adams.

He reviewed Mary Long's categories of head hair, pubic hair, and transitional hair. Going back over the many samples, he cited instances in which Mary Long changed classifications.

"All of a sudden she is caught in a trap," he said. "She has to change these pubic hairs, which she can definitely identify. All of a sudden she changes them to body hairs because they don't match up with anything."

Hovis reminded the jurors that Bugs Adams was more or less the host on the drinking spree.

"Mr. Sadler was the passenger in the pickup. He wasn't in charge of their evening, or their night out. He was sitting just drinking, presumably very, very drunk."

He insisted that the scenario in which Bugs Adams left the pickup and went into the house was more believable.

"Mr. Adams is the one that knew his way around Granite. Mr. Adams knew Mrs. Steele. Mr. Adams is the one that had her as his teacher. Granite is a tiny town. You might infer from the evidence that he might have been in her house a number of times before. It was dark. He knew his way in the back door. He knew where her bedroom was. Mr. Sadler didn't. Mr. Adams played in Granite as a kid. He knew the drainage ditch."

And he reminded the jury that it was Adams who pled guilty to murder in this case, not Sadler.

"Maybe the state should file charges for Mr. Sadler taking the money," Hovis concluded. "Presumably that would be some type of felony. But is he guilty of first degree murder? Is he guilty of rape? I think not."

"You're about to make the hardest decision that any of you have ever made in your life," Beam told the jurors.

"We are talking about convicting a young man of first degree murder and first degree rape. That's why it must be proven beyond a reasonable doubt, not merely by a preponderance of the evidence. And the evidence that you need to consider has to be reliable. And it has to be believable. You need to be morally certain of this man's guilt."

Beam said Williams had presented two scenarios—one at the beginning of the trial, outlining what the proof would be, and one at the close of the trial, reviewing the evidence presented.

The scenarios, he said, were essentially the same.

"But is that what actually happened?" he asked. "What you need to think is, what has the state of Oklahoma brought you this week with which to decide this case? The state has District Attorneys, special prosecutors, OSBI agents. They have investigators, and an unlimited amount of money. They've got Mary Long who can run God knows how many tests on God knows how many different things, and tens of people just like her at the OSBI. If they can't run a test, they just ship this stuff off to New York or wherever it needs to be shipped and have all kinds of tests run. They have everything at their disposal to prove a case."

Beam paused and lowered his voice. "My client is poor. He doesn't have any money. Mr. Hovis and I are appointed by the court to represent him. That's the kind of thing we are up against. You need to think: With all of that power, and all of those resources, why hasn't the state of Oklahoma brought you any more to decide this case than they have? They really haven't brought you very much, have they?"

Williams listened to Beam's closing argument with concern. Throughout his career, Williams had studied juries. He saw that Beam was making a strong argument and communicating it well.

Williams made notes, preparing to counter the inroads Beam was making into the state's case.

In the jury box, juror Bonnie Steiner was indeed feeling the effects of Beam's argument.

"Beam and Williams were such good orators. One could look at you and say, '*Believe me*,' and you would. And the next would say, '*Believe me*,' and you would. Their closing arguments were so very, very good. They were so even that it was real hard to decide."

"There are two different ways this could have happened," Beam continued. "There is the Bugs Adams way, where he points the finger at my client. And then there is our story. Now, Agent Goss over here went through a long scenario and a long explanation of exactly what our client told him in Woodward. Folks, I submit to you that's what really happened in this case.

"You got Bugs Adams who sat here, a guy that eats bugs off of the wall, and you've got David Wayne Sadler here. That's the two people you've got."

Beam reviewed the testimony of Bugs Adams. He pointed out that Bugs was crystal clear on what Sadler did, what Sadler wore, and what Sadler said. But Bugs could not remember anything concerning himself. He could not remember times. He could not remember places.

"That can only point you in one direction," Beam said. "That he's simply not telling the truth."

Beam told the jurors they should think about credibility.

"This guy, Bugs, was charged with murder in the first degree. The state was seeking the death penalty against him, too, just like my client. It's funny that all of a sudden he agrees to testify against my client. And what does he get in return? He doesn't get the death penalty. He gets a life sentence. That's why he's testifying. He's not a good citizen. He's been convicted of first degree murder! The man cannot be believed! He's a murderer!"

Beam pointed out that Bugs Adams weighed two hundred pounds. Sadler was small. Esther Steele had been described as a strong woman.

"There was one piece of evidence in this case that could have conclusively shown who raped Mrs. Steele," Beam said. "And I would say the same person that raped her killed her."

He reminded the jury of Mary Long's inability to pinpoint anyone specifically with the antigen tests, and that after the DNA test proved inconclusive, no further effort was made.

"Ladies and gentlemen, they did not try to find anybody else once the finger was pointed at David Wayne Sadler. The evidence that you've got—the physical evidence—are four hairs. Four little bitty hairs were found by Mary Long in the bedclothes. There is a real problem, folks, with those hairs."

One by one he named the fourteen people known to have been in the house before Esther Steele's body was moved.

"None of these people's hair was submitted for testing. Why? The state didn't want to test anybody else's hair. They already had David Wayne Sadler. They had four hairs. They didn't want to do anything else."

He pointed out the alternate tests Mary Long knew about but did not do.

"We've heard about blood for the last four days until I'm sick of it. There was blood on the sheets. Blood on everything. But was any of the blood in the house tested? No. It was not typed. Why? Because the state didn't need to do it. They already had four hairs and the testimony of an accomplice. That is all they thought about. They looked at this guy to the exclusion of all other people. Folks, that is not right."

He stressed that the only witness who testified that Sadler had blood on his hands also said he had a cut finger, and that every other witness testified that there was no blood on David Wayne Sadler. Nor did his grandmother find blood or semen on his clothes when she washed them. And, to the contrary, Bugs Adams had dried blood covering his legs beneath his pants.

"How did Bugs get blood underneath his pants unless he was the one that went into Mrs. Steele's house and killed her and raped her and got blood on his legs while his pants were off or his pants were down?"

Beam gazed into the eyes of the jurors, one by one, as he talked. "Our defense is real simple. Our client didn't do it. He did not rape her, and he did not murder her, and the state does not have the proof. They have not proved their case beyond a reasonable doubt."

Beam reminded the jurors of the story that Williams had told in jury selection, about the kid and the cookie jar, and the validity of circumstantial evidence.

"But the crumbs don't lead to Mr. Sadler," Beam concluded. "The crumbs lead to Bugs Adams."

Item by item, Williams demonstrated that the state's evidence had established every requisite of murder and rape in the first degree—breaking and entering in the commission of a robbery, and the use of force.

"How much force was used?" Williams held up the knife. "I guarantee you this probably will overcome any resistance. Just the look of it terrifies me."

He moved to the Styrofoam torso.

"You will recall the medical examiner testified that the wounds were inflicted with the knife at this particular angle." He struck the mannequin. "This wound at this angle. This angle. This angle. This angle. This angle. And that angle. So what about the angles? The person who did this was right-handed. And have you noticed this defendant during the trial? Have you noticed him writing on the yellow pad? Remember which hand he used? Right-handed."

Williams knew that one of the most damaging assertions made by the defense was that Bugs Adams was thoroughly familiar with Granite and the rock ditch, and that Sadler was not.

Using the aerial photograph of the house, he traced the route from where Bugs said Sadler left the pickup to Esther's back door, and the return path to the point where Bugs said he was picked up. Williams pointed out that the route was not complicated. Anyone locating the house from the front easily could follow the rock ditch to the back door.

"And where is the evidence?" Williams asked, taking another issue head-on. "That's the big problem. You heard how many man-hours and how many people were involved in trying to find the billfold. Trying to find the knife. Trying to find the socks. Trying to find the red cotton shirt. Ladies and gentlemen, it's my theory that the next day this defendant came out and retrieved this evidence. I submit that Sadler came out there and knew exactly where the evidence was, and he retrieved it, and it's not there anymore."

Williams was not sure how much weight the jury would give to Beam's portrait of a monolithic state rolling over his poor client, but he felt he should put that ploy to rest.

"I, as a state employee, as an Assistant DA for twelve or fourteen years, know how poor the state is. I have to think twice before I spend any money to get a transcript. The state does not have that much money, ladies and gentlemen. I wish it did. But it doesn't."

He answered the defense claim that Mary Long had not done her job.

"It would have been a useless gesture for her to have stuck that cervical swab in and sent it to Lifecodes. You saw and heard defense counsel read to you the letter from Lifecodes saying there was not enough sperm sent to detect DNA. That's all they had. You can't send any more than all you've got."

The dried blood under Bugs Adams's trousers also was a potentially damaging point. Williams argued that the blood might not have gotten there in the manner the defense suggested.

"Use your good common sense. If you go in a strange house at night with a knife, not knowing what in the world you're going to find, are you going to rape a woman by taking your pants halfway down?"

He moved on to Beam's attack on the quality of some of the state's witnesses.

"Now, I wish Billy Graham could testify in this case. But he can't. Why? Because he was not a witness. You take your witnesses as you get them. If you get them from Granite Reformatory, you get them from Granite Reformatory. If you get them as the state did, co-defendants, you take them as co-defendants. All I can do is provide you with the witnesses I have."

To this point, Williams had been responding to Beam's closing argument, speaking extemporaneously. He now segued into his prepared closing remarks.

He reminded the jurors of their answers to his questions during jury selection.

"I asked each and every one of you, 'If the state proves to you beyond a reasonable doubt that this defendant did, in fact, commit murder in the first degree, *can* you convict?' All of you said, 'Yes, I can.'

"My second question was, *'Will* you convict?' And every one of you looked me in the eye and said, 'Yes, I *will* convict.'

"Now I'm asking you to retire and convict this defendant. Find David Wayne Sadler guilty of murder in the first degree. Find David Wayne Sadler guilty of rape in the first degree. Thank you."

As Williams walked back to the prosecution table, a hush fell over the courtroom.

It was 7:19 P.M. Court had been in session, with only brief recesses, since 9:30 A.M. Everyone was tired after the long, emotional day.

Judge Markum spoke to the jurors. "Ladies and gentlemen, the case is submitted to you at this time."

He dismissed Barbara Turner, the alternate juror. The other jurors filed out of the courtroom to begin deliberations.

O.C., his family, Granite residents, and other close friends of Esther Steele stood at the back of the courtroom in glum discussion.

No one believed the state had proved its case. Beam's barn-burner of a closing argument had dismayed everyone.

Esther's sister Polly was in tears. She and Lenore decided they were too emotionally exhausted to wait for the verdict. They left the courthouse for the ninety-mile drive to Lenore's home in Oklahoma City.

As the wait for the verdict lengthened, O.C. felt helpless. He had lost what confidence he had ever had in the criminal justice system. He now felt it was just a game played by the lawyers, bearing little relationship to reality.

"They leave the victim, and the victim's family, completely out of

it. You don't have any rights. You can't get up there and say what
you want to say. There were a lot of things about Sadler they
couldn't bring out that people needed to know. Esther was not given
her due. And that's what makes me so angry about the whole damn
trial."

Williams came to the back of the courtroom to comfort O.C. and
the family. He told them that with a jury there was always reason for
hope.

Richard Goss had been talking with Barbara Turner, the alternate juror. He came to join Williams and Esther's family.

"The alternate juror said that if she were voting, she would have
to vote for acquittal," Goss reported.

The response to that was a chorus of "Oh, no!"

Williams was at his lowest point since the trial began. Goss's
report of Barbara Turner's opinion reinforced his own belief that
Beam had raised strong doubts with his closing argument.

"Realistically, the chances for the death penalty are bleak," he
told O.C. "We might yet attempt a deal with the defense and offer
to settle for a life sentence."

O.C. was reluctant. He wanted the death penalty. But he rea-
soned that a life sentence at least would prevent Sadler from going
free, as now seemed possible.

He did not want to make the decision alone. "Let me talk to
Lenore and Polly about it," he said.

As soon as Lenore and Polly arrived at Lenore's home in Oklahoma City, O.C. reached them by phone. He put the question to
them. They agreed that the offer seemed best.

O.C. told Williams the family would agree to a life sentence.

Williams took the offer to Beam.

But now Beam was moderately confident the jury would not go
for the death penalty.

He told the Sadlers the decision was theirs to make but that he
advised them against taking the deal.

Sadler and his family accepted Beam's advice.

Beam returned to Williams and declined the offer.

23 ▪ ▪ ▪

AT THE MOMENT THE JURORS FILED
into the small room to begin deliberations,
the majority agreed with alternate juror Barbara Turner that the state had not proved its
case.

One who disagreed was Bonnie Steiner. "I
had thought about it, and I had thought about
it. Until you serve on something like this, you
don't really know how difficult it is. But I sat
there, on the first day, and the second day,
and it finally came to me, yes, this guy is
guilty. He *did* this heinous crime, and he *can't*
be set free. I don't know what actually did it. I
just knew in my heart. I really felt it in my
heart that I was not wrong."

Knee to knee at the big table in the confined space, the jurors spent the better part of an hour absorbing a sheaf of printed instructions.

The first order of business was to elect a foreman. The only member with experience on a criminal jury was Barney Brown, the part-time lay preacher. He had impressed the other jurors with his quiet, commanding presence. He was elected.

The jurors discussed the elaborate instructions, what they could do, what they could not do. According to the rules, if they found Sadler guilty of murder in this first stage, then in the second stage—the punishment phase—they must assess either a life sentence or the death penalty. Those were the only choices.

On the rape, the choices for punishment were more flexible. They could recommend death or impose a sentence for a number of years, to run either concurrently or consecutively with the life sentence for murder.

The jurors lingered over the written instructions, reluctant to start deliberations. Everyone seemed to be feeling the weight of the responsibility.

Foreman Brown offered a suggestion. "Before we start discussion, let's take a quick vote and see where we stand."

Slips of paper were passed out. Each juror wrote down his or her first vote.

The slips were returned to Brown. He opened them, one by one, reading the votes aloud. "Not guilty. Not guilty. Not guilty. Not guilty. Not guilty. . . ."

Bonnie Steiner listened with dismay.

In all, Brown called out only three "guilty" votes. The rest were "not guilty."

Brown asked who had voted "guilty."

"I did," said juror Blane Archer. "But I'll change it."

Unknown to the others, Brown also had voted "guilty." But as foreman he did not want to influence other members of the jury that early in the deliberations. He had not revealed his vote. Bonnie Steiner was left with the impression that after Archer's quick switch, the first ballot was ten to two for acquittal.

She decided then and there that she would sit quietly and keep on voting "guilty." She hoped to keep her vote a secret. She strongly felt that she should not try to talk others into doing something they would have to live with for the rest of their lives.

Around her, those voting for acquittal began voicing their belief that the state had not made its case.

Steiner felt beleaguered. "That guy, Sadler! He came *so close* to going scot-free! And then at that point, this nice-looking, dark-haired young man spoke up."

The nice-looking young man was Otis Ray Martin. He also had voted "guilty." He also had been listening to the "not guilty" votes with great concern.

"I thought they were going to let him go. And I took that job seriously. I had sat there and listened to the evidence. My mind was made up when I walked into that jury room that this guy, if he wasn't there and did it, he was helping to do it, because you just don't throw away your clothes on a cold night."

Martin was disturbed enough to speak out. "You guys haven't been listening!" he said.

Martin then made a speech Steiner termed wonderful.

"He really got them to thinking."

Martin reviewed what to him was the most convincing evidence: Sadler was the one who had taken off his shirt and socks. Martin argued that not even a drunk would take off his clothes on a cold night. Not without a reason.

And Sadler had put on the green coveralls, strong indication that his own clothing was too bloody to wear.

Even more convincing, Mary Long had found hairs in the bedding that matched those taken from Sadler.

"But she said she couldn't be one hundred percent certain," another juror pointed out.

Several jurors agreed. They argued that Mary Long had said hair was not like fingerprints. Other people could have hair somewhat similar.

"How many of them would be wandering around Granite, Oklahoma, that time of night?" Martin asked.

The debate became general.

Foreman Brown had been keeping track: He had received only four votes for "guilty"—his own, Martin's, Archer's—now switched—and one from someone he had not yet identified.

Including his own as yet unannounced vote, the jury now stood nine to three for acquittal.

"Who was the other juror voting 'guilty'?" he asked.

"It was me," Bonnie Steiner admitted.

"Why did you vote 'guilty'?" Brown asked.

"I just believe he *is* guilty," she said, not wishing to say more at the moment.

Around her, an argument flared over Mary Long's terminology on hair comparison. No one could remember her exact wording. Foreman Brown felt that the exact term was essential. He brought the discussion to a halt.

"We'll return to the courtroom and ask," he said.

"The jurors have a question," Judge Markum told the courtroom. "We are not here for a verdict. I just don't want you thinking we are going to get a verdict, because we aren't right now. Let's bring them in."

The jurors returned. The clerk delivered foreman Brown's question to Judge Markum, who read it aloud: "Did Mrs. Long say in testimony that the hairs were comparable, or compatible?"

While the jurors waited, the transcript was searched. Court reporter Susan Hosford was directed to read the brief portion of Mary Long's testimony.

The word was *consistent*.

The jury's question left Williams even more disheartened. He believed the brief glimpse into the thinking of the jurors revealed that they were dwelling on the testimony of Mary Long, discussing it, not accepting it on face value.

To him, that was strong indication that the deliberations were going badly for the prosecution.

Foreman Brown became concerned over the repetitious phrases "I think this" and "I think that."

"What you think and what I think doesn't really enter into this," he warned the other jurors. "We have to make our decision on the evidence that's been presented, and that alone. Let's write it down so we can look at it."

He set up a small blackboard and divided the left and right sides with a line down the middle, top to bottom.

On one side he listed the pros the jurors made for conviction. On the other, he wrote down the cons.

On the side for conviction, the list grew steadily: The stories of both Sadler and Adams placed them in Granite on that night, drunk. Both agreed they went to Esther Steele's house. Both agreed on the purpose—burglary and/or robbery to raise money for beer. The versions disagreed *only* on which one went into the house.

Sadler was the one who lost his hooded sweatshirt and his socks. He was the one who changed clothes, put on the coveralls. Four hairs microscopically consistent with his had been found in Esther Steele's bedding.

On the side for acquittal, the list was shorter. Mary Long had admitted that the hairs could have been transported into the house by Adams wearing Sadler's sweatshirt.

But Sadler's claim that he gave Adams his sweatshirt and socks was not convincing. Why would Sadler give up his warm shirt and socks on a cold night? If Adams went into the house, why did he not use his own socks?

True, Adams was the one who knew the town. He was familiar with the rock ditch. Sadler was not. But as Williams had pointed out, the aerial photograph proved that the route to Esther's back door was plain, and Sadler would have had no difficulty finding it.

The prosecution side of the blackboard grew longer. Gradually, votes began to shift.

As the debate continued, Otis Ray Martin made another telling point: "As far as I'm concerned, one is just as guilty as the other. Either one of them could have stopped it. Neither one did."

The debate continued hour after hour and grew ever more emotional. More votes shifted, until the margin was nine to three *for* conviction.

Then another juror yielded.

The count stood ten to two for conviction.

But those two would not budge.

Juror Chester Simpson, who farmed just west of Arapaho, was thoroughly convinced that Bugs Adams was the one who killed Esther Steele.

"He had the blood on him," Simpson kept pointing out. "Sadler didn't have any blood at all on him. If I thought Sadler was the guilty person, I would be for the death penalty. But I just don't think he's as guilty as Adams."

The other juror still voting not guilty was Blanche Schapansky, who sewed for an Arapaho clothing factory. With five children of her own—four sons and a daughter—Blanche Schapansky heavily felt the responsibility of sending the young man off to prison or to the death chamber. As the debate grew ever more emotional, she gave way to tears.

"I just can't do it," she kept saying.

Bonnie Steiner was not inclined to argue with her.

"She felt just as strongly as I did. She was there the same as me. That was her right. I just never would have voted 'not guilty.' And she was saying she would never vote 'guilty.' "

Bonnie Steiner found the reality of jury duty far removed from abstract theory.

"When you read in the paper about some horrible crime, and they got the death penalty, you say to yourself, 'Good, good, good.' But when it gets right down to it, let me tell you! As a Christian, as a fellow human being! If not for the grace of God, there would be *my* child getting it. To actually be responsible for taking a life, no matter what the circumstances, is something that, right now, I think I'd have to say I doubt that I could."

Another juror experiencing difficulties was Eugene Merriman, a retired Sun Pipeline employee from Thomas. Fourteen long, tedious hours had passed since the day's testimony had begun with Mary Long on the stand. Merriman had not brought enough blood pressure medicine for a marathon. He was feeling dizzy.

Concerned, Bonnie Steiner switched from juror back to registered nurse and took his pulse. It was more rapid than normal.

At the end of four hours of sustained, emotional argument, the count still held at ten to two for conviction.

Mrs. Schapansky was crying. Simpson also was close to tears. But neither would yield to pressure.

At last foreman Brown halted the debate. "We'll have to report out as deadlocked," he said.

"They have deliberated four hours, and they say they are hopelessly deadlocked," Hovis said. "We request that a mistrial be declared at this time."

"Your Honor, I concur," Beam said.

"I object to a mistrial, Your Honor," Williams said. "And ask the jury to go back in and deliberate some more."

Judge Markum did not believe enough time had elapsed to call the deadlock hopeless. The law allowed him an option.

"I will read them the Allen charge," he said. "Gentlemen, will you take your seats? Is there anything you want to cover before we bring them in?"

"Are you going to bring them in, give them the Allen charge, and then send them back out?" Beam asked. "Are you going to make them continue deliberations this evening?"

"Yes," Judge Markum said.

Williams now believed the case was lost. He was not hopeful that the Allen charge—called in some legal circles "the dynamite charge" or "the shotgun charge"—would help. Under the Allen charge, a judge may place a limited amount of pressure on a jury to reach a verdict. The Allen charge was not permitted in some states. Oklahoma was an exception.

With a jury truly deadlocked, the special instruction seldom made much difference.

The jury returned to the courtroom.

"This case has taken approximately forty-one hours of trial time," Judge Markum told the jurors. "You have deliberated for approximately four hours. You report to me that you are experiencing difficulty in arriving at a verdict.

"This is an important case and a serious matter to all concerned. You are the exclusive judges of the facts. The court is the judge of the law. Now, I most respectfully and earnestly request of you that you return to the jury room and resume your deliberations."

Judge Markum explained that no one should surrender his honest convictions or concur in a verdict that in good conscience he or she believed to be untrue.

"This *does* mean that you should give respectful consideration to each other's views and talk over all differences of opinion in the spirit of fairness and candor. If at all possible, you should resolve your differences and come to a common conclusion that this case may be completed. Each juror should respect the opinion of his or her fellow jurors."

He told them to take all the time needed.

"I ask you to return to the jury room and again diligently and earnestly under your oaths resume your deliberations."

Judge Markum did not confide to anyone his greatest concern. He sensed that the jurors were deadlocked over the specter of the death penalty.

With the Allen charge, he now felt it possible, even probable, that they would resolve their differences and arrive at a guilty verdict on the first phase, then deadlock again on the second—or punishment—phase. If that occurred, the burden of deciding the punishment would fall on him.

And Judge Markum knew what he would have to do. He had thought it through. All the requisites were there. The rape, the stabbings. If the jury deadlocked on punishment, he would impose the death penalty. It would cost him sleep. But not as much as if he did not do it.

Bonnie Steiner, for one, felt the effects of the Allen charge keenly.

"Judge Markum made us realize that all these people—the lawyers, the detectives—had spent hours and hours and hours on this. People had come from all over to testify. And we had spent four hours and couldn't decide, when these people had worked for *months*. It made me feel really ashamed, that we could do better than that."

Foreman Brown had left the pros and cons on the blackboard. Discussion resumed. Once again he went back over the evidence.

Brown wanted the death penalty. He believed Sadler deserved it. But he began to see that the death penalty was beyond reach. Even some of the jurors voting "guilty" were strongly negative on the death penalty.

Brown switched discussion from the murder to the rape, hoping for agreement on the punishment for that. He pointed out that with a life sentence on the rape charge, to run consecutively, after Sadler served one life term he would have to serve the other. But some of the women on the jury surprised him. They wanted the sentences, if they were handed out, to run concurrently.

Debate continued for more than another hour.

Brown worked on Mrs. Schapansky, repeatedly going back over the evidence written on the board. Gradually it became apparent that her main concern was the punishment. She felt that once Sadler was convicted, the pressure on her would turn to imposing the death sentence.

"She just couldn't cope with it," Brown found. "She got all emotional, cried, and couldn't handle it. She just wouldn't do it."

After midnight, with no movement in the voting, Bonnie Steiner thought of a possible solution.

The burden of the death sentence seemed to be bothering everyone.

"If we can get a conviction, I promise I won't vote for the death penalty," she announced.

The relief was immediate.

But Otis Ray Martin was not happy with the compromise. "I think we're getting ahead of ourselves."

Bonnie Steiner agreed. "It isn't the right thing to do. But it's the only way we can get *any* verdict."

The next ballot was unanimous: guilty.

Brown again brought up the rape, trying for consecutive terms. Most of the men agreed with him: They proposed two life terms, stacked. But to Brown's continued surprise, the women wanted a lesser sentence on the rape.

The best agreement Brown could obtain on the rape was a fifteen-year term, to run concurrently.

The jury had now agreed upon conviction for murder and rape, with a life sentence for the murder and a fifteen-year term on the rape, with the sentences to run concurrently. With that compromise, the punishment phase of the trial became a pointless exercise. All decisions had now been made. But for the moment, that had to remain a secret among the jurors.

■ ■ ■

Juror Otis Ray Martin watched the defendant as the clerk read the "guilty" verdicts. For the first time during the week-long trial, Martin saw emotion from Sadler.

"He really didn't bust out and cry. But his eyes went to watering, and he started rubbing his eyes and sniffling. But on top of all that, he had a smirk on his face. A half smile."

Judge Markum was puzzled by the slip of paper containing the jury's verdict. Across the bottom, foreman Brown had written the notation "fifteen years concurrent" in the blank for punishment on the rape.

Judge Markum could only conclude that the jury had already agreed on a fifteen-year term for the rape, jumping ahead to a decision on the punishment phase of the trial. He had never heard of a jury doing that.

He also could infer that the jury had already settled on a life term on the murder, for how could a fifteen-year sentence run "concurrently" with the death penalty?

At that moment, Judge Markum knew that the trial was over and that he would not be called upon to impose the death penalty. The tension that had driven him through the week abruptly vanished. All energy seemed to drain out of him. He had to force himself through the remainder of the formalities.

"The record should reflect that it's now one o'clock," he said. "Ladies and gentlemen, you've been in court all day, or almost a day and a half, workwise. I want to get some feedback from you at this point as to whether you would like to go ahead and go into the second stage, or whether you would like to come back in the morning."

It was now Saturday morning. The next day would be Easter Sunday.

"Your Honor, I think we are agreed that we would go ahead and finish the sentence," foreman Brown said.

But it was not that easy. The court and the attorneys still had much preliminary work to do.

Judge Markum sent the jurors back to the jury room. He promised that the wait would not be long this time.

Hovis watched the jurors file out of the courtroom. "I bet they don't understand there's going to be another hearing," he said to Beam.

Judge Markum and the attorneys hammered out the instructions for the jury on the punishment phase.

Again Williams asked for admission of the photographs. "In the second stage, you can let them in as gory as you want," he argued. "That shows the atrocious—"

"It inflames the jury," Beam interrupted. "It just inflames, is all."

Once again Judge Markum said he would not admit the photographs.

When the preliminaries were completed, the jurors were returned to the courtroom. Judge Markum warned them that the punishment phase would take some time. He said he did not know how long.

Beam volunteered an estimate of two hours.

"That would probably be a maximum," Judge Markum said.

In the informality of the moment, Bonnie Steiner felt moved to speak from the jury box. "I'm personally rather concerned with Mr. Merriman," she told Judge Markum. "He ordinarily takes blood pressure medication, which he has not had, and he's feeling very dizzy. His pulse is a little more rapid than normal."

Judge Markum also was concerned. Merriman looked bad. The sixteen hours of emotionally difficult work he had just put in would have taxed a younger, healthy man. And now he faced perhaps two more hours of intense work.

Judge Markum again asked whether the jurors—and especially Merriman—wished to go on or if they would prefer to recess and resume deliberations later in the day.

The jury conferred, not leaving the box.

"He wants to go on," foreman Brown reported.

"Okay," Judge Markum said. "We'll start the second phase, and recognize Mr. Williams."

Williams said he was asking the death penalty for David Wayne Sadler because the murder of Esther Steele was especially heinous, atrocious, and cruel, and was committed for the purpose of avoiding and preventing lawful arrest and prosecution.

The members of the jury listened, knowing full well the death sentence would not be imposed.

Judge Markum and the attorneys suspected that this might be the situation. But most of those in the courtroom were caught up in the drama as Williams made his plea for the death penalty.

Sadler began to cry. He put both hands to his face. His body shook.

Some in the courtroom felt he was faking, seeking jury sympathy. But those seated close to him—members of the jury, the attorneys— saw tears.

Item by item, Williams incorporated the evidence from the first stage of the trial, reminding the jurors of the testimony from each witness, and its importance.

After Williams completed his opening, Beam approached the bench to make a demurral.

Once again jurors were sent to the jury room.

"I don't mean to belittle what happened," Beam told Judge Markum. "Certainly the lady was murdered, and certainly it's horrendous. But this particular murder was not especially heinous, atrocious, or cruel."

He cited precedents defining that legal terminology, and reminded Judge Markum that the state medical examiner had testified that no torture was involved.

Williams insisted that the phraseology was accurate. "If the court has looked at those photographs taken at the autopsy, and the court can tell me this is not serious physical abuse, I would accept a demurrer," he said.

Judge Markum reviewed his notes. "It's clear from the evidence we had six stab wounds." One by one, he enumerated them. "Further, we have suffocation. And Dr. Jordan's statement that death wasn't instantaneous, but that it would have taken some time. If it took three or four minutes, and Mrs. Steele laid there and watched, or felt, her life slip away, that is a torture situation."

On that basis, Judge Markum overruled the demurrer.

The jury was returned to the courtroom. Hovis incorporated testimony from the defense witnesses in the first stage of the trial.

Linda Sadler made another brief appearance on the witness stand.

Hovis asked her what type of person her son was.

"He's quiet," she said. "He's a loner, I guess. He was always pretty much by himself. He didn't have a lot of friends. He's a good boy."

"You said he didn't have a lot of friends?"

"No. He's never been very self-confident. Maybe if I had let him know more about how much I loved him, and needed him at home, maybe he wouldn't have ran around with some of the people he did."

Sadler's sobbing at the defense table became more audible.

"What type of home life has he had?" Hovis asked.

"Well, pretty much average, I think, until his dad died right after he turned thirteen. I could understand my girls pretty good. But boys, I couldn't. I mean fishing, hunting, stuff boys liked to do. I couldn't help him with a lot of that stuff. But he turned out. He's a good boy."

"You also have daughters?"

"Yes. I have a nineteen-year-old daughter and a thirteen-year-old daughter."

"Have they been in trouble of any kind?"

"No."

As Linda Sadler explained that Wayne had been much closer to his father, she also began to cry. The remainder of her testimony was frequently interrupted by sobbing.

"How did Mr. Sadler die?" Hovis asked.

"He was coming home from work, not on the main highway but one of the back paved roads. At the top of a hill he met another car, or a pickup. They were both in the middle, and they both swerved the wrong way. He was killed almost instantly."

"Prior to that, did Wayne have any type of a drinking problem?"

"No."

"What kind of effect did the death of his father have on him?"

"It was pretty bad. The night he died, I was at work, and Wayne was at his granddad's. I told Bill Greer I couldn't tell the kids, so he told them for me. And they took me home, and Wayne was standing out on the porch screaming, 'We don't have a daddy anymore.' And he was terrified. He was so scared I couldn't believe it."

She said as far as she knew, he started drinking when he was about seventeen, but that she did not recognize the problem until he was nineteen or twenty.

She insisted she never saw or heard of any drugs.

"Was he ever able to hold a job?" Hovis asked.

"No. He didn't mature as fast as most of his friends. I think that was partly because he didn't have a father, and I just didn't know how to raise a boy."

She said he had been picked up for drinking, and missing National Guard meetings, but had never before been in serious trouble.

Williams declined to cross-examine.

The defense called Hazel Sadler, who testified that her grandson had lived with her for much of his life.

"When he was small, they lived in the house with us for quite a while, and then he lived with me about a year here recently."

Hazel Sadler also began to cry. Linda Sadler and her daughters were sobbing in the gallery. The defendant was still weeping at the defense table.

"Did you notice any change in Wayne after your son was killed in the wreck?" Hovis asked.

"Yes, I did," Hazel Sadler said. "He's never got over his father's death."

"Can you tell the jury what type of a person Wayne is?"

"Wayne is a gentle person," she said. "He loves his family."

Again Williams declined to cross-examine.

"Your Honor, we rest at this time," Hovis said.

Williams rose to deliver his closing argument.

"I see the hour is ten after two in the morning," he began. "You're tired. I'm tired. We're all tired. I won't try to be long-winded.

"I know you felt, as I felt, for those two witnesses on the stand, the mother and the grandmother. But who caused the mother to cry? And who caused the grandmother to cry? The defendant.

"If we were to let murderers go just because they had families who care and cry, then we probably wouldn't convict anybody and give them the death penalty.

"That is not the standard here.

"If you give life imprisonment, then this defendant will go to McAlester. He gets three squares a day, and sleeps on clean sheets, and a warm room in the winter and cool in the summer. He gets medical bills paid, and an occasional visit from the family. Contrast that to the cold grave Mrs. Steele is confined to. That's not justice. That's not at all justice.

"I ask you to go back and return the only verdict possible. Assess the death penalty."

Beam also promised to be brief.

"One thing that Mr. Williams brought up, he makes it sound like if you don't give David Wayne Sadler the death penalty, you're somehow letting him off the hook.

"My question is, what purpose will it serve to kill him? It won't bring Esther Steele back. It's not going to help anyone."

He said prison was not a country club.

"Prison is a terrible, terrible place to be. He's twenty-two years old. You can look at him there. He's not very strong. He's frail. He's

not very smart. He has lots of problems. Sending him to prison is
going to be a terrible experience for him.

"Those are your two choices. You've got life imprisonment, or
you've got the death penalty. The state has already shown you
which sentence you should give my client. It's inconceivable to me
that you could give him, or that any sentence would be appropriate,
that would be more severe than that which the state has already
plea-bargained and given to Phillip Pat Adams."

Again Beam talked of reasonable doubt. Again he argued that the
circumstantial crumbs led toward Bugs Adams, not Sadler.

Beam reminded the jurors of testimony that Sadler was mild,
meek, withdrawn.

"He's not some mad dog killer like the state would make him out
to be. He's not some remorseless person. He's been sitting over here
crying for the last thirty or forty minutes."

Beam assured the jury that Sadler's tears were real.

"I'm sure he's scared to death. I would be if I was in his shoes."

Beam closed by reminding the jury that with the two felony convictions, Sadler was going to prison for life, a terrible punishment.

"It does not serve a purpose, ladies and gentlemen, to kill this
twenty-two-year-old boy. It serves absolutely no purpose. Thank
you."

Williams reminded the jurors that during jury selection each of
them had agreed to assess the death penalty if it was merited.

"I submit this is a proper case," he said. "Adams didn't kill Esther
Steele. The defendant did. Who says? You say, you twelve people.
Adams didn't rape Esther Steele. Who did? The defendant. Who
says? You twelve people. You convicted him of murder in the first
degree. You convicted him of rape in the first degree."

He said the evidence left no doubt there was serious physical
abuse, and that the murder was especially heinous, atrocious, and
cruel.

Again he stabbed the Styrofoam torso. "Stab wounds inflicted as I'm showing you on this dummy is definitely serious physical abuse."

When he had finished the stabbing, he turned back to the jury and lowered his voice. "Ladies and gentlemen of the jury, go to the jury room, think about all of the evidence. Pray together, if you must. Cry, if you must. But there is only one verdict in this case, and that is death."

Ordinarily Williams would have stopped there. But the dramatic appeal from the defense led him to offer a personal note—a self-revelation completely uncharacteristic of him.

"When I was three years old, I was in a car accident," he told the jurors. "My mother was killed. It hurt my father. Hurt me. My father became an alcoholic. He left my aunt and my grandfather to raise me. I didn't turn out too bad. Just because you have a tragedy in your life does not excuse you for the culpability of murder. Go back there and do justice. Thank you."

The jury returned to the small jury room for the last time. Foreman Brown, Otis Ray Martin, and several others still wanted the death penalty. But the deal had been made.

Only one ballot was required. The jury quickly returned to the courtroom with the sentence of life imprisonment.

By the time closing formalities were completed and the jurors had been thanked by the court for doing their duty, it was 3:00 A.M. The final day of the trial had lasted eighteen hours.

Exhausted, Williams left the courthouse and returned to his car for the drive to his home in Watonga. Someone had thrown a damaging liquid all over his car. The Lincoln had to be repainted.

Out in the Texas Panhandle, Mary Long drove northward into a spring blizzard. The blinding snow slowed her to a crawl. Her hometown of Stratford lies eighty miles north of Amarillo, almost as far into the Texas Panhandle as one can go without bumping into the Oklahoma Panhandle.

When she arrived, the snow was so deep neighbors had to help her reach the home of her parents.

She found no evidence of the wedding shower she expected. The house was dark and empty.

"I was there in my mom and dad's house, all by myself, until they called later that night and told me my dad had died. He had been so sick. I'll never forget it, because it was such a terrible day."

24 ▪ ▪ ▪

DAVID WAYNE SADLER AND PHILLIP PAT Adams are serving life sentences in separate facilities three miles apart in the rolling, wooded farmlands an hour's drive south of Oklahoma City. Both institutions are models of a prison concept that has replaced the walls, gun towers, and cell blocks made familiar by movies and television dramas. Here the world of the prison inmate is limited to a tight cluster of buildings resembling a busy anthill. The atmosphere is more that of a crowded, low-budget community college designed by an architect with a penchant for economy, function, and small structures. Confinement is assured by a surrounding expanse of open space and, in the near distance, double fences eighteen feet high, amply padded by concertina razor wire. At the center of each compound, guards keep watch from a tall structure resembling an airport control tower. The fences are well lit by night, and electronic sensors detect any movement. Officers can be dispatched immediately to the scene of suspicious activity. All access to the inner "yard" is through the administration buildings, where baffles of electronically operated metal doors keep tight rein on traffic. Each door cannot be opened unless the others are closed and locked. Entry and exit to the interior is a slow, closely monitored process.

Pat Adams has been an inmate at the Joseph Harp Correctional Center eight miles east of Lexington for the last four years. On a day in July of 1993 he was called away from his work for an interview. He was waiting in the Delta Unit. He displayed propriety, was the perfect host. He showed the way into a vacant dining hall and locked the door against interruptions.

Here he is still called "Bugs." But those who saw him on the witness stand five years ago, testifying against Sadler, might fail to recognize him today. Gone is the overweight, cocky slob who so alienated jurors. Gone are the abundant illiteracies that once graced his voluble speech. Through exercise and weight lifting, he has trimmed down to a muscular one hundred and eighty-five pounds. Recently he received his high school equivalency certificate—an impressive attainment for an eighth-grade dropout generally recognized as a poor student from kindergarten on.

Under other circumstances, Esther Steele no doubt would have been enthusiastic over his belated, bootstrap academic success and the way he has turned his life around. Apparently he finally put to use some of the potential she saw in him.

Ironies abound.

"Science was my best subject," Bugs said in telling of his accomplishment. "Mrs. Steele got me interested in it. I've helped some of the other inmates in science and math."

Now he is bald on top, with a thick, dark, carefully trimmed fringe at the sides. His face is round and apple cheeked, reminiscent of a younger Buddy Hackett. He speaks with an easy, ingratiating sincerity that tends to disarm a listener.

In short, five years in prison seem to have shorn Bugs of many rough edges. He has developed a much more presentable personality.

"He has come a long way," said one of the correctional officers supervising Delta Unit. "I've watched him do it."

His turnaround began two years ago with a suicide attempt.

Bugs was not reluctant to talk about it.

"It just seemed like I was never going to get out of this place," he explained. "It all looked hopeless. So I took ten ampules of Haldol."

Medical authorities confirm that such an overdose of the tranquilizer should have been sufficient.

"He almost succeeded," the correctional officer said later. "I was here when he did it."

The suicide attempt placed Bugs under special counseling. He credits the counselors with inspiring his new attitude toward life.

"People will help you, but you've got to let them help you," he explained. "I'm working toward starting a new life when I get out of here. A job. Maybe marriage. Kids. Somewhere out of state, where people wouldn't know me, and I could start over."

He works in the industrial shop, making drawers for desks. He explained the function of Delta Unit, where he is assigned.

"It's like a family. Or maybe a military unit. If one of us is in trouble, we're all in trouble. So we take care of each other, help each other."

He still insists that he remained in the truck that night while Sadler went into the house, that he knew nothing of the murder until the following day, and that he is guilty only of pointing out Esther Steele's house, making him an accomplice in a burglary, nothing more.

"I deserve to be in here," he said. "But I don't deserve to be in here for the crime I'm in here for."

He will be eligible for pre-parole in the year 2001. But like most of the nine hundred and ten inmates in the Joseph Harp Center, he is trying to move the date closer through an appeal.

A few months ago, he was called upon to testify about a prison incident. The experience placed him in contact with a lawyer. After talking with Bugs about his case, the lawyer suggested that an appeal might be based on insufficient legal counseling before plea bargaining.

Now Bugs is convinced that he did not receive adequate legal counseling before he entered his guilty plea.

"I was scared, freaked out when I was arrested," he said. "If I had known then what I know now, I would have gone ahead with the trial."

He shrugged off a suggestion that he probably would have received the death penalty from a jury.

"They didn't have anything on me. Only what I told Sunderland and Goss at Fort Sill. And that would have worked *for* me. That was the truth. All I want is to get my sentence knocked down to about thirty-five years."

If that were done, Bugs would soon be eligible for parole. He believes he might qualify.

"I have no write-ups in my jacket, no problems."

Appeals have become a prison cottage industry. Almost every inmate has litigation pending action.

"We get them by the ton," said a spokesperson for the Oklahoma Attorney General, with perhaps understandable hyperbole. Most of these prison-generated appeals patently lack merit. But they must be taken seriously. The high courts have so decreed, and no one can forget that a handwritten appeal from a fellow named Miranda a few years back set the judicial system on its ear.

An appeal of a murder one guilty plea might appear to be an exercise in futility. But Bugs could get lucky.

He stoutly denied that Pearl Johnson was first selected as the robbery victim on the night Esther was murdered.

"She was like a mother to me," he protested.

Then why did he pull into that specific alley to urinate, when there were other places more remote?

"Habit," Bugs said. "We used to run around with her son David. We always went into that alley to take a leak."

Bugs confirmed the memory of Esther's niece, Betty Monday, that he did yard work for Esther.

This was perhaps a significant revelation. Even with all of their work, Goss and Sunderland never discovered this connection. The family had tended to think that perhaps Betty was mistaken, that "Esther would never hire anyone like that."

Bugs said his work for Esther came two or three years after he was in her room in school.

How did she treat him?

"She was always real nice."

Then why did he select her house to rob?

"I just thought Wayne would go into her house and get some money. I didn't intend to do her any harm."

With Esther's well-known open-door policy, and generosity with soft drinks, he must have been familiar with the interior of her house. Did he coach Sadler in the burglary, describe the layout?

"No," Bugs insisted. "I didn't coach him."

Then how did Sadler, drunk, manage to make his way through the dark house, following a horseshoe route past the kitchen, dining room, living room, and down the hall to her bedroom, all without disturbing furniture?

"I don't know," Bugs said. "I wasn't there. We never talked about it."

Perhaps Bugs's dramatic self-improvement should not have come as a surprise. He has always seemed to have a ready answer for everything. That requires considerable intelligence.

He was apologetic over his earlier flip-flop on agreeing to an interview. Early on, he had agreed. Then he reneged, changing the terms. He wrote that although it was true he could not accept money while in custody of the Department of Corrections, he could accept payment through power of attorney.

"I am anxious to come to a mutually agreeable financial arrangement," he wrote. "This is nothing I plan to make enough money to retire on, or anything of the sort. I am just convinced that my story is of interest to a lot of your readers, and am willing to share that with them."

But after receiving a reply refusing payment and pointing out that future pardons and parole boards no doubt would not look with favor on his attempt to profit further from the crime for which he is doing time, he again changed his mind.

"Your first letter just freaked me out," he explained. "I hadn't heard anything about a book." He said he had intended to use the money to retain the lawyer for the appeal.

Bugs first served time at the James Crabtree Center near Helena in the northwest part of the state. Because of his plea bargain, he entered the prison system a full year before Sadler.

After conviction, Sadler also arrived at Crabtree. For a while both were confined in the same facility.

A correctional officer at Crabtree reported that he overheard Bugs making a threat to kill Sadler.

Bugs denied making the threat. But because of the accusation, he was transferred to the Joseph Harp Center, halfway across the state from Sadler.

Bugs said he feels no animosity toward Sadler.

"Now I forgive him. Back then, I didn't. Now I just feel sorry for him. He's a person who needs a lot of help, just like I did."

Once again, Bugs insisted that Sadler is lying about what happened that night. He again insisted that he stayed in the truck and had nothing to do with the rape and murder.

"Someday we'll both stand before God," Bugs said. "And God knows who did it."

On January 7, 1993, the Oklahoma Court of Criminal Appeals affirmed David Wayne Sadler's 1988 conviction. Three judges signed the majority opinion. A fourth wrote a concurring opinion.

On February 17, 1993, the Oklahoma Court of Criminal Appeals denied Sadler's petition for a rehearing. This action formally ended Sadler's five-year mandatory appeal in the state courts. Throughout that time, his attorney had advised him against submitting to an interview, pointing out that anything he said might be used against him if he won a new trial.

With that precaution no longer needed, Sadler agreed to an interview.

He was waiting in a holding cell at the Lexington Assessment and Evaluation Center, three miles west of the Joseph Harp facility. The two institutions are separate, with different wardens and staffs. Although both are considered medium security, the Assessment Center is more claustrophobic. The thick metal doors slam louder and the electronic locks thunk with more authority. The baffles are obtrusive, sequential reminders of their effectiveness and purpose. The extra security is no accident. The reception center processes all inmates coming into the system, covering the entire spectrum from nonviolent offenders serving short terms to murderers destined for death row at McAlester.

The holding cell where Sadler waits is six feet by ten, with metal walls and door and a Plexiglas window looking out onto a security corridor. A correctional officer is seated at his post across the corridor, twenty feet and two electronically operated doors away. The cell contains only Sadler and two folding chairs. The solid walls subdue the institutional sounds, leaving the interior as quiet as a recording studio.

Sadler was transferred to the Assessment Center a year ago, after four years at Crabtree. Since his arrival, he has been working in the kitchen. His five years in prison have left him lean. But no longer could anyone term him starvation thin. With his thick chestnut hair, high prominent cheekbones, close-trimmed dark beard, and well-proportioned features, he could be called handsome. His eyes remain most salient. They are pale blue, relentless, impenetrable, even hypnotic. His arms are decorated with prison tattoos.

Physically, he appears to be in good shape. Mentally, he may not be faring so well. As he talks, his hands work incessantly, kneading the flesh of his arms, his legs. He keeps shifting position in his chair as if unable to sit still. With each question, he hesitates a long moment, and often it appears strong emotion is on the verge of breaking through. But that never happens. Sadler still speaks with the cold, calm, objective demeanor that first won the attention of Goss and Sunderland in the initial investigative interview in Mangum, six years ago.

Sadler said he had nothing to add or to alter in his original version of the murder. He insisted that what he told Goss and Sunderland at Woodward was true, that he waited in the truck while Bugs Adams went into the house.

"If I'd done the right thing, and gone to the police right after it happened, maybe I wouldn't be in here," he said.

He admitted that prison life is wearing on him.

"When I was first here five years ago for assessment, after I talked with a psychiatrist they put me on Sinequan. Now they've taken me off of it."

Sinequan is a psychotherapeutic agent commonly used for the treatment of psychoneurotic patients with depressive and/or anxiety states and manic-depressive disorders.

He believes he is doing just as well without it.

"There's a shock in coming into a place like this," he explained. "You need something to help. And there's a shock when you leave and go back out into the world. It works both ways."

He said that after five long years of waiting, the affirmation of his conviction by the Court of Criminal Appeals in January came as a terrible disappointment.

His attorney, Assistant Appellate Public Defender Cindy G. Brown, had believed chances were good that either the verdict would be overturned or the case would be remanded for a new trial.

Sadler said she had conveyed her optimism to him.

The court decision was further frustrating because the court agreed with Brown on several important points.

Among other challenges, Brown had cited the missing DNA report, the slim corroboration of the testimony from Bugs, the question of a Miranda rights violation in the Woodward confession, and the suggestion of special prosecutor Williams, in his final argument, that Sadler had returned to the scene of the wreck and removed evidence, when nothing supported his statement.

"There is no question that evidence was suppressed," the court agreed on the DNA issue. But the court added: ". . . we fail to see how the outcome of appellant's trial would have been different if he had had access to this report earlier."

The court upheld Judge Markum's ruling that contact had been broken in the Woodward interview and that the session was renewed on Sadler's instigation. The court also agreed that the remarks of prosecutor Williams went beyond the realm of fair comment, but added, "We cannot say that the error affected the outcome of the case."

"I'm filing a federal appeal now," Sadler revealed. "The federal rules are different. The state kept that DNA thing from us. That hurt our case. If the DNA thing had worked, it would have showed who raped her. It would have showed that I didn't do it."

Sadler also said he feels that the matter of the palm print on the inside front door facing should have been pursued.

"They never did anything with that."

He termed the testimony of Anthony Hinch, his cellmate for three days in the Mangum County Jail, as a lie from beginning to end.

"I never spoke a half dozen words to him."

"Then how could he have known about what happened to your grandmother, if you didn't tell him?"

"I don't know," Sadler said. "Maybe someone told him. One of the deputies around there."

"Your high school football coach, Mike Smith, said to tell you hello. He said to tell you he still thinks about you. He had a lot of good things to say about you."

Again, for a moment, emotion seemed to be struggling to break through. But when Sadler spoke, his tone was matter-of-fact. "I was never much good at football. I was too light. It was baseball that kept me in school. I really liked baseball."

Mangum teachers had expressed their dismay that Sadler's

younger sister, Katrina, had dropped out of school during the spring. They said she was an intelligent student and had good potential. When this was conveyed to Sadler, he nodded abruptly. "I've told her that when I get out of this place, I'm going to take her over my knee if she doesn't get back in school."

Sadler's own efforts for further education have been temporarily stymied. After enduring a long waiting list at the James Crabtree Center, he completed college courses in English, history, and psychology through Northwestern Oklahoma State University at Alva. Then came his transfer to the Lexington Assessment Center.

Now he is back on a long waiting list.

"The classes are small," he said. "There's about a three-year wait to get into them."

He said he still has trouble with reading.

"I'm working on it. I read everything I can get my hands on."

He also denied that Pearl Johnson was first selected as the robbery victim the night Esther Steele was murdered. His response eerily repeated words heard less than an hour before from Bugs Adams.

"She was like a mother to me," he protested.

"In one of your presentence hearings, a psychiatrist who examined you said he was genuinely moved. He said you'd had a terrible childhood, perhaps a damaging childhood. Do you feel that was true?"

Again the long hesitation, the hint of emotion trying to break through. "I don't know anything about that," Sadler said.

"Goss and Sunderland believe you went into Mrs. Steele's house to rob, got in there, and simply got carried away by a deep-seated anger. Have you ever felt anger like that? Is anger a constant thing with you?"

Sadler pondered a long moment, staring into the middle distance. Across the corridor, correctional officers were crowded around the security doors at shift change. Two officers hurried past with rifles at port arms. The entire area was in lockdown until the guns were brought from the tower and safely stored away.

"I think most people should have more anger than they do," Sadler said. Again he paused. "That's the honest answer."

"There was a report that not long after you came into the system, your cellmate was found dead one morning, asphyxiated. Did they hassle you much over that?"

Sadler winced and shook his head in exasperation. "That was rumor."

"That was what?"

"A rumor. It was started by a deputy sheriff." He named the deputy. "Nothing like that ever happened. But he told it around. My family heard it. He later told that I'd killed two or three people in here. He's trying to turn me into a Charles Manson or something. I've only got four write-ups in my jacket. The worst is for fighting."

The report of the asphyxiated cellmate had been widely circulated, but it had proved impossible to track down. The Department of Corrections said no such fatality occurred in the system in that time frame.

"Back when you were drinking so heavily, did you ever have blackouts?"

"Sometimes," Sadler admitted. "The next day, I wouldn't know how I got from one place to another. I'd have bruises and cuts, and I wouldn't remember where I got them."

"Those who used to drink with you say that sometimes when you were really drunk, you'd ask people to hit you, and they would, then you'd get up laughing."

Sadler shrugged. "I don't know anything about that."

"Did you have a blackout the night Esther Steele was killed?"

Sadler shook his head negatively. "No. I remember giving Bugs my shirt and socks. I remember waiting in the truck."

"Did you take the threat Bugs made against you at Crabtree seriously?"

Sadler nodded affirmatively. "I've never seen it, but I've heard he has a temper, that he goes into rages."

"Here it is six years later, and we still don't know what happened that night. You have your story, and Bugs has his. You say Bugs went into the house. What do you think happened? Could Mrs. Steele have awakened and recognized Bugs? Could they have exchanged words? Could Bugs have become enraged and killed her?"

"That's possible," Sadler said.

He seemed reluctant to speculate further.

The late Joe Harp, for whom the correctional institution was named, had been a longtime, much-admired warden at the Granite reformatory. One day, after listening to an inmate's lengthy tale of injustices, Harp turned to an associate with an observation: "Isn't it simply amazing how so many innocent men wind up in this place?"

Correctional officers are familiar with a phenomenon: The majority of prison inmates continue to proclaim their innocence long after denial serves any practical purpose. They may brag about other capers, but not the one for which they are serving time. They have told their story of innocence so many times that they appear to believe it themselves.

But Esther Steele is dead, horribly murdered, and today either Bugs Adams or David Wayne Sadler—or perhaps both—is still lying.

After six years, with Sadler and Adams both serving life terms, the question of who was the actual killer continues to haunt everyone involved in the case, from the detectives and lawyers to her family and the jurors.

O. C. Kruska has spent many hours brooding over his sister's death. He remains convinced that both Sadler and Adams went into the house, and that both participated.

"They grabbed her and took her down in that one spot," he believes. "She never got out of that bed. Never. Both of them had to be there. She was too tough and she was too strong."

He is certain that if Esther had gained her feet, the entire bedroom would have become a battleground.

Yet he has never been able to explain to his own satisfaction how two drunks could have made their way through the house without disturbing the furniture.

"That just blows my mind," he concedes.

The long ordeal of the murder and trial sent him into a period of clinical depression.

"If you've never been through something like that, you don't know what people are talking about when they say depression," he said. "It's pretty tough."

The emotional and physical strain precipitated a heart attack. He is still recovering from that.

Nor is the long ordeal yet ended. Recently a Victim Services Agency was organized in Oklahoma to track prison inmates and to keep victims and/or families informed. O.C. maintains contact with the agency, ready to testify when Adams and Sadler come up for parole.

He is prepared to describe once again all the horrors of the murder.

"I think about it most of the time, anyway," he said.

Sunderland and Goss continue to believe the story told by Bugs Adams. They think Sadler went into the house alone.

"Sadler's mean," Sunderland said. "You can tell that by looking at him. The cold eyes I consider what the typical killer would have."

From his experience as warden and criminal investigator, Sunderland does not hesitate to make a prediction.

"Sadler's going to be in trouble the rest of his life. He'll come out and kill again."

Sunderland retired from the OSBI not long after Paula's death.

"I was pretty devastated," he said.

Today he is administrator with Community Services Corporation, a private sector prison system in Oklahoma. He thinks private prisons may be the solution to overcrowding and revolving-door crime.

"Our pay scales are lower than the state's," he explained. "We work with smaller staffs. We can handle inmates with less expense."

His oldest daughter, Memory, is married to a Tulsa fireman, and they own a furniture store in Collinsville, just to the north of Tulsa. His son Shawn is a policeman in Yukon. His son Shay is finishing up his Ph.D. in agronomy at North Carolina State.

Stephanie Toole, the eldest of Paula's two daughters, is a junior at Oklahoma State University. Megan Toole, the only one of Sunderland's children left at home, just completed her junior year in high school. In the spring of 1993, she was state champion in the high jump.

"I'm really proud of her," Sunderland said.

The partnership of Sunderland and Goss ended with Sunderland's retirement. They keep in touch, and see each other occasionally.

Goss is still with the OSBI, now as senior inspector. He remains a resident agent in Lawton.

Goss believes that when Bugs was arrested at Fort Sill, and confessed, all his defenses were down. He feels that what emerged from Bugs was essentially the truth.

"Maybe you just had to be there, and see Bugs when he was telling it," Goss said. "It's hard to explain. There was *sincerity* in it, is what I'm trying to say."

In November 1991 Richard Hovis was elected Associate District Judge. He still believes that his former client Sadler was telling the truth and that it was Bugs Adams who went into the house.

"Mary Long's testimony, from what I knew about it, pretty well eliminated Sadler as the rapist," Hovis insisted.

He said he remains troubled by several areas of the Sadler case, most especially the results of the OSBI polygraph tests.

"If Sadler ever gets out, I'd like for him to take an independent polygraph," Hovis said. "Just so I would know."

■ ■ ■

Stephen Beam also believes that the antigen tests pointed to Bugs Adams as the rapist and tended to eliminate his client, Sadler.

He said he felt the OSBI should have resolved the inconsistency of the antigens instead of forging right ahead.

"To me, Adams's makeup is more that he would be able to fake being upset, in order to get himself out of this deal. To me, Sadler's makeup is such that if someone questioned him about this, he would get *more* withdrawn. Maybe it's not necessarily a coldness and a calculatedness. It's just that he's withdrawn, and sullen, and afraid. That's more the idea I got from him."

He pointed out that Bugs Adams's own testimony shows that he instigated the evening, decided where they would go and who they would visit, right up to the time of the murder.

"Adams was the leader. I've thought so from the first time I talked with Wayne Sadler, and got a feel for what he was all about."

But Beam remains troubled that Sadler was the one who changed clothes and put on the green coveralls.

"That's hard to deal with," he said. "It really is."

Special prosecutor Charles Williams still believes that Bugs Adams was telling essentially the truth.

He cites the fact that Bugs Adams passed his polygraph test, and that Sadler flunked.

"I'm a firm believer in the polygraph as an *investigative* tool," Williams said. "Of course, it depends on the expertise of its operator. I believed in that, and I don't feel the OSBI manipulated the results."

Williams credits Sunderland and Goss for developing the case well from such slim physical evidence. And he points out that the contributions of Richard Goss continued all the way through to conviction, as an advisory witness helping him with the prosecution.

"Thank God for Richard Goss," Williams said.

Williams has retired as Assistant District Attorney in Blaine County. He has moved to Yukon, just west of Oklahoma City. There he is enjoying his leisure while considering possibilities for a new career, perhaps in a different vein.

"I've told them I don't want courtroom work," he said. "I feel I've had enough of that."

In 1990 the University of Cincinnati College of Medicine reported on a study of forty jurors serving in cases involving violent crime. Twenty-seven of the forty suffered posttrial psychological symptoms, including sleeplessness, anxiety, headaches, stomachaches, heart palpitations, and depression.

The report pointed out that this result should not be surprising, considering that the jurors were plucked out of their everyday lives to hear graphic testimony and to rule on a defendant's fate, perhaps involving life or death.

None of the jurors in the Sadler trial reported the severe symptoms mentioned in the Cincinnati study. But most admitted that the trial—and the unanswered questions—continue to haunt them.

"In one way it bothers me, and in another way it doesn't," said Chester Simpson, the long holdout. "I think both of them were guilty. It didn't bother me that Sadler was given that sentence. I just didn't think he was any more guilty than Adams."

And he added: "I often wonder what the real story was. I would like to know if I was right or wrong. I just did what I thought was right."

Juror Otis Ray Martin said he looked upon the trial as a job that had to be done, one that he hopes he will never have to do again.

"I took that job seriously," he said. "I was nervous, but I guess it was kind of a good nervousness. I never lost a minute's sleep over it."

Juror Bonnie Steiner said she still feels the weight of the decision.

"I think we did what was right, what was expected of us. But it was such a struggle. Such a struggle! And we all have to live with this the rest of our lives."

In Granite, the effects of Esther's murder still linger but, with the passage of time, have become diffused.

"This is not the village of long ago," one resident observed. "People are now clannish, secretive, afraid to converse, to open up."

Like any small town, Granite has always known contentious politics. But in the years since Esther Steele's murder, the acrimony has escalated.

As Charles Jones predicted, his tenure as police chief was limited. His policy of strict enforcement was met by increasing opposition and complaints to the City Council. He resigned in March of 1989. He still resides in Granite, and can joke in vernacular about the experience: "Lots of folks around here don't like me no more."

Terry Rhine received a total of one hundred years on the drug charges, and he plea-bargained for a life term for the rattlesnake venom murder. The sentences are to run consecutively. Even with liberal parole policies, Rhine will be away a long while.

Before his departure, Rhine threatened the lives of Jones, parole officer Paul Wayne Morris, and their families.

They are kept informed of Rhine's whereabouts.

"He has reason to be unhappy with me," Jones pointed out. "If we hadn't got him on the drug bust, they wouldn't have got him on the murder."

After resigning as police chief, Jones completed requirements for his master's degree in counseling. Today he works with a firm called New Horizons, in the mental health field, serving a large area of western Oklahoma.

"We do counseling and therapy work," he explained. "I'm a family therapist. I go into the homes and work with children who are emotionally disturbed, at risk of being taken out of the home. Sometimes they're abuse cases, neglect, and so forth."

Jones expressed deep satisfaction at putting Rhine away. He said he believes the drug traffic in Granite has lessened considerably.

But he added, enigmatically: "We didn't get the really big ones. Maybe someday."

He would not say more. But rumors persist that some Granite residents continue to be players in regional drug traffic.

After Jones resigned, the political atmosphere became even more hectic for a while.

In the wake of a nonproductive drug bust, the targeted couple sued the city for damages. Later, a police chief was summarily fired. He sued the city for a lack of due process. For a time the town was awash in litigation. The town's bond rating was in jeopardy. Council meetings became shouting matches.

Only recently has the tide ameliorated somewhat. Much of the ill feeling and bitterness remain. So intense have been the issues that most of those involved have forgotten that the entire sequence of events started with Esther's murder.

Afterword . .

L. D. WILLIAMS, CHIEF OF POLICE AT the time of Esther's murder, today serves as mayor of Granite. The actor, William D. Post, Jr., died in September of 1989. Doris Broiles Post continues to live in Granite, near her family.

Daisy Brown moved from her home in Granite to an apartment in Lubbock, Texas, to be near her daughter, Nancy Beth Tabor.

"She has her good days and her bad days," Nancy Beth reported. "She is still bothered by what happened to Esther. She has never fully recovered from it."

Increasingly troubled by the rheumatoid arthritis and asthma that have plagued her since childhood, Jan Wingo Locklear sold the

Granite Enterprise to her friend, Tena Hahn. In October of 1993, Tena sold the newspaper to Diana J. Suender—the daughter of Bill and Joyce Manning—who moved to Granite with her husband and three children from Las Cruces, New Mexico.

For a time, Bill and Joyce Manning had become somewhat disenchanted with life on their Northern Cross Ranch.

"We've had about all the peace we can stand," Joyce joked.

Joyce wanted to live nearer her grandchildren before they, too, were up and gone. Bill could not hire labor for work that needed to be done on the ranch. Now, with three grandchildren nearby and a weekly newspaper in the family, peace may not be so oppressive.

Ernest Craig, who ran the Granite Variety Store for many years, died in 1992. Gertrude Hawkins, who was driven home from church by Esther on the night of the murder, also died in 1992.

Palmer Briggs observed his hundredth birthday in April of 1993, unsuccessfully resisting efforts of friends to toss him a party.

Penny Kruska Hook and her husband, Richard, moved in 1990 to Algeria, where Richard was engaged in oil exploration. With the Shiite disturbances in the spring of 1992, Penny and the children returned to Houston, while Richard continued to commute to his work in Algeria. In 1993, Penny and the children again moved to Algeria. Again all foreigners were threatened with death. At year's end Penny was back in Houston, househunting. A new addition to Penny's family, another daughter, was named for two favorite aunts, Abigail Esther.

Many recent accomplishments of Esther's former students and Audubon Club members would have brought her pride and delight. But of all who came under her influence, perhaps none has gone further, conceptually if not academically, than Holland Ford of Johns Hopkins University.

In June of 1992, Holland was leader of the team of astronomers who announced the discovery of a black hole in galaxy M51, twenty million light-years from Earth.

Holland and his brother Mark grew up only two doors away from Esther. They were members of her Audubon Club and received the full treatment. As always, Esther awakened certain curiosities.

Today Mark is an attorney in Tulsa. He became curious about Greer County history. On visits home he often talks with Palmer Briggs about the early days, and he digs into original sources, assembling historical material on the region—and especially on Comanche Springs, purchased from Palmer by Mark's father.

Today Holland is a professor at Johns Hopkins. He and his colleagues are following up on the black hole discovery, exploring the significance of a tantalizing X-shaped image in the photograph. The scientific ramifications of this big X may be enormous.

Holland is busy with this and other things. His plan for fixing the myopia of the Hubble telescope was adopted. He was invited by NASA to attend the launch of the repair team. In addition to teaching, he is spending considerable time on a mountaintop in Chile, searching with other scientists for the elusive cold, dark matter that may—or may not—make up the bulk of the universe.

Holland confirms that he is following as exciting a life as he ever could have imagined.

"And it all started right there in Granite," he said. "Two doors down from Esther."

Esther's influence remains evident in other ways. Although Granite continues to hang on economically, in the spring of 1993 a "Vision for Granite" program projected an ambitious future for the town. Volunteers set to work investigating the feasibility of refurbishing and reopening the old Main Street hotel and, possibly, the Sulphur Springs resort on the east side of the mountain. Projected plans go beyond cleanup and fixup into renewing the town's basic infrastructure—replacing sidewalks, renovating downtown buildings, revitalizing the television cable service, improving the water and sewer facilities, recycling, and investigating what needs to be done about health care and affordable housing for the elderly.

The program calls for ninety volunteers in the various phases. But there is no doubt where Esther would be at work. Outlined are goals to provide Granite with an educational system of unusual excellence, tailored to the expressed career choices of the students. Goals that Esther sought so passionately all of her life now seem to have been adopted by the entire community.